**COULD
SHOULD
MIGHT
DON'T**

COULD
SHOULD
MIGHT
DON'T

•

HOW
WE THINK
ABOUT THE
FUTURE

NICK FOSTER

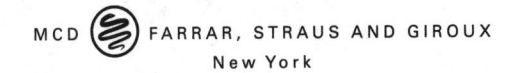

MCD · FARRAR, STRAUS AND GIROUX

New York

MCD
Farrar, Straus and Giroux
120 Broadway, New York 10271

EU Representative: Macmillan Publishers Ireland Ltd, 1st Floor, The Liffey Trust Centre, 117–126 Sheriff Street Upper, Dublin 1, DO1 YC43

Copyright © 2025 by Nick Foster
All rights reserved
Printed in the United States of America
First edition, 2025

Grateful acknowledgment is made for permission to reprint lines from "Kennedy," written by David Gedge and performed by The Wedding Present. Use licensed by permission of David Gedge.

Library of Congress Cataloging-in-Publication Data
Names: Foster, Nick, 1976– author.
Title: Could should might don't : how we think about the future / Nick Foster.
Description: First edition. | New York : MCD, Farrar, Straus and Giroux, 2025
Identifiers: LCCN 2025003257 | ISBN 9780374619350 (hardcover)
Subjects: LCSH: Future, The. | Forecasting—History.
Classification: LCC CB161 .F58 2025 | DDC 115—dc23/eng/20250218
LC record available at https://lccn.loc.gov/2025003257

The publisher of this book does not authorize the use or reproduction of any part of this book in any manner for the purpose of training artificial intelligence technologies or systems. The publisher of this book expressly reserves this book from the Text and Data Mining exception in accordance with Article 4(3) of the European Union Digital Single Market Directive 2019/790.

Our books may be purchased in bulk for specialty retail/wholesale, literacy, corporate/premium, educational, and subscription box use. Please contact MacmillanSpecialMarkets@macmillan.com.

www.mcdbooks.com • www.fsgbooks.com
Follow us on social media at @mcdbooks and @fsgbooks

10 9 8 7 6 5 4 3 2 1

CONTENTS

PREFACE vii

JUST IMAGINE 3
THE METRONOME QUICKENS 9
A RELUCTANT FUTURIST 29

COULD
OH, WOW 47
SCIENCE FICTION 52
THE ROOTS OF COULD FUTURISM 58
COULD FUTURISM IN PUBLIC 64
COMMERCIAL COULD FUTURISM 78
HEROIC FUTURES AND BACKGROUND TALENT 87

SHOULD
"BETTER" 103
BELIEF 109
ON PREDICTION 117
EMPIRICAL FUTURES 132

NUMERIC FICTION 141
THE FUTURE IS ACCRETIVE 151

MIGHT

FUTURES PLURAL 167
THINK TANKS 176
STRATEGIC FORESIGHT 181
THE LIMITS OF IMAGINATION 193
REGURGITATIVE FUTURES 203
WAGGING THE DOG 212

DON'T

CRITIQUE, CAUTION, AND FEAR 231
ALGORITHMIC ADVERSITY 242
TOXIC POSITIVITY AND SOLUTIONISM 252
DEPENDENCIES, IMPLICATIONS, AND ENDS 262
EXTRAPOLATORY FUTURES 280

AND SO . . . 301
THE FUTURE MUNDANE 305
THERE'S PLENTY OF FUTURE LEFT 323

THANK YOU 335

PREFACE

When set against the grand arc of civilization, both you and I will very shortly be dead.

In all likelihood, our lives will represent little more than barely perceptible twitches of a needle in the vast machinery of humanity. I can't know where you are in your life, but I'm currently in that alluring period known as my "late forties," and as such, I've started absent-mindedly browsing the Porsche website and suffering unprovoked pains in my back and shoulders. I'm gradually drifting away from cocktails and nightclubs, and feeling the inescapable pull of documentaries and early nights. I've come to the unsettling realization that countless world leaders are now younger than I am, and I've started to think more about how many years I might have left rather than how many have passed. Sickness and suffering have also started to poke their unwelcome noses into more of my business. I've experienced the death of my mother and witnessed the health struggles, financial turmoils, and emotional burdens of my family, friends, and colleagues. Given current estimations (and making broad assumptions about your location), you and I should both expect a living window of around eighty years on Earth. A tailwind of good healthcare and evolving medicinal interventions might extend this window somewhat, but the pair of us will definitely, inexorably, and inevitably end up dead.

But for now we are here, in the vibrant, bustling space we call "the present," surrounded by all the things we know and love, and with all the things we've experienced trailing out behind us. Now, let's cast our gaze forward and imagine a vast barren desert stretching almost infinitely ahead. On the horizon sit a couple of brightly colored flags fluttering in the breeze that represent the ends of our earthly journeys. If you squint you can almost see yours dancing in the distance.

So what do you think lies in between here and there? When you peer into that vast, uncharted expanse, what do you see? What do you see for yourself, for your family, and for your friends? What paths will you take and what decisions will you make? How far will your money go? Where will you live? What will your home be like? Where will you go on holiday and how will you get there? What might be in your pockets, on your dinner plate, or in your bag? What will you worry about? Where will you work, and who might be in charge?

It's likely that this desert is filled with huge amounts of uncertainty, and the further out we look the more blurry things become. This is the space in which I've spent my career, and it's the space we'll explore together in this book.

**COULD
SHOULD
MIGHT
DON'T**

JUST IMAGINE

Close your eyes for a moment and think about the future.

Welcome back. Now, what did you see?

Were you standing in the middle of some kind of fantastic city, surrounded by towering glass structures? Were there self-driving cars zipping through the streets and all sorts of robots scurrying this way and that? Were there swarms of delivery drones in the sky and blindingly quick monorails threading their way silently between the glistening buildings? Perhaps it was late at night, and the city was awash with purple and blue neon lights. Were there gigantic 3D holograms projecting up into the sky? I bet there were.

Or did you see fantastic new gadgets? Perhaps you were wearing some sort of goggles or magical contact lenses, or maybe you had an intelligent digital assistant whispering helpfully in your ear? Maybe your imagination went a bit further and you pictured some sort of colossal space station? A gargantuan, interconnected superstructure made of pods, nodes, and cells gleaming against the blackness of space. Maybe there was some sort of shuttle approaching one of its air locks, delivering visitors and supplies from Earth? Maybe it was stopping off on its way to a new civilization on the Moon, or even farther afield.

There's a chance that your imagination took you to somewhat darker places, where the images were significantly less appealing and the background music was decidedly gloomier. Perhaps you saw a barren Ozymandian wasteland, baked dry by the unrelenting sun. Violent storms demolishing buildings, flash floods tearing through neighborhoods and thin, shriveled crops wilting beneath moody skies. Maybe you saw a future defined by political upheaval, uncontrolled technological overreach, increasing division, and unrest? An overwhelming polycrisis of suffering, struggle, and stalemates, with endless handheld camera shots of shouting mouths, shaking fists, and shocking violence?

But hang on, maybe you saw something a bit more hopeful? A more equitable place where everyone is accepted for who they are. A place of calmness and tranquility, where people greet each other with a polite smile or a friendly nod. What about a world beyond plastics and petroleum, the end of national borders and oppressive public policies, or a future filled with limitless sources of clean energy? Is that where your imagination went? Did you find yourself in a landscape of rolling green hills dotted with pristine wind turbines and acres of solar panels? Or did you see a future filled with astounding medical technologies, artificial limbs, amazing biological implants, incredible drugs, and life-changing therapies?

Perhaps you were thinking of a future economy of some kind? Did you see the meteoric rise of a new market or the decline of one of today's megacorporations? Did your imagination conjure the end of a particular industry or the collapse of a popular ideology? When you thought about the future, were you excited, impatient, or terrified? Did the future you envisaged feel better or worse than today? Do you even know what "better" looks like? Could you stand up and describe it in detail for the rest of us? Maybe you're anxious about the future? Maybe you're concerned about money, or the success of your business? Will your industry even exist in twenty years, and will you be able to earn a living? Maybe artificial intelligence will take your job, do it faster, cheaper, or more reliably, or perhaps turn it into something unrecognizable? Are you saving enough? Will banks even exist in the future, and if not, what might take their place? Should you be hoarding gold coins or stashing US dollars? Would it be better to invest in property or fill a digital wallet with bitcoin? And what about the kids? What about your nieces, nephews, or grandchildren? What about *their* grandchildren? What will *they* do? What might *their* future look like?

Now, stop and think for a second. Where did those ideas, questions, and images come from? How do you think they got into your brain? Did you create them yourself from scratch? Be honest, now. Is there a slight chance that you pulled some of them from *Blade Runner* or *Total Recall*? Perhaps you were simply remembering an engaging expert you saw on television last week or a TED Talk that your friend recommended? Maybe it was that clever economist you heard on a podcast a while ago? It's hard to remember, isn't it? How about that sci-fi book you read over the summer—could that be it? Could it have been a scene from your favorite show on Netflix, or that scary-sounding technology your neighbor mentioned when you bumped into him walking his dog? It could have been the financial advisor you saw last year, and all that stuff she was saying about your retirement. Or what about those slick strategy guys from work, the ones with the half-zip fleeces who produced that expensive-looking document? They must have had *something* worthwhile to say, right? And there was that article you read on *The New York Times* website—maybe that was it? Or maybe it was just something you've *always* felt. Maybe it's a dream you've had since childhood, or an image from a picture book that you read in your bunk bed. Is that where those ideas came from?

There's a high chance that your thoughts about the future are a composite of all of those things (or at least some of them), and I'm almost certain that what you imagined wasn't yours and yours alone. When you imagine the future, you're much more likely to see a collage of ideas created by countless other people humming away in boardrooms, labs, and studios across the globe than something of your own making. Every day, in every country, in every industry and every society, immense amounts of effort and investment are trained on giving the future some sort of shape. Take the big technology companies, for example. In 2022, Meta, Amazon, Apple, Netflix, and Google collectively spent $177 billion—the equivalent of the GDP of Kuwait—on research and development. While not all of this work can be considered "futurism," it's certainly an indicator of how much these organizations (and hundreds of organizations like them) devote to shaping, exploring, and planning for the future.

Much of this kind of work is hidden from view, but a

significant amount finds its way into the public sphere, either as declarative visions of the future or more often embedded within new products, corporate strategies, or acquisitions. These get presented to us in the form of press releases, product launches, and pitches, which set the tone for how we think about the direction of industry, and point us at the futures they want us to see. Alongside these corporate efforts are the future stories told to us by our governments, analysts, economic organizations, and lawmakers. These are presented to us as stump speeches, manifestos, election pledges, investment proposals, financial outlooks, data projections, and leadership visions, which begin to shape the narratives and priorities we all reach for when considering the future of politics and society. These contributions are significant but are utterly dwarfed by the formidable juggernaut of our popular media. Millions of hours of film, TV, podcasts, documentaries, and news footage relentlessly feed us concepts from every one of the multitude of screens that now fill our lives. In parallel, mountains of written material in the form of novels, articles, essays, and commentary reach out at us from bookstores and websites, libraries and newsletters. If that wasn't enough, our religious and cultural organizations also elbow their way into the party, adding their own weighty and uncompromising takes to the long list of future narratives jostling for position in our brains.

Some of these ideas are overt, strident, and declarative, while some are subtle, subversive, and hidden. Indeed, some of the concepts you have about the future were embedded within you from birth, long before you had a chance to question them. The result is a dense, swirling, impenetrable fog of opinion that suffocates and stifles our ability to create our own independent ideas about where things might be heading. Our lives have become utterly saturated with these endless speculations, and thinking about the future has become one of the most deep-seated collective obsessions of our time. You'd be forgiven for believing that such a dominant preoccupation was hardwired into our very souls. But it wasn't always so.

THE METRONOME QUICKENS

The world is so futuristic now, and I feel in the way of it.
—NATE BARGATZE

The impetus to consider the future typically springs from some form of provocation—some significant event or challenge that crops up and compels us to reframe the world and ponder what might lie ahead. Anything from a brooding conflict to a reflective moment on a beach can encourage us to lift our eyes up toward the horizon, but as we look back through history, a pattern emerges with startling clarity: one of the most powerful of these provocations is the emergence and development of new technologies. Don't worry, this isn't one of *those* books that fawns and gushes over the boundless merits of innovation, but the emergence of new technologies does seem to have an undeniable knack for provoking new lines of thought, or at least accelerating ideas from elsewhere. For centuries, the introduction and adoption of everything from sharp sticks and permanent inks to roaring steam engines and minuscule microchips has acted like rocket fuel for our imagination. These interventions have expanded our horizons, revealed previously unconsidered possibilities, and posed fresh challenges to the status quo that have endlessly shaped and reshaped the ways in which we think about the future.

Humans have been crafting tools and technologies for as long as we've walked the Earth, but around 12,000 years ago—as the Ice Age drew to a close and the Neolithic Period began—humanity passed a key milestone in our orientation toward the future. Prior to this, human life was largely built around nomadic subsistence, and was presumably shaped by immediate needs, local environmental conditions, and a rudimentary understanding of seasonal cycles. As our roaming ancestors began to settle down and cultivate portions of land, the stockpiling of supplies for survival through the winter and the planting of crops for the following year became essential considerations, and it's likely that people began to think about the future more intentionally. Based on discoveries of ancient burial sites, monumental architecture, and ceremonial objects, it seems that these Neolithic societies also developed their own beliefs and traditions related to the future, which included shamanic rituals aimed at improving fertility, ensuring protection from natural disasters, and appeasing deities. These ancient civilizations also began recording seasonal changes and the movements of celestial bodies, and in around 4000 BCE, societies in Mesopotamia developed humanity's earliest calendars, which suggests that more structured notions of the future followed accordingly.

The Bronze Age began around 3300 BCE and lasted for over two millennia, during which time technological advances understandably focused on mining, metallurgy, casting, and toolmaking. Religious and spiritual beliefs continued to dominate how people thought about the future, and many cultures developed societal systems that incorporated notions of fate, destiny, and the afterlife. Rituals, sacrifices, and ceremonies were performed in order to placate gods and spirits or to secure favorable outcomes for the future, such as successful harvests, victory in battle, or protection from nature's wrath. The evolution of shamans into oracles also occurred during this period, with a more pronounced focus on prophetic abilities and acts of divination as a means to unpick the mysteries of what lay ahead. The people of this era also created artworks depicting mythological beings, divine figures, and fantastical creatures, speculating further on what might lie beyond the present and on the shape of the afterlife.

The Iron Age arrived around 1200 BCE, and with it the emergence of iron tools, weapons, fortifications, coinage, transportation, and trade, yet throughout this period of significant technological progress, the future continued to be defined by religion and focused on the whims of gods and supernatural forces. In parallel, Iron Age communities developed a keener understanding of the cycles of nature through their agricultural practices, creating festivals and ceremonies to mark important milestones, and using prayer to help give their future some shape. Significant social change also came through the establishment of major trade routes such as the Amber Road, which stretched from the coasts of the North and Baltic Seas to the Mediterranean. These industrial highways allowed not only for the exchange of goods, but also for the mixing of cultures, which, most likely, included the sharing of ideas about the future.

As the historical clock ticked over to the Common Era, a great many things began to shift, and our orientation toward the future became more formalized. The concept of fate became a central feature in the Roman mindset, suggesting that certain events were predetermined or preordained by their sprawling array of gods. While individuals could strive for personal success during their lives, there was an underlying sense of inevitability and an acceptance of one's destiny in Roman culture. The emergence and popularity of literature in Roman and Greek civilizations also allowed for speculation about the mechanisms of the future to spread, such as in Virgil's sprawling poem *The Aeneid*, wherein the Trojan hero Aeneas receives numerous prophecies and omens from ghosts, gods, and creatures that appear to foretell his future. These prophecies served as reminders of the characters' roles within some sort of grand, predetermined scheme, portraying destiny as a complex interplay between divine will and mortal actions and highlighting the tension between individual agency and the forces of fate.

From the fifth century, we transitioned into the Middle Ages. Outlooks on the future continued to be dominated by religion, and most citizens believed in some sort of supernatural plan for humanity, but the Middle Ages also generated periodic waves of crippling apocalypticism. Real-world upheavals such as plagues, famines, and wars seemed to confirm references found in biblical texts such as the Book of Revelation, which led to further speculation on the underlying machinery of the future. Toward the end of this era we also saw the introduction of stories about the future that explicitly focused on technology. The medieval philosopher and Franciscan friar Roger Bacon attempted to imagine the possibilities of "artificial" technologies as early as 1260, with his letter entitled "Concerning the Marvellous Power of Art and Nature and the Nullity of Magic." Bacon was deeply influenced by the experimental thoughts within the *Secretum secretorum*, a tenth-century Arabic text on decorum, statecraft, magic, and invention, which he falsely believed to have been written by Aristotle. In his letter, he makes a pitch for a more clearly imagined future, complete with vivid descriptions of fantastical machines and incredible inventions. He writes, "A chariot can be made that moves at an unimaginable speed without horses . . . and an instrument for flying can be made, such that a man sits in the middle of it, turning some sort of device by which artificially constructed wings beat the air in the way a flying bird does." More brutal, perhaps, is the apparatus he describes "by which one man could violently draw to himself a thousand men against their will." At the end of this portion of the letter, Bacon starts to sound like a contemporary entrepreneur during a *Shark Tank* pitch, dismissing any request for details and asking us to focus more on the "spirit" of the thing, writing, "These things were all made in antiquity, and it is certain they have been made in our times, unless it be the flying machine, which I have not seen, nor do I know anyone who has, though I do know a wise man who has thought of a way to carry out such a device."

A couple of hundred years later, the German goldsmith Johannes Gutenberg made a significant dent in our technological timeline with the development of what we now refer to as "movable type." Up to this point, there were two ways to produce a book: you either copied the whole thing out by hand, or you meticulously carved the text of every page into large wooden blocks, a process that allowed for some level of reproduction but left no room for editing or reconfiguration. Gutenberg instead took a modular approach, developing small, metal pieces for every character of the alphabet that could be rearranged at will. Perhaps unsurprisingly, this technology was initially used to create copies of the Bible, but before long the technique was used in the reproduction of secular texts, including legal documents, scientific treatises, literature, educational materials, and political pamphlets. The mass production of books—and the associated spread of knowledge and information—undoubtedly increased general literacy and the dissemination of new ideas, particularly in the fields of philosophy and logic, a development that utterly terrified those in positions of power. What followed was the Enlightenment era of the seventeenth and eighteenth centuries, which marked a significant shift in the shape of human thought, and an emphasis on reason, evidence, and progress. This period witnessed major advancements in science and technology, including noteworthy discoveries in physics, chemistry, astronomy, and medicine, which fueled optimism about the potential for further progress and a curiosity about the years to come. Philosophers such as Francis Bacon and René Descartes advocated for a move away from superstition and religious dogma in favor of a more rational and empirical approach to understanding the world and a shaping of the future through scientific inquiry and innovation.

The Industrial Revolution of the eighteenth and nineteenth centuries further transformed humanity by ushering in unprecedented levels of technological advancement, economic growth, and societal development. The rapid pace of innovation and urbanization during this period prompted people to consider not only the immediate effects of these changes, but also the long-term implications of progress and the social and environmental consequences of industrialization. Authors such as William Morris and Edward Bellamy wrestled with these kinds of questions, and presented alternative visions of society that challenged the inequalities of industrial capitalism. Utopian socialists such as Charles Fourier began proposing grand blueprints for future societies within which everything about how we work, live, have sex, and negotiate beekeeping duties was radically restructured in order to address the inequalities brought about by the surging influences of industry. Speculative fiction also blossomed in this period from the minds of authors such as Mary Shelley and Jules Verne, who examined the possibilities and potential outcomes of emerging technology by exploring themes of space travel, robotics, and speculative biology, prompting deeper thoughts about where each of these disciplines might be heading.

Before we get fully up to date with this timeline, it's worth reminding ourselves that technological progress operates a bit like compound interest, in that every new idea spawns further innovations, and each new thing builds upon the achievements of the past. Once someone has created the internal combustion engine, for example, the next generation can start from that point and begin thinking about a gearbox. Once engines and gearboxes exist, the next group of inventors can devote their careers to thinking about turbochargers, adding their contribution to the huge amount of work that has already been completed. Consequently, the pace of technological development tends to accelerate, with each successive generation witnessing more rapid changes than its predecessors. If we were able to find some effective way to plot our technological milestones since the Neolithic Period, we'd see a fairly flat line for many thousands of years where not much happened. Over time, as technology began to pile on itself, the progress curve began to steepen, but, as transformative as the Enlightenment was, it still took over two centuries to get from Gutenberg's printing press to agricultural innovations such as Jethro Tull's seed drill. Since the late nineteenth century, however, the tempo of innovation has accelerated dramatically and driven this technological progress curve into a near-vertical ascent.

Every decade since the Second World War has delivered an impressive parade of transformative technologies, and communities all over the world have experienced associated changes in their understanding of life, culture, society, and industry. As the 1940s drew to a close, the world began repurposing technologies that had originally been developed for combat—from jet engines and radar to synthetic fabrics and medicines—leading to a surge of publicly available innovation and a general feeling of optimism about the future in many Western countries. The automation and mechanization technologies of the 1950s changed how we built our world and introduced new models of leisure, travel, and economic prosperity. The mass adoption of color television and FM radio in the 1960s introduced us to the notion of "youth culture" and fundamentally changed our models of family, relationships, fashion, and sexuality. The 1970s saw the emergence of space travel, VCRs, MRIs, and LCDs, which arrived amid a swirling tide of political and social activism, civil rights protests, and the second wave of feminism. The microprocessor revolution of the 1980s made computational power widely available, while our television sets fed us the Cold War, corporate culture, parachute pants, and pop music. In the 1990s, the development of mobile telecommunications and the World Wide Web connected businesses and individuals at an unprecedented scale, and Nintendo, PlayStation, and MP3s changed how (and where) we entertained ourselves. The 2000s witnessed an explosion of new forms of media and social networks that reshaped our concepts of community, advertising, and interpersonal connection, only to swiftly trigger a collapse of trust and leave deep scars in our social fabric. The equity and inclusivity upheaval of the 2010s rewrote our understanding of gender, sexuality, and race, as our global political community struggled to navigate the Arab Spring, Occupy Wall Street, #MeToo, and Black Lives Matter movements. Today, surging developments in machine intelligence appear poised to fundamentally reframe many aspects of our lives, in ways we're yet to fully comprehend.

Let's pause for a second to remind ourselves that all of these changes occurred within the span of a single human lifetime. My father, now in his eighties, has experienced a world both before the invention of vinyl LPs and after the introduction of ChatGPT. Barely a hundred years ago we were emerging from the devastation of the First World War. The global population was around a quarter of its present level, penicillin had yet to be invented, and less than half the homes in America had electricity. That's an extraordinary amount of change, occurring at a density and scale we've never had to wrangle with before, and it's affected both the pressure we feel to consider the future and our ability to do so. The science fiction writer William Gibson captured this mood well in his 2003 novel *Pattern Recognition*: "Fully imagined cultural futures were the luxury of another day, one in which 'now' was of some greater duration. For us, of course, things can change so abruptly, so violently, so profoundly, that futures like our grandparents' have insufficient 'now' to stand on. We have no future because our present is too volatile."

There's something that feels insightful and a little unsettling about that language. It's become difficult to think about the future because it feels like we have "*insufficient now to stand on.*" The never-ending daily onslaught of change we are all experiencing seems to destroy any semblance of foundational solidity, making it hard to get a grip on things before they change beneath us. A significant part of my professional life is focused on keeping abreast of all sorts of change, from new technologies to evolving language, habits, materials, techniques, politics, products, and tastes. I dedicate hours of my week to reading about this sort of thing, yet even I'm struggling to keep up. There's simply too much to wade through. Our generation is experiencing technological and societal change at a rate and magnitude not felt by our ancestors, and the effects of this change can be bewildering. Alvin Toffler defined this feeling as "future shock" in his seminal 1970s book of the same name, describing a psychological state of dislocation and disorientation experienced by individuals—and entire societies—that is brought about by "too much change in too short a period of time." But, like it or not, here we find ourselves, pinned to the front of this thundering locomotive of change, with the wind roaring in our ears and tears streaming down our cheeks. But how do we feel about the ground we've covered, and where do these tracks point, exactly?

Speaking at Howard University in 2016, Barack Obama commented, "If you had to choose one moment in history in which you could be born, and you didn't know ahead of time who you were going to be—what nationality, what gender, what race, whether you'd be rich or poor, gay or straight, what faith you'd be born into—you wouldn't choose 100 years ago. You wouldn't choose the fifties, or the sixties, or the seventies. You'd choose right now." This kind of positivity is perhaps not surprising from a president whose slogans were "Change we can believe in," "Yes, we can," "Hope," and "Forward," but he might have a point. Extreme poverty is plummeting, from 35 percent of the world's population in 1987 to under 11 percent in 2013. We've witnessed a 40 percent reduction in child labor from 2000 to 2016. Life expectancy is rising on every continent, and child mortality has fallen by more than 50 percent since 1990. Global income inequality is also decreasing, more people are going to school for longer, and literacy levels have never been higher.

If we pick the right numbers, it appears that the human race is doing better than ever. But somehow it just doesn't *feel* that way. Everywhere we look, the world appears to be telling us that things are actually getting *worse*, and we're not short of examples that seem to prove it. Chronic diseases such as obesity and diabetes are on the rise, and 1.7 billion adults are currently overweight. In developing countries, there are now more autocratic leaders than democracies, and the trend is moving quickly in that direction. Perhaps no example of the critical state of things is more vivid than that of anthropogenic climate change, which has become the overarching, international concern of our time. Undeniable evidence of the detrimental effects of our prior actions is everywhere, and climate change is affecting our lives at a faster rate than we can handle. Once-in-a-lifetime meteorological events occur almost weekly, and our governments and industrial leaders seem unable or unwilling to tackle the enormous challenge with sufficient rigor. Forest fires, floods, droughts, runaway atmospheric temperatures, extreme winds, and species-level extinctions have become commonplace news stories. Even the most optimistic climate projections are now focused on mitigations rather than solutions, and individuals feel increasingly powerless to address the changes coming our way.

Every society has traditionally looked toward its young people for hope about the future, but we appear to be witnessing a significant erosion of that tradition. Today's young adults—referred to as Generation Z or Gen Z by demographers—are utterly surrounded by depictions of the future, but in contrast to the optimistic future tales I grew up with in the 1980s, or those my parents grew up with in the 1950s, today's youth are engulfed by a smothering blanket of anxiety. A typical young adult averages around nine hours per day on their phone, much of which is spent doomscrolling their way through media that is increasingly negatively biased. A 2023 study by the *Journal of Human Behavior* examined 5.7 million clicks from 105,000 news articles and found that each additional negative word increased the click-through rate by 2.3 percent, and in a world where clicks equal revenue, it's no surprise that these sentiments find their way into ever more of our content. Bad news sells, and it's clearly attracting the eyes, ears, and attention of young people. This brooding, perpetual concern about the future is also having measurable effects on Gen Z's mental well-being, leading to a phenomenon that is broadly termed "ambient adolescent apocalypticism." Recent studies found that 34 percent of Gen Z are worried about the future and 45 percent are concerned about the stability of their future employment. Young people are collectively experiencing a moment of deep unease about what might be coming next. They're looking to the future, and they don't seem to like what they see.

So, are we doing fantastically well, or are things worse than ever? Should we be proud of what we've achieved or embarrassed at where we find ourselves? In truth, of course, the full picture is incredibly complex, perhaps impenetrably so. Both Barack Obama and our melancholic young people might be simultaneously correct; it depends on what we're looking at, how we measure it, and what we omit. There's simply no practical way to gather a full tally of these variables to reveal whether humanity has headed north or south on the great chart of progress, but whatever direction we head next is ultimately up to us, collectively. We have an immense amount of agency as a species—certainly more so than any other—and our future is largely ours to define in whatever form we choose.

Let's assume that a unifying ambition for all humans is the ongoing success of our species. If we can agree on that overarching principle—at the very least—then we clearly, undoubtedly, and undeniably have plenty of work to do. As I mentioned, the pace of change over the last century has been nothing short of breathtaking in almost every measurable respect, and "change" looks set to remain a defining theme of human existence as far ahead as we can see. Technology is hurtling onward at staggering speeds, thrusting its nose into ever more of our business whether we want it to or not. Previously slow-moving and reliably stable natural environments now feel erratic and precarious, and cracks are appearing in a great many of our bedrock convictions about society, culture, governance, and money. Intriguing new ways of thinking are also beginning to emerge that could upend, reprioritize, restructure, and reorder many aspects of the world as we know it. These adjustments could bring about life-changing opportunities for many of our struggling communities or accelerate already problematic levels of division and disparity, depending on how and where they're deployed. In the coming decades we're likely to see fundamental shifts in the ways we communicate with one another, in the detection and treatment of illnesses, in how we make things, where we live, how we consume, how we fight, how we entertain ourselves, and how we learn. If we *do* care about the success of our species, then finding ways to productively think about these things beyond near-term horizons feels like the right thing to do, the responsible thing to do, and the commercially sensible thing to do. The short-term bias that dominated the last century is only now revealing the full spectrum of its impact, and the issues it's created seem increasingly intractable and difficult to unpick. Given this reality, a shift toward a longer-term, future-oriented mindset, one packed with imagination, creativity, responsibility, and considerations, seems not only useful but *essential*.

I think most people know this.

But even so, it's rare that a rigorous, structured orientation toward the future forms the central pillar of our thinking, and it's almost never integral to the ways in which most organizations, industries, or governments are built. Even given the significant amount of uncertainty we all feel about the future, this kind of consideration remains on the fringes of almost every serious conversation, nudged out of the way by other, more pressing or nearer-term concerns. In any business, the incessant pressure to find clients, balance the books, chase sales, respond to orders, pay debts, ship products, execute plans, and deliver results utterly dominates day-to-day affairs, and many organizations struggle even with these fundamentals. There's rarely enough time or money available to invest in anything else, so futures work tends to be restricted to only the very wealthiest of companies, and even then, only very occasionally. Likewise, the day-to-day pressures felt by governments—be that shaping headlines, winning votes, defending decisions, or fighting any number of fires—can act as headwinds for long-term thinking. Any consideration for the future is typically relegated to simplistic manifesto slogans or snappy policy statements that are plastered onto podiums, pin badges, and bumper stickers, and whose ambitions rarely extend beyond a single presidential or prime-ministerial term. It seems that democratically elected leaders have become uninterested in embarking on fifty-year transitions or proposing generational investment programs, preferring instead to focus on quick wins and immediate results to capture or keep the attention of voters. Indeed, there's an uncomfortable reality brewing that long-term political and societal efforts seem increasingly confined to the world's dynastic autocrats, who have the ambition to undertake such things and are free from the pesky inconvenience of elections and campaigning.

So, when you close your eyes and think about the future, where does all that stuff come from? Surely somebody must be making it. Well, of course they are, in overwhelming quantities, but just as with an all-you-can-eat buffet, quantity doesn't often equate to quality. A lot of futures work is mistimed, misinformed, imbalanced, willfully shallow, poorly aimed, and sloppily executed, and that's predominantly due to where and why it was created, and by whom. Our list of future ideas is all but endless, and we all seem to enjoy discussing the merits and pitfalls of individual examples. It seems we've become incredibly comfortable discussing and debating the "what" of the future, but I don't think we spend enough time trying to make sense of *how* we think about the future, which feels important, especially now. I've been interested in exploring these topics for most of my life, and have therefore found successive homes within the bellies of big companies with the time, space, and budget to spend on such efforts. I've been involved with thinking about the future of domestic products, from washing machines to electric razors; I've explored robotics, prosthetics, and wearable technologies; I've worked with teams of people trying to figure out the future of computers and space travel, and have led efforts to tackle some of the planet's largest challenges, from waste and recycling to energy generation and climate change. These projects have been endlessly rewarding, but in reality, it's hard to say I've ever felt like an integral part of the organizations that commissioned them. In my experience, future-focused work has always been cleaved off into some sort of "lab," "innovation center," or "workshop," which is often housed within a separate building, accessible only by a special key card. There are good arguments for separating future-oriented work from the throbbing heart of a business—so that it isn't dragged down by the gravitational pull of everyday pragmatism, or to protect it from prying eyes—but this habit of "othering" futures work is one that I find increasingly troubling. Over the years, I've been on the receiving end of a fair amount of resentment and hostility from engineers, designers, and executives working in the main body of these organizations who feel like they're doing all the difficult, "real" work (and making all the money) while we sit in our fancy high castles, dreaming up impossible things that never seem to change very much.

I can see their point, mostly.

Before I took my first in-house role at Sony in 2005, I worked for a couple of design agencies in the UK. As a designer-for-hire I was often required to take part in "future explorations" or "innovation sprints" for a wide variety of organizations, from toothpaste companies to luxury car manufacturers, and while chatting with these clients over post-workshop drinks, I began to recognize depressing patterns in their motivations for undertaking this kind of work. Rather than striving to build a coherent perspective on the future, to help their company start a new chapter or to build a culture robust enough to withstand an impending change, all too often this work was positioned as an exercise in vanity, a puff piece for a trade show or a magazine article, or simply to create some sort of pantomime of innovation to retain key talent or soothe an anxious leader. Worse still (and this happened on multiple occasions), the projects were simply commissioned to eat up spare budget at the end of the fiscal year, or to act as some sort of fun exercise to allow the leadership team to cut loose a little, the creative equivalent of a boozy holiday party. I found this incredibly demoralizing, but it's perhaps symptomatic of the place we find for futures work, and the importance that we attribute to it.

It feels abundantly clear to me that we should all be thinking more about the future, that we should dedicate more time to this kind of work and make that work significantly more thorough, and perhaps you agree—but here we are. We appear to have largely pigeonholed long-term thought about the future into the folder marked "nonessential." A fun, optional indulgence for when you have a little spare time or some leftover money. Rather than forming a meaningful central pillar in how organizations think, futures work is almost universally seen as frivolous, superficial, and flimsy. How can it be that we're surrounded by such momentous change, such technological evolution, such societal upheaval, and such existential complexity, yet our collective ability to generate rational, balanced, detailed ideas about where we're headed remains so utterly underpowered and underprioritized? The fact that I can listen to award-winning podcasts, read books by Pulitzer-winning authors, open globally renowned magazines and newspapers, watch presentations from CEOs with PhDs, or meet marketing teams with million-dollar budgets and still hear lazy references to flying cars, hoverboards, *The Jetsons*, and *Star Trek* is not just embarrassing, it's a disgrace.

But how could we change this? How could we rethink the world so that a bias toward the future feels not only enticing but essential? How can we make the development of a well-defined perspective on the future feel as commercially important as sales, partnerships, investments, and returns? How can we find ways for companies, governments, and society at large to feel motivated to meaningfully invest in this kind of work, and then act upon it?

It feels as if a key factor in getting to that point is to aim for a significant increase in the quality of our thinking about the future. If futurism continues to feel clichéd, unrealistic, escapist, self-assured, preachy, vacuous, and generally subpar, it's unlikely that this kind of work will ever attract those in power, but if its output improves, perhaps its audience will grow and the conversation will get richer. I believe the next generation of futures work needs to feel more considered, professional, and grounded. It needs to fit into the ongoing flow of life and embrace its inherent complexity, variability, and ambiguity. It needs to meet the scale of uncertainty it faces with equal amounts of discipline and detail. It has to be actionable, relatable, understandable, empathetic, reasonable, responsible, and engaging.

In a word, it needs to be significantly more *rigorous*, and this is where you come in.

A RELUCTANT FUTURIST

Suppose I'm on an island all alone . . . I'm drawing diagrams in the sand, all by myself, naked, wearing a goatskin hat . . . and I'm seriously pondering the future, all by myself. Am I a futurist? Can I be a futurist under those conditions? I'm pretty sure that I'm not. I'm not a futurist, and the reason is I don't have anyone to tell about it.
—BRUCE STERLING

While a number of people spend significant time thinking about the future, either as a part of their job or out of general, everyday inquisitiveness, a much smaller group of people choose to call themselves "futurists." These people explicitly frame their lives around explorations beyond the here and now, and typically think at longer timescales than most other people. But who are futurists, exactly? Where do they come from, and what do they do? At what point do you call yourself a futurist? Should *you* become a futurist?

The term "futurism" seems to have first appeared somewhere in the mid-nineteenth century, and was originally used to represent a particular theological stance that focused on the more apocalyptic, eschatological sections of the Christian books of Revelation, Ezekiel, and Daniel. Later, it was adopted by various artistic movements and political ideologies that typically eschewed conservatism and embraced all things associated with change (which we'll explore a little more later). Today, futurism has become something of a catchall term that covers a vast array of mindsets, disciplines, and approaches, but the associated noun "futurist" appears to have evolved to represent a very specific type of person, a very specific list of activities, and a very specific set of underlying beliefs.

For years I've resisted calling myself a futurist—and I don't describe myself as a futurist today—but occasionally I've found myself trying the label on for size, turning around in front of the mirror to look at it from all angles and attempting to see how well it fits. If I'm being truly honest, I've only ever added "futurist" to a longer list of titles in an attempt to help soften the blow somewhat, hiding it among the foliage of my résumé, and hoping to somehow diminish its dominance. In 2021 I was honored (and, quite honestly, more than a little surprised) to accept the title "Royal Designer for Industry" from the Royal Society of Arts. When I was asked to define my field of work for the inevitable press announcement, I finally chose "Futures Design" after much troublesome internal debate, because I couldn't quite bring myself to write "Futurist." My career has been focused on exploring emerging technologies, thinking across long time frames, and helping people make decisions about what they might make over the decades to come, so by any measure I must be pretty close to being a futurist. If that's the case, then why do I feel so uncomfortable saying it out loud?

Why does it fit so awkwardly with me? Why am I *embarrassed* by it? What is a futurist anyway?

Within popular culture I don't think we've made sense of this role, or if we have, it's not something we seem to take very seriously. It feels superfluous and unnecessary somehow, and to many people it probably represents yet another obscene symptom of our overfunded, overprivileged consultant culture. When compared to a builder, doctor, welder, or farmer, "futurist" feels like a bit of a joke—at least it does to me. Aside from my general discomfort with the term, it also appears to have become something of a cliché. Whenever I've been introduced to someone as a futurist, there's firstly the faintest glimmer of an eyeroll (which people manage to hide with varying degrees of success), before the conversation typically falls into one of three distinct channels.

First, people seem convinced that I adore science fiction. They're confident that I'm profoundly acquainted with the works of William Gibson, Margaret Atwood, Isaac Asimov, and Philip K. Dick, and am able to meticulously dissect the minute details and philosophical underpinnings of these sacred texts. There's a prevailing assumption that I'm an enthusiast of franchises such as *Star Wars*, *Dune*, and *Star Trek*, or that I have a deep-seated passion for space travel, off-world colonies, rockets, androids, and robotics.

Second, there's an assumption that I'm a technology junkie. People seem to think that I'm obsessed with programming, automation, and computer science, and can passionately discuss obscure details of the underlying structures of the Android operating system. There's an expectation of deep technological know-how, obsessions with mathematics, microprocessor history, cryptography, communication protocols, and network infrastructures.

Finally, and perhaps most frequently, people expect me to have a strong strain of idealism, or to be armed with a clearly defined vision for the future. They're eagerly waiting for me to make confident predictions about where we're headed and effortlessly deploy data and statistics to bolster my convictions. People are confident that I'm a campaign-minded, mission-driven, and politically motivated visionary, and they expect me to have strong opinions about exactly which decisions the world should make, and in which order.

But none of those things is true for me. Not really.

I've seen people's noses wrinkle and their brows furrow in disappointment when I explain this (or more often, when they notice my blank expression staring back at them midway through a conversation). As you'll learn through this book, there are a significant number of people shaping your future who don't fit this mold, but there's still clearly something *expected* from futurists, some sort of core scaffolding that needs to be in place for the title to be held valid. Be honest, if someone said they were bringing a futurist to your picnic, what would *you* expect?

•

I'm now a citizen of the United States of America, but I know I'll always feel somehow British. No matter how long I live here, I think I'll always pronounce the *h* in the word "herbal." My life began in Derby, a small, damp city nestled at the base of the Pennine hills that would likely be of little importance were it not for its pivotal role in the Industrial Revolution. Throughout the eighteenth century, Derby blossomed into one of the major hubs of England's technological boom, driven by experimental individuals with wonderful names like Jedidiah Strutt, Richard Arkwright, and John Bloodworth, each of whom built textile mills in the region and established Derby's reputation as a good place to make stuff. This continued through the nineteenth and twentieth centuries, and the city grew into an important hub for the production of trains and aircraft engines; but unfortunately, like many industrial cities across the Western world, Derby suffered during the latter part of the twentieth century, falling prey to the fierce pummeling forces of international competition, ill-conceived privatizations, and large-scale corporate mismanagement. This city, with its tumbling warehouses, empty factories, and derelict mills was my introduction to the world, and it felt more like a reflection of a broken past than any sort of crucible for the future.

As a child I was definitely interested in science and technology, but growing up in the 1980s it was hard not to be: the stuff was absolutely everywhere. I vividly remember tuning in to watch space shuttle launches on TV, and I saw the *Challenger* break into a billion pieces as newscasters struggled to make sense of the images being beamed live from Florida. Television shows like *Tomorrow's World* and *Horizon* introduced me to new technologies every week. Cordless phones, portable TVs, laptop computers, compact discs, and voice-controlled light bulbs were each presented with balanced, straightforward, and somewhat stuffy descriptions of how they worked and what they might allow us to do. Computers, microchips, and gadgets featured in almost every television show in the '80s, from *MacGyver* to *Knight Rider* and *The A-Team*—but I think you'd struggle to call these works of "science fiction." Space fantasies and melodramas such as *Doctor Who*, *Dune*, and *Star Wars* all emerged throughout my childhood, and utterly captured the imaginations of most of my school friends—but I was never really interested in them. (Don't tell anyone, but I actually first watched *Star Wars* in the mid-1990s.) These types of science fiction books, TV shows, and movies seemed so abstract and silly to me, and when it came to sci-fi, I was far more interested in films like *Back to the Future*, *Innerspace*, and *Short Circuit*. In truth, these feel more like "gadget pictures" than "science fiction movies," and on reflection, what unifies them is that they are all set on Earth and feature normal people like you and me. They put little bits of the future in the hands of ordinary folks and asked, "What would you do in this situation?"—which I found significantly more engaging than things happening in different galaxies light-years away.

Science fiction—at least the quintessential, canonical, archetypal stuff—hasn't ever been a resource I reach for. It's not how I see the world, and it's certainly not my primary reference when thinking about the future. Over the years, well-meaning friends and colleagues have sought to convert me, pressing sci-fi books into my hands or urging me to watch their favorite movies or TV shows. I've found some of them to be interesting or thought-provoking and some have been fun, escapist joyrides, but a great many of them I've found to be vacuous, adolescent nonsense. For me, science fiction fills a gap, but I don't find it particularly inspirational, and as a genre it hasn't yet provided me with any sort of meaningful guidance in my work.

So, what about computers? It's true to say that today all of our lives are utterly dominated by computer technologies, from the clever boxes in our pockets to the huge, underpinning infrastructures that ensure our toilet rolls are delivered on time. As Georgina Voss said, "Software might not have eaten the world, but it has given it a good chew." The world has undoubtedly evolved significantly since the creation and mass adoption of these tools, and I consider myself lucky to have experienced much of that transition firsthand. I remember my school acquiring its very first computer and most of us not knowing why it was there or what to do with it. The big, beige box lived on a trolley in the library, and a group of the school's quieter boys would spend every lunch break tapping away at its chunky keyboard. A couple of years later, the school had a dozen computers that were housed in a dedicated room, and computer lessons appeared on our schedule shortly afterward. I would occasionally play around with rudimentary programming (mostly to make rude words scroll across the screen by typing "10 print 'boobs' / 20 goto 10"), but that's about as far as I got.

Aged eighteen, I left home to study design at a university near London. At the beginning of the four-year course, my classmates and I would spend hours meticulously drawing engineering layouts with pencils and inks, but as my degree neared its conclusion, we'd almost entirely shifted to computer-aided design, nearly all of us had a desktop computer of our own, and CDs of pirated design software made their way from room to room in brown envelopes. Over the last couple of decades, I've worked for major technology companies including Nokia, Sony, and Google, all of which have made a significant dent in our world through the careful application of computing technologies. But it's not the computers themselves, nor the silicon technologies and software within them, that have ever interested or excited me. I've always been much more curious about what these things can do—or more importantly, what they might *mean*. When technology intersects with people it comes to life. It changes the way they do things, where they can do them, and with whom. This is the part that many people miss in conversations about technology and the future, and where I've found the discussion almost always gets significantly richer—the part where we talk about people and impact rather than gigaflops and terabytes.

The final trait of our clichéd futurist is the presence of a deeply rooted sense of idealism and a strident sense of purpose. In thinking about where we're all headed, an ability to spot trajectories and understand change is undoubtedly useful, but any kind of *certainty* about the future has always felt startlingly hubristic to me. Conviction about the future—whether pointing toward some sort of ambition or away from some sort of threat—tends to lead toward a mission-driven type of futurist who has a well-defined "ultimate state" in mind for the world. This kind of singular dedication to a cause can be impressive, but I've never felt that this was a job for me, or that I even had *permission* to think at that kind of scale. It might be my working-class roots showing, but I've always felt more like a contributor than a leader. As I've aged, I've become more comfortable with my own opinions, agency, and confidence, but I've also come to realize just how flimsy, naive, and ill-considered the majority of this kind of thinking can be. It's all too often built around isolated ideals that deliberately overlook the intricate machinery underpinning the systems we navigate, and as a result this type of mindset often feels achingly romantic, but lacks sufficient rigor to resist even the most basic of questioning. No matter how many times I look within myself, I know I'm not on any sort of mission and I don't believe I have a calling. I'm not pushing any singular technology, ideology, or ultimate destiny for my species, and I'm troubled when others do so.

I'm proud to have forged a successful future-oriented career without this bedrock of obsessions and fascinations, but it's not been straightforward. Over time I've built a workable knowledge of all the things listed above to get me through countless dinner parties and client meetings, but these aren't the topics that define me. They're not where I came from. They're not *in my bones*. So, given this realization, why do I do it? I don't seem to fit the profile, nor do I meet people's expectations, and I regularly feel as if I'm swimming against the tide, so why do I devote my time and effort to thinking about the future? Why do I care about it, and why has this formed the majority of my life's work?

Well, there's a curiosity in me. It's as simple as that.

As a child I had an almost uncontrollable urge to pick at Christmas gift wrapping, to try to discover what hid inside. Today I want to crack open the future just to see what might ooze out. I love to help people bring their ideas to life. I enjoy the complexity of it and the discussions that come from my provocations. I love those first few moments when attempting to understand a new technology or idea, when trying to discover what I call the *grain* in it, to experience how it works, where it wants to point, and what might be possible if we can get it to play along. I like to think about whether cinemas will survive or fail, what old people will do when their retirement funds run dry, what the next generation of music might sound like, how we might continue to power our homes and put food on our tables, or what we might feed our pets in years to come. I get a kick out of thinking about what a holiday will consist of in a couple of decades, what a phone might be able to do, what kinds of people might go hiking, how our cities will feel, or who might be in power. The darkness ahead of us intrigues me. It sometimes seems like I can see little pinpricks of light flickering out there, or small fragments of clarity moving toward us through the gloom. I can't help myself. I find it intoxicating. It's *curiosity*, that's the thing, and it's all I can do to rein it in.

As I hope you'll come to realize, becoming involved in futures work needn't necessarily mean conforming to any sort of standardized pattern, nor contorting yourself to fit into a predefined box. Indeed, there's a strong argument to be made (and one that I support) that there needs to be significantly more diversity in the global community of futurists, people who will bring a broader spectrum of opinions and ideas to the table and help us break the repetitive imagination cycles we so often find ourselves trapped in. However—and I want to be clear here—it's not for everyone. The overwhelming majority of futures work frequently feels directionless, uncertain, conjectural, and hypothetical, and much of it is little more than what I call "shruggy hunches." This work is dominated by loose ideas that need to be loosely held. It can't easily be peer-reviewed, tested, or measured in any meaningful ways, which can prove endlessly frustrating for some people. Likewise, the impact of futures work often occurs so early in a project that it's long forgotten once the project has come to fruition, which can make it all feel rather thankless. But if you do feel the urge to point yourself at this kind of work, I offer you strong encouragement. Go for it, let's see what you can do.

If you already work as a futurist, or are explicitly focused on producing foresight, projections, or long-term explorations, then perhaps this book can help you reflect a little. There might be things in here that could help you rethink how you approach your work or reframe your conversations, but this book isn't really aimed at practicing futurists. It hasn't got any methodologies, matrices, or pyramids for you to scrawl on whiteboards. There are no diagrams or frameworks or magical techniques to somehow make you better at "doing the future." There aren't any predictions, statements, or projections about the future in here either. I'll make no claims about what I think will increase or decrease, what the future will consist of, or what we should invest in.

What I aim to do with this book is to take a step back,

in an attempt to reset things a little and reflect on what we might be doing before diving into any sort of detail. With this ambition, I've aimed to write a book for someone like you: an ordinary human living on Earth with a curiosity about what might be coming next. As a consumer of futurism (which you undoubtedly are), you have a right—and indeed a duty—to question the ideas being pitched at you, to ask where they come from, who made them, and how you fit in them, and to demand significantly more clarity and detail in what you see and hear.

If this kind of work is going to get better—and as a somewhat selfish extension, if I'm ever to get comfortable with the term "futurist"—then we need to hold the output of these people to account. People who spend their lives thinking about the future can be an odd bunch, and there's often an air of confident superiority to their work. It can frequently feel as if they're party to conversations, insights, ideas, and discussions beyond the grasp of mere mortals, and as a result, audiences can often feel overwhelmed with uncertainty and self-doubt, recoiling shyly away from the towering intellects and bold confidences reaching toward them. In truth, while a lot of this stuff might appear highbrow and intellectually rigorous on the surface, it's often of surprisingly poor quality. All too often, futurism sells you fantasies, reaffirms your biases, or stokes your nightmares, and we all deserve much, much better.

As audiences, we need to get comfortable demanding more detail, more discipline, more precision, and more thoroughness in what we see and hear from those pushing future ideas in our direction. But that will take confidence.

With this book, I hope to arm you with that confidence, and a keenness to lean into this endless stream of content with a critical eye and an inquiring mind. I want to help you break through the cacophony. I want you to better understand futurism when you see it happen in front of you or when you catch yourself doing it. I hope to give you a few pointers to pick holes in what's presented to you and to offer ways to understand whether something might be missing.

As much as we might like to ignore it, push it aside, or focus on other things, the future will definitely appear. There's no direction any of us can run that will let us dodge the weekend. The future is everywhere, it's in everything, and it's coming for us all. Unfortunately, hundreds of thousands of people have spent many centuries filling the future with ideas, projections, stories, and beliefs that have made it much too bloated and unwieldy for us to wrap our heads around. For every thought there's a counterthought, for every idea there's a rebuttal, and for every believable projection there's some annoyingly conflicting data. Like trying to consider the constituent parts of a galaxy or discuss the entirety of modern literature, the future just doesn't fit into our heads in any manageable way. It presents a level of overwhelming complexity that's sure to make even the most well-adjusted people feel a little anxious.

But what if we pulled out of this swirling maelstrom a little? What if we were able to resist being dragged into discussing the merits or pitfalls of individual ideas, quibbling about singular projections or obsessing over specific stories? What if we zoomed above all the noise and tried to get a feel for the bigger picture at play? Are there any thematic consistencies or patterns we can identify that could at least help us break this expanse into more manageable chunks, so we can know roughly what we're dealing with before we get sucked into the details? I think there are.

My life has been primarily focused on design—and this book will take a largely design-oriented view on the world—but my career has been spent deep within global-scale organizations, surrounded by communities of entrepreneurs, designers, scientists, engineers, investors, and policymakers. Throughout this career, I've sat on both sides of the table, as both a producer and a client; I've been a part of major futures groups on three continents; I've studied and taught in futures academia; and I've attended countless lectures, seminars, and discussions. Over time this saturation has revealed a few underlying patterns to me. It seems that every thought about the future—irrespective of its source or ambition—fits into one of four distinct domains, each of which has its own strengths, weaknesses, benefits, and drawbacks. In reality, just as with any kind of thematic categorization, these ways of thinking all overlap and collide, and their boundaries are more blurry than crisp. You shouldn't think of them as isolated from one another, but perhaps by viewing them as the four corners of a map, you can better understand the shape of the territory within.

So let's jump in and take them one at a time: Could, Should, Might, and Don't.

COULD

THE COULD FUTURISTS

Theirs is the realm of wishful thinking.

They harbor fantasies of incredible new worlds.

They enjoy future devices, product concepts, and vision videos.

They devour science fiction.

They hope to be considered visionaries.

They are hopeful, wide-eyed, and excitable.

They begin their sentences with "What if . . ."

They are unbounded by timelines and think at generational scales.

They are frustrated by pragmatism, rationalism, and skepticism.

They are solutionists and utopianists, their glass always half full.

They are comfortable blurring the lines between fact and fiction.

They are overwhelmingly male.

OH, WOW

The first stop on our journey to break this world into more digestible pieces is perhaps the most obvious and overt of them all. A little earlier I asked you to imagine the future, and it's my assumption that a whole host of ideas and images came rushing into your mind. But if I ask you to conjure the word "futuristic," I'm betting that something curious happens. The word "futuristic" behaves differently somehow, bringing forth images of exotic technologies and outlandish change, reflecting a dogma that I refer to as "Could Futurism." If you grew up around the influence of Western society, this is the futurism you're likely most familiar with, as it appears regularly in almost every form of media. It pops up as talking heads, it spreads itself across countless column inches of newsprint, it peeks out in podcasts, radio shows, and interviews, and sneaks into the conversation at conferences, lectures, and after-dinner talks. You'll often see a Could Futurist earning pundit-dollars on prime-time TV, sitting on the studio couch talking about technology in vague and lofty terms as the hosts sit enthralled, slowly shaking their heads and marveling at his fantastic tales. *Think of all the things that could change! It's incredible how different everything could be! Just imagine the world if this happened!*

Could Futurism focuses squarely on the positive, transformative nature of our emerging world. It's full of optimism and a gleeful imagination that can be incredibly alluring. It sits comfortably in our popular culture, as it's often exciting, titillating, and occasionally incendiary, or, to use appropriate media lingo, it's "good content." Deliberately designed to induce strong feelings—typically of excitement and an eagerness for progress—Could Futurism is often intentionally simplistic. It delivers punchy sound bites and easily understood concepts—the sorts of things anyone could remember and retell in a bar. Could Futurists typically have a knack for creating engaging narratives, and some of them are masterful storytellers, finding ways to make complex ideas simple, digestible, and relatable. When we consume popular content about the future, these characters are usually at the front and center, delivering just enough real information to be compelling but adding layers of editorial comment and imagination designed to reel in the viewer and keep them enraptured and engaged. Could Futurism is transactional in nature rather than critical or complex, and it needs you to be interested. It's driven by the desire to elicit a response, and you're familiar with this type of futurism predominantly because it *actively seeks you out*.

Could Futurism is, above all things, overwhelmingly technocratic. It views the world through the twin gazes of science and industry, and defines all types of change in those terms. It's filled with robots, self-driving vehicles, vertical farms, subterranean monorails, space colonies, artificial foods, 3D printers, bionic implants, holograms, gene editing, and virtual reality, because these technologies act as neatly packaged transformative hangers upon which its proponents can craft a compelling story. It presents these technologies as keys to unlock new possibilities and places technology at the center of any proposed transformation, creating an engaging hybrid of business and entertainment in the process. Could Futurism works particularly well in our sound-bite culture and suits our decreasing attention spans, often packaging nuanced ideas into crisp, memorable missives that can be easily shared as tweets or giddy LinkedIn posts. This type of work often stumbles around clumsily when confronted with complex questions about society, policy, or economics, as the conversation becomes too subtle, intricate, and layered for it to digest. It much prefers the big ambitious statement, the striking visual stimulus, or the single provocative proclamation.

This variety of futurism also has a curious relationship with time; it's often noncommittal about schedules, pointing at some notional version of the "the future" that could be ten or fifty years hence. Conversely, Could Futurism also has a habit of making strident predictions about the future and pinning its transformations to well-defined deadlines. You're no doubt familiar with these sorts of prophetic outpourings: *By 2050, we'll all be eating artificial meat* or *Africa will be the center of the VR economy by 2040*. This is a tactic typically adopted when a story needs some pep, some shockingly close date or an arrestingly high figure to proclaim when an intricate idea needs condensing into a headline or a character-limited post. What's frequently absent from Could Futurism is any notion of intermediate steps from the present, and in many regards, it represents a rejection of incrementalism in favor of large, transformational gestures. It prefers to present the future at maturity, fully developed and mass-adopted, but this forces us to ask, If we're all to be eating artificial meat by 2050, what might 2040 or 2030 look like? What steps will society, industry, and technology go through to reach this end state? Could Futurism rarely engages in this level of detail, and there's a hefty dose of freewheeling approximation at its heart. Any efforts to dive into pragmatism or dip even slightly below the exciting surface are dismissed by Could Futurists as unwelcome, troublesome needling.

Could Futurism represents an unshackled way of thinking about the future, but while it often loudly boasts about its staggering imagination, even a cursory survey of its output reveals just how repetitive it can be. If you type the word "futuristic" into a Google Images search, you'll be rewarded with a disappointingly homogenous collection of pixels, with the same images repeating over and over—CGI renderings of cybernetic humans, glossy bipedal robots, and baffling concept cars, all lit in deep purple, vibrant blue, or dazzling white. Ethereal glass cities, flying vehicles, and monorails occupy the background, while the foreground is filled with transparent screens, retinal scanners, and impenetrably detailed computer interfaces. These images (and their associated ideas) echo over and over again, apparently vivid but dissuading any real interrogation of their detail. This homogeneity is also true of stock photography resources and (as they're trained on existing media) our emerging generative AI tools. Any search or prompt for anything "futuristic" yields the same old tropes, further cementing them into our collective imagination and restricting our ability to dream of anything new. It's curious that these images somehow still feel representative of the future, yet we've been stuck in these loops of thinking for decades. For example, the bipedal *Maschinenmensch* robots featured in Fritz Lang's *Metropolis* were created almost a century ago, yet they are barely distinguishable from the images of glossy humanoid robots that can be seen atop any number of contemporary articles about the rise of AI.

At its core, Could Futurism takes an inherently positive stance, largely viewing technology as an emancipatory force, enabling—above all things—some ill-defined notion of *progress*. It's become a highly visible and easily recognizable pillar in our collective perspective on the future, and for many people it represents the extent of their thinking. Could Futurism exists to show us alternative worlds, to build excitement, and to represent the momentum of ambition, and in one particular branch of the arts, it's found the ideal feedstock for its work.

SCIENCE FICTION

In 1963, the esteemed author Arthur C. Clarke declared that "a critical reading of science fiction is essential training for anyone wishing to look more than ten years ahead."

Well, I suppose he would, wouldn't he?

It's difficult to talk about Could Futurism without talking about science fiction, such is their intertwined and codependent nature. Many of the companies I've been a part of over the last twenty years gleefully embrace science fiction when describing the shape of the work they're undertaking, the products they're developing, or the intended outcomes they're seeking, but what is science fiction exactly, and why does it hold such a powerful force over popular futurism? We should probably begin by acknowledging that the term "science fiction" is something of an oxymoron: science is concerned with proof, facts, and testable, repeatable outcomes, whereas fiction is concerned with creativity, invention, and imagined situations. This is perhaps little more than a cute observation, but this oppositional duality is what can make science fiction incredibly interesting, engaging, and fun. It pokes at the status quo and imagines what else might happen, if only we could squeeze scientific truth into a new shape of our choosing.

It's actually quite difficult to cleanly define science fiction. It doesn't fit into a neat thematic bucket, and its boundaries are notoriously ill-defined and fuzzy, mingling with fantasy, fairy tale, and horror, and overlapping a little with the worlds of wizards, orcs, and warlocks. It's odd, for example, that we consider Luke Skywalker's landspeeder to be a piece of science fiction but Aladdin's flying carpet to be a work of fantasy. The two seem fairly similar, at least in principle. We shouldn't assume that science fiction is solely focused on the future either. Many key science fiction texts are set in alternate pasts, parallel versions of the present, or entirely nonterrestrial time frames. Regardless of this taxonomic uncertainty, science fiction literature has become incredibly popular, generating over half a billion dollars in revenue every year in the United States alone, and in some territories such as the UK, sales are growing significantly. In truth, these numbers are likely much higher, as science fiction has a vibrant culture of self-publication, and operates far below the radar of traditional industry analysis. Many literature critics turn their noses up at science fiction, often dismissing it as silly, niche, or escapist, but it remains wildly popular. Frank Herbert's 1965 science fiction epic, *Dune*, has sold in excess of 20 million copies, which is significantly more than Jane Austen's enduring classic *Pride and Prejudice*. Science fiction also plays a strong role in the much larger comic book industry, which now accounts for around $15.5 billion in yearly global sales. Both books and comics have played a major role in bringing science fiction to popular acclaim, but these industries pale into insignificance when compared with the most immersive, pervasive, and persuasive format of all: cinema.

It's curious that one of the world's earliest films—and certainly one of the earliest known moments of cinematic progress—is a work of science fiction. In 1902, George Méliès created *Le voyage dans la lune* (translated as *A Trip to the Moon*), a whimsical eighteen-minute adventure film that follows six members of a Parisian astronomy club on a mission to the lunar surface. The 1902 film may have no sound, but it's a joyful creation—a fast-paced hybrid of animation and stage play, complete with painted sets, jump cuts, acrobatics, and elaborate costumes, which makes the whole thing feel utterly charming and dreamlike. After its premiere, the film became a huge success in France and around the world, running uninterrupted at the Olympia music hall in Paris for several months and becoming a headline attraction at theaters in Germany, Canada, and Italy. *A Trip to the Moon* was so popular in the United States that it was copied (in acts of willful piracy) by other experimental filmmakers, including Thomas Edison, much to the disapproval of Méliès.

In the early years of mass-consumption cinema, science fiction films were often considered niche productions, with cheaply produced sets, questionable prosthetics, and low-grade special effects, but these B movies proved to be surprisingly popular with audiences. Pulpy titles such as *The Phantom Creeps*, *Zombies of the Stratosphere*, and *Flying Disc Man from Mars* featured at cinemas and drive-ins across America, and parallel sci-fi film industries quickly sprang up all across the globe. By the late 1950s, audiences were becoming more interested in scientific progress due to the post-war technology boom and the space race, resulting in a steady increase in the genre's popularity and associated box-office success. In the 1960s, the genre became cemented in mass culture with the release of films including *The Time Machine*, *Barbarella*, and Stanley Kubrick's masterpiece, *2001: A Space Odyssey*, quashing the notion of science fiction as a specialist niche art form and thrusting it into the spotlight of mainstream appeal. In the 1970s, science fiction took a decidedly bleak turn in parallel with the changing shape of global politics and public opinion. As audiences wrestled with the very real specters of stagflation, the Cold War, Watergate, multiple energy crises, and countless global conflicts, science fiction broadly followed suit with movies such as *The Omega Man*, *Westworld*, and *Soylent Green* . . . until a weird little space picture took everyone by surprise.

On May 1, 1977, the first public screening of *Star Wars: Episode IV—A New Hope* took place at Northpoint Theatre in San Francisco. Initial responses to test screenings had been muted, and the movie wasn't predicted to be much of a success. The board at Fox Studios weren't convinced that a Buck Rogers–style science fiction movie would fill theaters, so they decided to restrict the film's initial distribution in order to limit their losses. However, it quickly became clear that George Lucas had created something special. His simple tale of good versus evil set a long time ago in a galaxy far, far away proved to be hugely appealing to audiences desperate for some form of escape from the grim world outside. *Star Wars* made over $195 million in 1977, pulling in over four times as much as the second-place movie of that year, and in the process fundamentally transformed not just the position of science fiction within popular culture, but the very approach to crafting visual entertainment.

A few years before filming began on *A New Hope*, George Lucas discovered that the special effects department at Fox Studios was barely functional. He approached Douglas Trumbull, who was best known for creating the visual effects for *2001* and *Silent Running*, to help, but Trumbull was already committed to working on Steven Spielberg's *Close Encounters of the Third Kind* and instead suggested his assistant John Dykstra. Lucas and Dykstra gathered together a modest crew of college students, artists, and engineers in a warehouse located in Van Nuys, California, birthing a collective that became known as Industrial Light and Magic. The team worked tirelessly on all manner of visual effects for *Star Wars*, creating countless spacecraft, interior models, and props, and developing entirely new techniques to help the images on screen feel more vivid, believable, and engaging. The results were transformative, and ILM quickly established itself as the go-to team for science fiction realism, developing hundreds of scenes for classic movies including *E.T.*, *Back to the Future*, *Total Recall*, and *Jurassic Park*. The pioneering work of ILM cemented the role of visual effects in science fiction, and to this day these effects—driven by significant leaps in computation, animation, and rendering software—have contributed to the growth and popularity of the genre. The era of shaky sets, rubbery costumes, and crude models has now largely made way for photorealistic computer renderings, digital studio environments, and real-time CGI prosthetics, and science fiction productions now feel incredibly immersive, well resolved, and believable.

In recent years, sci-fi cinema has largely left its niche roots behind and evolved into the dominant cultural and economic powerhouse in Hollywood. Over the last decade, seven of the highest-grossing movies at the American box office have been science fiction films, which has both increased the reach of sci-fi ideas and encouraged the production of even more content. Advances in the production and distribution of this kind of content have also increased the prevalence of sci-fi shows on streaming channels like Netflix, Hulu, and Apple TV+. It's hardly surprising, then, that these productions have begun to dominate society's outlook on the future, embossing their stylistic choices and subjective obsessions into our collective consciousness and elbowing out other ideas in the process. The sheer cultural density of science fiction has undoubtedly exerted a gravitational pull on our imagination, shaping what the general population believes could be possible, what our priorities should be, and how the future will ultimately arrive.

THE ROOTS OF COULD FUTURISM

Nearly all creators of Utopia have resembled the man who has toothache, and therefore thinks that happiness consists in not having toothache.
—GEORGE ORWELL

As dominant as it is, science fiction isn't the sole cultural force fueling our appetite for Could Futurism. Throughout history, countless models, movements, and moments have cultivated a giddy optimism and insatiable desire to manifest the future driven by all things new. In reality, science fiction sits atop a much larger artistic and social movement that has fundamentally shifted the ways in which we think about the present and shaped how we view the future: the sprawling multidisciplinary phenomenon known as Modernism. It would be foolish to try to give an expansive treatise on the origins, scope, and effects of Modernism here, but let's at least try to hit the high points.

Until the nineteenth century, artistic expression (such as painting, music, theater, writing, sculpture, and architecture) was largely concerned with the servicing of deities, and artworks typically focused on representing or glorifying angels, gods, theistic characters, and stories from sacred texts or folkloric narratives. Following the Enlightenment (say, the eighteenth century give or take a few decades on either side) and the significant progress of technology, science, and industry brought about by the Victorian era (1837–1901), these attitudes and approaches began to gradually break down. An increasing number of radical critiques of the values and traditions of Western culture began to emerge, and the dominance of religious ideologies began to diminish, leading to a profound reexamination of the purpose, methods, and outputs of art.

As the nineteenth century made way for the twentieth, a new breed of artists, creators, and theorists began to emerge, with a desire to break with the past, reject established tradition, and push forward with human progress. At its heart, Modernism was interested in experimenting with technique as much as subject, and it's important to understand that "Modernism" represents a broad umbrella term—more of a mindset than a single aesthetic or movement. Monet's *Waterlilies* is an example of Impressionism and Picasso's *Guernica* is a work of Cubism, yet both are leading works of Modernism. What ties them together is a rejection of past traditions and techniques, and a steadfast focus on exploring the new.

While it's barely related to contemporary futurism, it's worth briefly mentioning a very particular form of Modernism here: Futurism—the version with a capital *F*. A little over a century ago, Italian design was dominated by a singular visual and architectural aesthetic, a variant of Art Nouveau known as *stile Liberty* (named somewhat curiously after the London department store), which revered Baroque opulence and warmly embraced lavish excesses of ornamentation. In 1908, in the outskirts of Milan, a neatly mustachioed Italian poet named Filippo Tommaso Marinetti crashed his car as he swerved to avoid two cyclists. Though he escaped serious injury, the accident left a profound impression on Marinetti, prompting him to question what he saw as the outdated, historically oriented designs of the day. Instead, he became obsessed with speed, technology, automobiles, airplanes, and the burgeoning industrial attitudes springing up across Europe, believing that these innovations offered humanity the means to bring about profound change in the world. In 1909, he published his first Futurist manifesto (one of many) on the front cover of the French newspaper *Le Figaro*. The sprawling thesis was a somewhat incendiary text that called for an end to art's relationship with the past; the destruction of museums, libraries, and academies; the glorification of war; the celebration of patriotism; and scorn for women. Over the following years, Marinetti and a growing number of followers published increasingly incendiary manifestos, and explored new techniques in painting, writing, sculpture, and music that celebrated the dynamism of movement found in both the natural and mechanical worlds.

The emergence of these Modernist ideals represented freedom from the clutches of conformity and tradition, which led to a subsequent explosion of creativity, expression, and sprawling thoughts about the future. Around the same time as Marinetti and his cohorts were laying out their Futurist manifesto, similar—but ideologically opposed—immersions in Couldness were happening in postrevolutionary Russia. Throughout the 1920s, the Constructivists—and particularly those in and around the legendary Vkhutemas art and technical school—were busying themselves by radically imagining what Soviet society could look like, now that all the rules had changed. The architect and artist Vladimir Tatlin created stunning plans for a huge, spiraling tower to be built from iron, glass, and steel in the city of Petrograd, a gargantuan endeavor that would have utterly dwarfed the Eiffel Tower. The monument was never built, but Tatlin's decidedly modern proposition set down the challenge for those who would follow. In 1921, Anton Lavinsky's "City on Springs" made the bold suggestion of elevating all buildings above the ground on sprung trusses. In 1928, the Vkhutemas student Georgii Krutikov took things even further with his thesis on "The City of the Future," offering up the sensational "Flying City," which placed living quarters in the sky and left all the work on the ground, with residents commuting between the two in personal flying capsules.

A little less fanciful, but equally influential, was another bastion of Modernism that emerged in the small German city of Weimar around the same time. The incredibly talented yet seemingly perpetually grumpy architect Walter Gropius had an ambition to create a multidisciplinary school that would unite arts and crafts with modern industrial techniques. In 1919, he created a place to do just that, which he named the Staatliches Bauhaus. What resulted was an arresting series of seminal projects, artworks, and products that embraced a forward-looking aesthetic characterized by simplicity, functionality, and the innovative use of materials. The output of the Bauhaus—comprising furniture, lighting, ceramics, graphic design, textiles, architecture, photography, and typography—forms a backbone to the ways in which many of these disciplines are taught to this day, and the Bauhaus principles of material honesty and formal purity can be seen in everything from industrial design to architecture and software development.

Throughout the twentieth century, Modernist ideals became more formalized, widespread, and normalized. Architects including Le Corbusier, Oscar Niemeyer, and Frank Lloyd Wright created stunning new buildings—often incredibly engineered structures wrought from highly technical materials—that introduced new forms of construction and created new spaces for living. Authors such as Virginia Woolf, Bertolt Brecht, and James Joyce embraced the creative freedoms that came from Modernism, writing novels and plays that broke from traditional structures and linguistic norms. Similarly, the bold graphic styles created by the Soviet Constructivists led to huge shifts in graphic design, including the introduction of typographic grids, sans serif fonts, and rule-breaking asymmetric layouts.

Modernist themes also found themselves welcomed in the worlds of cinema, dance, design, sculpture, photography, and philosophy, and Modernism has become the defining expressive characteristic of our time. The sprawling, algorithmically generated visions of architects such as Rem Koolhaas, Frank Gehry, and Zaha Hadid, the exploratory, experimental music of Kraftwerk, Brian Eno, and Aphex Twin, the huge sculptures of Anish Kapoor, Antony Gormley, and Olafur Eliasson, and the products of Apple, Muji, Vitra, IKEA, Dyson, and Braun all owe a huge debt of gratitude to the emergence of the Modernist mindset.

Modernism effectively set the table for Could Futurism, creating a population well attuned to radical ideas about the future, the rejection of the old in favor of the new, and a desire to move forward in some continual state of *progress*. At its core, Modernism represented a rejection of duty to the ideas of the past, which freed up significantly more time to look forward. In parallel, it encouraged experimentation and eagerly rushed toward the warm embraces of technology, science, and industrialism. The explorations of Modernists undoubtedly shaped the design and art of a generation, but perhaps its most powerful legacy is how it taught us to *think*. It bred in all of us the notion of newness as a positive attribute, particularly newness driven by technological and scientific advancement. Science fiction was one outcome of this seismic shift in our way of thinking—which set the benchmark for how a great many of us view the future—but the thematic ideals of Modernism also extended beyond art and design and into industry and government, where they began to shape ideas about authority, science, nationalism, and urbanization. Companies and governments alike grew keen to share their forward-looking, technologically driven visions of the future with the public to assert their positions at the forefront of technological progress and bring people together to champion the achievements of their nation.

COULD FUTURISM IN PUBLIC

Public celebrations of technical prowess have been around for a surprisingly long time, acting as a means to celebrate technological breakthroughs, promote the manufacturing capabilities of a region, or simply to beat a patriotic chest. Back in 1791, Prague hosted the first World's Fair, which invited people to come together to marvel at the sophistication of Bohemian industry. France too has a history of hosting gatherings celebrating its own industrial aptitude, culminating in the French Industrial Exposition of 1844 in Paris. In 1851, the first World Expo was held in the Crystal Palace in London under the rather pompous title "The Great Exhibition of the Works of Industry of All Nations." The Great Exhibition, as it's more often called, was an extraordinary undertaking that ran for over five months, received guests including Karl Marx, Michael Faraday, Charlotte Brontë, Charles Dickens, and Lewis Carroll, and had the world's first soft drink, Schweppes, as its official sponsor. Aside from shining a spotlight on existing industrial capabilities, events such as the Great Exhibition also served to show the public what might be coming next, often in immersive and energetic detail. In 1939, New York City hosted a World's Fair, an event that expressly focused on themes of social progress through technology and aimed to lift public spirits following the economic shock of the Great Depression. Alongside the usual array of national pavilions celebrating the output of individual countries were a number of dedicated zones featuring the technical and commercial achievements of the day and vivid depictions of the future. In the center of the Transportation Zone sat the General Motors pavilion, an expansive installation that

General Motors—Futurama—Artists standing among models of buildings (Manuscripts and Archives Division, The New York Public Library. "General Motors—Futurama—Artists standing among models of buildings," New York Public Library Digital Collections. Accessed January 12, 2025. https://digitalcollections.nypl.org/items/5e66b3e9-26b9-d471-e040-e00a180654d7)

included *Futurama*, a huge model of a future city that attracted over 30,000 people per day and became one of the major attractions of the event.

The creation of the exhibit was led by the esteemed designer Norman Bel Geddes, who had begun his career designing stage sets for theater productions in Los Angeles and New York, before turning his hand to domestic product design. His subsequent concepts for streamlined vehicles, elegant ships, and Modernist architecture largely defined the aesthetic language of the 1930s and clearly caught the eye of executives at General Motors, who commissioned him to create their exhibit for the fair. *Futurama* presented the corporation's futuristic vision of an America built—unsurprisingly—around the automobile. The diorama they created was absolutely vast, covering over an acre with more than 500,000 individually designed buildings, a million trees of thirteen different species, and approximately 50,000 model cars. It presented a world where every landscape challenge could be overcome with humanity's ingenuity, where people were brought together through a sprawling network of expressways that connected every corner of the nation into one cohesive whole. Technology—primarily in the shape of the automobile and the freeway—once again played its favorite role as the great enabler, feeding the imaginations of the attendant crowds, whose moving seats trundled high above the model, giving them a god's-eye view of the future laid out below, and unfurling a long list of "coulds" before their very eyes.

Presentations and immersive experiences such as *Futurama* defined and then cemented a way of thinking about the future for a large proportion of the American population. The future became a place for brave imagination, a place for lofty dreams, audacious visions, and idealistic expressions, a new world created through unwavering optimism and the transformative application of new technologies. From the mid-1950s to the mid-1960s, the United States experienced a significant increase in this kind of future positivity, largely driven by its postwar economic boom. In parallel, progressions in automation, materials science, and engineering were also accelerated by America's role in the space race and the formation of NASA in 1958.

In the same year, the ingenious American designer and illustrator Arthur Radebaugh launched a comic strip titled "Closer Than We Think!" that was featured in publications owned by the *Chicago Tribune–New York News* network, and found an audience of around 19 million readers at its peak. Every Sunday, families across the country marveled at his beautifully illustrated designs for solar-powered cars, jetpack mailmen, warehouses staffed by robots, and undersea freeways, each accompanied by a small paragraph of explanatory text extolling the virtues of that week's particular miracle. The overriding tone of these images was one of possibility and productivity, which presented technology as the great unlocking force leading the nation toward a brighter tomorrow. Similarly, the exquisitely named Athelstan Spilhaus also created a comic strip in 1958 that found its way into over a hundred newspapers across the United States. Spilhaus was an oceanographer and geophysicist, but he had an ambition to make scientific knowledge fun and accessible for children, to explain how things worked and, importantly, what technology might enable in the future. When he met President Kennedy in 1962, JFK told him, "The only science I ever learned was from your comic strip." The possibilities of America's technological future seemed boundless, and this mindset folded directly into a culture concurrently embracing mass media in the forms of radio, TV, and cinema.

In 1962, the animation studio Hanna-Barbera released *The Jetsons*, a frothy animated sitcom set in 2062 that closely mirrored the studio's prehistoric hit, *The Flintstones*. The show featured a traditional nuclear family living in Orbit City, a sprawling metropolis of malls, walkways, and towering buildings constructed in the late 1950s Googie aesthetic. Each episode of *The Jetsons* pitched a vision of the future dominated by convenience and leisure, enabled by countless magical machines, technological wonders, and elaborate contraptions. The family patriarch, George, worked for just one hour a day, two days a week, while his wife, Jane, looked after the kids, shopped, and cooked the family dinners. The series was the first show on ABC to be broadcast in color, and it proved to be a hit with audiences. Although only twenty-four episodes were produced in 1962, *The Jetsons* had a profound impact on public perceptions of the future, and the original series remains a touchstone for many futurists and innovators today. A second and a very short third season were produced more than twenty years later, along with an ill-fated feature-length movie in 1990. The franchise finally ended with the 2017 film *The Jetsons & WWE: Robo-WrestleMania!*, which nobody seems to talk about very much.

Three years after the Jetsons' debut, Irwin Allen launched

Lost in Space, a reimagining of the 1812 novel *The Swiss Family Robinson* that featured a family adrift in deep space, battling alien foes with ray guns, gadgets, and their trusty robot companion, Robby. The following year, Gene Roddenberry introduced the world to *Star Trek*, a weekly TV series that featured similarly escapist notions of interstellar travel, robotics, alternate societies, and automation, which proved so popular that the franchise continues to thrive to this day. Inevitably, this type of media found its way further afield, gracing screens both big and small, and filling the pages of magazines and newspapers across the world. The entertainment created during this period ultimately formed the bedrock temperament for audiences worldwide, solidifying the future as a place brimming with boundless potential, a place of possibility and change driven by innovation, where new models of society and civilization could thrive.

This golden era of Could Futurism is perhaps best exemplified by the launch of a huge project of immense ambition that attempted to bring science fiction, entertainment, and experiential futures together into a single, inhabitable whole. Walt Disney's Experimental Prototype Community of Tomorrow aimed to take the narrative ambitions of science fiction and make them real, creating a city of the future known acronymically as EPCOT.

From the outset, the EPCOT project represented an immense piece of optimistic imagination, a complex and ambitious hybrid of World's Fair, science fiction fantasy, and utopianist dream. In the late 1950s, Walt Disney was flying high; he'd created masterpieces including *Snow White*, *Pinocchio*, *Dumbo*, and *Bambi*—but he wanted more. He wanted to produce something more than entertainment, more than theme parks, more than cartoons. Walt Disney wanted to be remembered in the same breath as Henry Ford, and to do something that really changed people's lives. It was during this period that he famously quipped, "Fancy being remembered around the world for the invention of a mouse." Following the success of Disneyland, Walt and his team received accolades not only for its entertainment value, but also for the design and planning of the site. Emboldened by this success, Walt began developing an epic new project, scoping out an opportunity with the insurance and real-estate tycoon John D. MacArthur, who had a vast 6,000-acre tract of land for sale in Palm Beach, Florida. This allowed Walt's imagination to run wild. He planned to use 400 acres of the plot for a new theme park and the rest for a "city of tomorrow"—an idyllic pastoral land where children could play out in the open, a community free from crime, poverty, and traffic. It was to be Walt's crowning achievement: a futuristic, idealistic, autocratic company town.

Unfortunately for Walt, the MacArthur deal fell through. Roy Disney (Walt's brother, and the financial head of the organization) objected to the surrounding residents and businesses profiting from Disney's success, and when he attempted to negotiate for additional land as a buffer, the Palm Beach deal was scrapped. By 1963, Walt and his team were deeply involved in designing multiple attractions for the 1964 World's Fair in New York, but Harrison Price (a research economist at Disney) continued to look for suitable locations for Walt's dream, scoping out plots in Washington,

DC, Baltimore, and New Jersey. Later that year, while flying over the swamps of Orlando, Walt declared that this would be the place to bring his utopian dream to life. In the following months, his team began secretly buying up vast areas of land, eventually amassing over 27,000 acres—twice the size of Manhattan—and soon enough the secret was out.

By 1965, the first plans began to appear from a development team led by Marvin Davis, the legendary mastermind behind the layout of Disneyland. The site would be split into three parts: a theme park to the north, the world's first operational jet airport to the south, and Walt's enormous planned community in the center. Designed to be home for around 20,000 residents, EPCOT would cover 5,000 acres and be a little over three miles in diameter. Built around the same hub-and-spoke design used for Disneyland, the city would separate traffic into three layers. The first two would be subterranean, with trucks and freight on the bottom and cars on the floor above. At surface level, priority would be given to pedestrians, and above them the entire city would be connected by elevated monorails and automated people movers. At the center of the city would be a huge, air-conditioned urban center to house businesses and commercial outlets, with the thirty-story Cosmopolitan Hotel towering at its hub. Disney's utopian ambitions stretched even further than the physical design and architecture of the city, aiming to also shape the community and social structures of the residents. No one would own land or homes in EPCOT, and no one would have municipal voting rights. All adults living in the city would be employed at the theme park, the shopping center, the airport, or the Disney Industrial Area, a business facility intended to house offices for corporations including GE, Westinghouse, and Monsanto. The entire property would operate on a bespoke communications network called WEDCOMM—something akin to an analog internet—that would be constructed and operated by RCA.

As the plans for the Florida site took shape, it became evident that Walt's true passion lay not in the theme park but in EPCOT. In October 1966, he commissioned the construction of a scale model of the city, and produced two films in which he talked about the vision in his friendly and approachable "Uncle Walt" style. Standing proudly in front of vast aerial illustrations in a neat gray suit and black tie, he proclaimed, "EPCOT will always be a showcase to the world for the ingenuity and imagination of American free enterprise." This was to be the crowning achievement of Walt Disney's vision for America—an idyllic city built upon family values, a blueprint community of tomorrow that would continually evolve and innovate long into the future.

However, on December 15, 1966, aged just sixty-five, Walt Disney succumbed to lung cancer and died. Shortly afterward, his brother Roy announced that the company would scrap the EPCOT effort. When the Walt Disney Resort opened on October 1, 1971, EPCOT was nowhere to be seen. Three years later, the EPCOT project was revived by the Disney organization, but since its opening in 1982, it has been something of a confused mess, operating somewhere between an educational entertainment venue, a contemporary World's Fair, a technology showcase, and a movie-franchised theme park—a far cry from Walt's utopian city of the future. In the early 1990s the Walt Disney Company announced the construction of a small town called Celebration on the original Florida site, a planned community that employs some of Walt's original ideas but represents only a tiny slice of his ambitious EPCOT vision. Disney's attempts to not only conceive of a bold vision of the future but also to usher it into existence are perhaps admirable, but the failure to achieve this conversion—even with the political, financial, and societal momentum of an organization like Disney—starkly underscores how expansive the chasm between ambition and reality can be. In spite of this, grand, immersive public visions of the future continue to prove enduringly popular, either as a means to champion the transformational power of technology, or for elected leaders to fan the flames of national pride.

•

In 1994, the British prime minister John Major and his Conservative government began making plans to mark the nation's transition into the twenty-first century. Major's team conceived of a somewhat modest affair intended to showcase the historical achievements of the United Kingdom, champion its present-day capabilities, and cement its role in the future. Just as with the 1951 Festival of Britain, the centerpiece of the event would be housed within a large dome, and the architect Richard Rogers began drawing up plans for a site on the banks of the River Thames. However, in 1997, a general election saw Major's government ignominiously ousted from power by Tony Blair's Labour Party, which won more than double the number of seats of the Conservatives and shuffled the priorities of the UK.

Blair was comparatively young for a prime minister, and his dynamic and image-savvy approach to leadership represented something of a new direction for Britain. Keen to mark the end of eighteen years of Conservative rule and the start of a new chapter for the country, he began looking for opportunities to redefine Britain's role in the rapidly changing world. He radically expanded the scope and funding of the original celebratory project, and soon afterward construction of the Millennium Dome began. From the outset, the project struggled to capture the imagination of a cynical British public, and it rapidly became a symbol of what many saw as Blair's out-of-touch and overly optimistic "New Labour" outlook. Once completed, the Dome comprised fourteen distinct zones grouped into three grandiose collections named "Who We Are," "What We Do," and "Where We Live." Each zone featured displays, sculptures, and immersive experiences intended to illustrate Britain's commercial prowess and glittering future, but in order to reduce the financial burden on the public each exhibit was also co-funded by a major industrial group, leading to that uniquely grim cocktail of artistic expression, government oversight, and corporate sponsorship. Visitors were treated by the Mind Zone, sponsored by BAE Systems and Marconi; the McDonald's "Our Town Story" exhibit; and the Learning Zone, brought to you by Tesco. You get the idea.

I somehow found myself with a free ticket to the Millennium Dome in the spring of 2000, so I took a train to Greenwich to see what all the fuss was about. What I found was an underwhelming and ramshackle collection of corporate fantasies and promotional material jumbled together in a huge, drafty tent, with small groups of people milling about, looking for something interesting to do. The Dome attracted barely half of the 12 million forecasted visitors—significantly fewer than had attended the original Festival of Britain—and the project is widely regarded as a spectacular failure. When it closed at the end of the year, the original exhibition elements were either sold or dismantled (with much of the content shipped to Disney World), and the Dome was repurposed as a live music venue, a far cry from the "beacon to the world" that Tony Blair had originally promised.

Perhaps the most recent attempt to create an immersive public futures experience is the Museum of the Future in Dubai, a glittering government-sponsored project whose website confidently proclaims, "This is where the future lives." The large, eye-shaped building sits proudly on the fourteen-lane Sheikh Zayed Road and features oversized Arabic calligraphy carved into its exterior. As an architectural achievement it's undoubtedly impressive, but its contents are surprisingly drab and disappointingly familiar. The building has six floors of exhibits, and the museum owners claim that each "is like a film set from a future that you can inhabit, explore, and interact with." The top three levels focus on immersive environments, the first of which is a classic space fantasy that transports visitors to a base on Mars in 2071 complete with robots, holodecks, and virtual spacesuit fitting rooms. The second level purports to explore the natural future of Earth, and the third is a somewhat bizarre exploration of the future of wellness. Each of these spaces appears to be more an expression of science fiction aesthetics than anything else, filled with projected animations, interactive lighting displays, and thousands of glowing LEDs, which seem less like a genuine public exploration of the future and more geared toward offering up enticing backdrops for Instagram posts. Following these three immersive levels, the museum descends into familiar technocratic territory, featuring all the usual whizzbang candidates we've all seen a thousand times before: robots, delivery drones, automated vehicles, jetpacks, and cyberdogs—a disappointing parade of the same old escapist "coulds" over which we are supposed to coo and swoon with very little exploration of "whys" or "hows."

After more than two centuries of attempting to engage the public in meaningful discussions about the future through such such installations and ambitious projects, it seems we are collectively unable to deliver anything beyond escapist fantasies or experiential extensions of the science fiction entertainment industry. The Museum of the Future is more representative of something deeply rooted and deeply depressing about our culture, but I can't figure out which is worse: that those in positions of leadership and power think that such mediocre and repetitive pablum is interesting and stimulating, or that the public appears to agree. It seems that engaging the public in meaningful, rigorous conversations about the future remains out of reach, but what's more concerning is that the escapist, bombastic tropes of this kind of Could Futurism continue to find a welcome home in professional circles. The same messages, mindsets, and obsessions we see in these entertaining but shallow public experiences have been injected into boardrooms, strategy sessions, conferences, and planning meetings, and have ultimately shaped the ways in which each and every one of us thinks about our collective future.

COMMERCIAL COULD FUTURISM

Here's my advice: any time anyone tells you what something could *do, ask them why it isn't.*
—TOBIAS REVELL

In contemporary industry, the hub of any piece of Could Futurism is often occupied by a single individual who takes the role of storyteller, visionary, commentator, pundit, or provocateur. Many Could Futurists actively cultivate a reputation for bold recklessness; indeed, they often luxuriate in moments of performative temerity and integrate it deep within their personal brands. They're mostly self-employed, and many of them have built impressive empires and amassed armies of devotees through strident essays, energetic public appearances, and stirring posts on social media. One example of such a character is David Shing—he prefers that his followers call him Shingy—who for many years held the role of "digital prophet" for the fading internet giant AOL. Shingy made a name for himself in the early 2000s as an edgy character with big, back-combed hair, painted nails, and statement spectacles who frequently appeared onstage at public events to talk about the future (and presumably AOL's role within it). It's easy to mock futurists like Shingy—indeed, many people do—but he's representative of the kinds of characters who appear to be enduringly popular in commercial circles. If you've been to any kind of conference about technology or the future, you've no doubt come across them. Having marched confidently out onto the stage, dressed in the T-shirt-and-suit-jacket uniform of the professional public speaker, they wait for the lights to dim, steeple their fingers in messianic contemplation, and pause for silence before making a single, provocative statement.

The content produced by such characters can be genuinely engaging, acting like an inspirational sugar rush and flooding audiences with futuristic endorphins. It works well projected onto huge screens, and often features eye-watering statistics, bombastic future ideas, and renderings of incredible imagined worlds. At the end of a packed agenda filled with hours of presentations and speeches, Could Futurists are often brought in to help things end on a high note, offering a juicy, thought-provoking jolt to wake audiences up in time for the canapés and cocktails. It's titillating, escapist stuff, and at its core it's good entertainment. The captivating tone of this work hasn't been missed by our media either, and you've undoubtedly seen these people in any number of documentaries about the future. You've seen them standing with their arms folded in the middle of Tokyo's Shibuya Crossing, crowds swarming all around them. You've followed them through polytunnel greenhouses as they run their fingers through hydroponic crops in slow motion. You've seen them standing next to scientists in huge laboratories, nodding along sagely while their narration rides over the inspirational music soaring in the background, and you've listened to their heartfelt monologues about the future, delivered from the top of a sand dune at sunset, just before the credits roll.

The ambition of this kind of work is purportedly to inspire an audience, to feed uplifting ideas into brains and exciting images into eyeballs. It's often framed as aiming to "start a conversation," but it rarely goes very far beyond the headlines or deals with any irksome, gnarly practicalities. The professional Could Futurist also has a knack for christening novel technologies, phenomena, or mindsets, often by creating buzzy rhyming couplets or viral brands to sum up complex ideas, technologies, or movements. The veteran onstage futurist Faith Popcorn (born Faith Plotkin), who claims to have a "documented 95 percent accuracy rate" in her predictions, has a long legacy of producing such things, introducing the world to neologisms such as "cocooning," "AtmosFear," "anchoring," "99 Lives," "icon toppling," and the "vigilante consumer." This kind of pithiness might seem simplistic and reductive, and more than a bit daft, but it is quite a bit harder than it may seem, and it regularly brings these Could Futurists into contact with broader media outlets beyond the worlds of science, engineering, or technology. Whenever a future-focused story makes its way into the news cycle, they're often called upon to act as pundits or commentators, which gives them a great platform to proffer outlandish statements about how things could be radically different if only we were able to unleash a particular capability. When people say, "We were promised flying cars," these are typically the people doing the promising.

Could Futurism also dominates the world of trade shows, those cacophonous orgies of energetic capitalism that are held annually in vast, drafty hangars constructed for such things. These events exist primarily for manufacturers and suppliers to meet with customers and clients, with the former doing whatever they can to attract the latter. Given their inherent chaos—where time and attention are precious commodities to be fought over—stallholders have long experimented with "curb appeal" techniques designed to catch the eye of hurried attendees. Until disappointingly recently, this mostly revolved around sex. Many exhibitors relied on the tried-and-true tactic of hiring scantily clad young women—euphemistically known as "booth babes"—to drape themselves over the products on display in an attempt to attract an audience of lusty buyers and journalists who were, historically, almost always male. Thankfully, this practice is declining, but it's been broadly replaced by Could Futurism—images, models, animations, and videos of energetic manifestations of the future, which thrust audaciously out of exhibition stands and beckon passersby with their striking appearance and sexy curves.

This is perhaps nowhere more prevalent than at the apex predator of technology trade events, the Consumer Electronics Show, which takes place amid the razzle-dazzle of Las Vegas every January. As expansive as it is exhausting, CES is a vast affair that sprinkles every conceivable gadget, device, and nascent technology over 2 million square feet of carpeted exhibition hall, with each manufacturer vying for its share of customers, clients, and column inches. The competitive nature of such a show—which in 2025 featured over four thousand exhibitors—means that companies are constantly seeking something enticing to draw people in. Something outlandish—preferably something brightly lit and moving—can capture the eyes of passersby, just as the neon signs outside draw people from the highway into the casinos. At a show like CES you'll see all sorts of movies, simulations, models, and prototypes leering out of the exhibition stands, trumpeting the latest technological trends and hoping to grab the attention of the exhausted punters ambling past. NFT smartwatches, blockchain cameras, ironing boards with AI, couches with VR, autonomous lawn mowers, facial recognition kettles, 3D-printed makeup . . . it doesn't really matter, as long as it's something surprising, engaging, or arresting. Unfortunately, this type of content begins to dominate how the show feels to those in attendance, elevating these garish propositions to headline status and creating an impression of maturity that barely exists beyond the pantomime. Perhaps more concerningly, this content often reaches outside the show itself, offering up engaging images for news crews to point their cameras at before presenters begin their coverage. As such, they often become the driving narrative of the event and begin to represent how we collectively view the state and direction of consumer technology. CES exists in the public eye largely through the lens of Could Futurism, represented by extreme, whimsical, and experimental work, as opposed to the more grounded, normal, everyday fare that is stashed away in the back of almost every stand, and probably represents the vast majority of products at the show.

Another example of Could Futurism you're probably familiar with is the concept car, which—given the shift toward automation and electrification in recent years—has also started to appear at CES. Concept cars present themselves as directional rather than intentional, and feature technologies that reach beyond the presently achievable. Rolling doors, holographic in-car entertainment systems, spherical tires, hydrogen fuel cells, color-changing bodywork, biometric sensors, and onboard drones conjure up a world of unbridled creativity in which the possibilities of imagination are allowed to run free. While these vehicles appear gorgeously well-resolved, almost all concept cars are models instead of functioning vehicles. Under the paint, fabric, and plastic wrap, they're impressively artisanal creations, often hewn from clay that's been pushed, scraped, and carved into enticing new forms by huge teams of skilled craftspeople. Hundreds of hours of precision model making are sunk into every concept-car project in a simulation exercise designed to convince the viewer of a level of engineering maturity that doesn't actually exist. These figureheads purportedly exist to help an automotive brand describe where it's headed and the principles it cares about, to test new ideas with potential customers, and to act as a means to explore new territories. At least that's the theory. In practice, they largely function as thirst traps. Seductive futuristic pornography designed to drive clicks and draw crowds rather than to define or display any meaningful product development efforts. These models of future vehicles or exotic devices can be compelling in themselves, sitting on plinths or podiums under bright spotlights, but manufacturers have learned that presenting a future idea within a story can help bring it to life and in the process make it significantly more appealing. Even at the earliest consumer trade shows, attractive actors were often paid to walk through carefully scripted sequences, swooning over refrigerators, washing machines, and kitchen appliances that boasted incredible new features (as teams of stagehands pulled levers, activated lights, and pushed secret doors from within).

As film and television technologies improved and became more available, these live performances could be captured and presented elsewhere as news, editorial content, or promotional material, complete with plummy voice-overs explaining what was going on and why it deserved your attention. In 1956, General Motors commissioned the director Victor Solow to produce a short film for Motorama, their traveling annual show. The piece, titled *Design for Dreaming*, is a whimsical, extended musical number that follows a young woman (portrayed by the dancer Tad Tadlock) who is magically whisked from her bedroom to the glitzy exhibition by a masked man in a tuxedo. After swooning over new Corvettes, Pontiacs, Oldsmobiles, and Buicks, our heroine inexplicably finds herself wearing an apron, and is transported into the Frigidaire Kitchen of the Future. This portion of the movie is pure fantasy, with a stage set that features card-operated computers, automated cake bakers, ultrasonic dishwashers, and so much "push-button magic" that our leading lady is "free to have fun around the clock." This short film has become a cult classic, and is a precursor to what became known as a "vision video," an enticing form of media that includes elements of storytelling, prototyping, advertising, brand building, prediction, and prophecy. Though the objects and technologies in these visions were almost always nonfunctional models—brought to life through clever stagecraft and visual effects techniques from the science fiction movie industry—they proved to be incredibly powerful and incredibly useful. Given the complex, capital-intensive nature of computer product development, the vision video became a particularly valuable tool for the tech titans of the 1980s and 1990s. Companies such as IBM, HP, Sun Microsystems, and even notoriously tight-lipped Apple spent significant sums of money crafting future visions of productivity, entertainment, and communication. These short clips—made to feel like movie scenes or advertising reels—showed what a new product might look like, how it might work, and what it might do. This allowed companies to test their thinking with internal teams or focus groups to gauge interest in an idea before committing to costly and time-consuming product development.

Today, the vision video is so prevalent and pervasive that it's evolved into a genre of its own, with familiar tropes, structures, and narrative conventions. Vision videos typically adopt a problem-and-solution format, showing how future technology might deliver a timely and satisfying answer to a familiar and relatable question. As a result, they are almost always focused on some form of productivity and are typically centered on notions of simplicity, convenience, and performance. They're neat, tidy, and self-contained—or what the futurist Scott Smith describes as "flat-pack futures": easily assembled visions that follow a simple set of basic instructions and yield broadly similar outcomes. Thanks to the increasing availability of video capture, postproduction, and editing tools, it's never been simpler to add an animated screen to a model, to prototype an app with impressive fidelity, or to create photorealistic products with CGI. Social media channels (in particular video platforms like YouTube, Vimeo, and TikTok) have also allowed vision videos to spread far and wide. Even small companies can now produce compelling and convincing vision videos showing where they dream of heading and what they might make in the coming years. When done well, a vision video can be an effective way to present your company as forward-thinking, invested in the future, and creative, yet all too often they simply reflect internal organizational fantasies or attempts to drum up interest in a brand or a product through the creation of science fiction–inflected tidbits.

Could Futurism is without doubt the most familiar and broadly consumed of our four branches of futurism. It comprises a highly effective arsenal of tools for attracting an audience, for getting people to sit up and listen, to click, to engage, and to comment. It isn't dry and dull like science papers or technical reviews. It offers an inviting hand, it tells us engaging stories, and it wows us. It focuses on improvement, betterment, progress, optimization, audacity, and augmentation, proposing and illustrating staggering improvements in the things we care about. Once you recognize the tropes of Could Futurism, you can't stop noticing it. It's everywhere, it's viral, and it requires very little technical knowledge to engage with. This is its core strength, but it's also a considerable and often overlooked weakness. Could Futurism can be ephemeral, momentary, and simple to dismiss. It exists in a hopeful dreamworld, and can be naive and willfully positive in unhelpful ways, masking huge levels of complexity that lurk just below its thin skin. It can feel unattainable—and is often created with that ambition—resulting in a gnawing feeling of the future being perpetually "over there" somewhere, a faraway land filled with breathtaking technologies, impossible ambitions, and mythical heroes.

HEROIC FUTURES AND BACKGROUND TALENT

*We can see your future—and you're looking
so good in your Levi's®.*
—MARKETING EMAIL

Contemporary Could Futurism typically finds its roots in a piece of emergent technology, a new scientific discovery, or an intriguing new way of thinking, but in order to grab an audience it requires some form of storytelling. Indeed, there's a strong argument that all futures work represents an act of storytelling, because the future doesn't actually exist yet. We can't touch the future. We can't pick it up, turn it over in our hands, or feel its weight, so instead we find ourselves telling stories.

Whether presented as a movie, a novel, a stage play, a proposal, a demo, or a vision video, a story can help an audience understand what a new idea represents, where it might point, what it might look like once completed, or what it might help them achieve. But the act of storytelling brings its own baggage to the process, and whenever anyone tells a story, they naturally find themself falling into some sort of framework. Through our education and experience, we're all aware that a good story needs a beginning, a middle, and an end, or some sort of act structure to follow. There needs to be an issue, problem, or conflict to drive tension, and some way of illustrating how the problem might be altered, overcome, or solved. There needs to be some sort of arc or evolution, and perhaps an underlying moment of reflection. The story also needs a time and a location, and perhaps most importantly it needs characters. Throughout history, almost every conceivable character has been created, including nonhuman or even nonsentient beings, but in the output of Could Futurists, one character consistently looms large: the hero.

Since before the development of recorded language, every generation has shared stories that feature heroes. Norse mythology relished its tales of Hothbrodd, who killed Odin's son Balder, the Romans had brave prince Aeneas, who defended his city against the Greeks, and as a teenager I had John McClane, who freed Nakatomi Plaza from the grip of the criminal mastermind Hans Gruber. Heroes are a wonderful, enticing, and energizing concoction. They help us imagine just how significant the impact of a single person can be. They give us someone to cheer for, a focus for our aspirations, and perhaps someone to learn from, but heroic tales can be more than a little formulaic. Over time, countless academics, psychoanalysts, narratologists, and literature theorists have picked over our innumerable heroic works to uncover a series of eerily recurrent patterns. In 1871, the anthropologist Edward Burnett Tylor explored the origins of myth and religion and highlighted commonalities in human storytelling. In 1936, Lord Raglan (Fitzroy Somerset) defined twenty-two common traits of god-heroes in *The Hero:*

A Study in Tradition, Myth, and Drama. In 1949, Joseph Campbell introduced the concept of the "monomyth" to describe a universal narrative framework that suggested that all mythic stories are variations of a single, archetypal structure. Today, this enduring idea is more broadly known as the "hero's journey," a model for heroic storytelling that we've all encountered and that feels comfortable and familiar.

The first act of any heroic tale is typically some sort of call to action—some visitation from a messenger or the acknowledgment of a significantly problematic issue (a bomb on a bus, a kidnapped child, or a treacherous monster, for example). The second act is defined by a significant test, some seemingly insurmountable issue that the hero must dig deep within themselves to solve (defusing the bomb, rescuing the child, or slaying the monster). The third act of the cycle is marked by some form of return, where the hero comes home with a changed heart (reuniting with an estranged partner, learning the true meaning of family, or finding personal redemption). Not all heroic tales repeat this pattern exactly, but they certainly tread in similar steps.

One place where these archetypal heroes exist in abundance is in works of science fiction. From Ellen Ripley and John Anderton to Han Solo, Katniss Everdeen, Sarah Connor, John Carter, Marty McFly, Princess Leia, Captain Kirk, Buck Rogers, and Tony Stark, the list of strapping sci-fi heroes is almost endless. Just as with all heroic tales, these characters typically find themselves in extreme situations and use technology (or their superhuman abilities) to achieve an outsize impact or resolution. As science fiction plays such a dominant role in the Could Futurism mindset, the products, situations, and societies proposed by Could Futurists also become awkwardly encumbered by heroism. Their vision videos, future concepts, and hypothetical propositions often feel grandiose and eye-widening, featuring characters and situations that feel utterly alien to the vast majority of us. If asked to render the future of VR, for example, Could Futurists tend to gravitate toward imagery that features beautiful architects developing plans for vast, towering skyscrapers, neurosurgeons performing infinitely complex brain procedures, or propulsion engineers spinning three-dimensional diagrams of jet engines around in cavernous clean rooms. Their lead characters sit in spotless laboratories using glossy white robots to squeeze pipettes into petri dishes, working hard to discover cures for cancer or creating new sources of energy. Their impossibly attractive families live in expansive penthouses and laugh together while cooking dinner with gorgeous grandparents in spotless kitchens. These characters and the lives they lead are aspirational, impressive, and motivational, but these are not the ordinary people we see when we look in the mirror: they're who we'd *like* to be. In truth, their lives are largely irrelevant to us and represent little more than escapist Walter Mitty fantasies.

Put more bluntly, they're *myths*, because that's just not how the world works. These are not the people who will use these future products, and these are not the things they will do with them. If we look at the facts, around 13 percent of US households currently have at least one VR headset; they can't all be designing cities, performing surgery, or developing jet engines. Indeed, according to recent studies, around 70 percent of them are playing games and the rest are watching YouTube. And it's not just the people in these future visions who feel mythic; the products that Could Futurism gravitates toward also represent heroic expressions of achievement. The concept vehicles that dominate our auto shows aren't sensible family SUVs or affordable hatchbacks; they're almost always sports cars or high-end luxury vehicles. When we're shown the future of emerging devices, we're not shown midrange stuff or affordable products for teens; we're almost always shown professional-grade, best-in-class devices delivering the highest possible performance.

While it's tempting to think about the future as a transformative place filled with heroic technologies, idealized families, and game-changing executives, it's likely to be much more humdrum than that. Just look around you. Look in your tote bags, your glove compartments, your cupboards, and your kitchen drawers. Look at what you bought on Amazon last month, look at your credit card receipts, look in the cardboard boxes in your basement or spare room. Our world is filled with—indeed is *dominated by*—ordinary, everyday, middle-of-the-road things. Every year, organizations hand out countless marketing, engineering, design, and enterprise awards for humdrum things like air-conditioning units, trash cans, spectacles, and fish-finger packaging. Toyota's revenue is four times as large as Ferrari's, Kimberly-Clark has become a more valuable company through selling diapers and toilet paper than Prada has by selling high-end fashion, and in 2024, the global market for socks reached over $49 billion—more than double the value of the VR market.

Of course, it's understandable why people would choose to portray the very best version of their idea, why they would deliberately feature unusually successful characters, and why they would illustrate a new technology embedded within a premium product. It's the same reason why Samsung pays David Beckham to advertise their phones. It's why Beyoncé has bottles of Pepsi on stage at her concerts, and it's why Nike focuses its messaging on products like the $260 Ultrafly sneaker while quietly making most of its money from selling the Air Force 1, a shoe that sells in Walmart and has remained largely unchanged since 1982. Advertising has long understood the power of aspiration, and it wields that power over all of us, daily. The firms producing advertisements understand that when an audience sees aspirational people having aspirational experiences with aspirational products, they start to believe that the product will help them get a little closer to the life they crave. Maybe this new thing could help them be sexier, richer, or more productive? Maybe their friends, colleagues, or lovers would find them funnier, smarter, or more attractive? Maybe wearing this pair of sneakers will let them run as fast as Usain Bolt? When people portray the future as a place filled with premium products that are owned and used by immaculate people in exquisite homes, they're simply following this tried-and-true methodology. These are what I call "trickledown futures," and they represent expressions of aspiration and ambition rather than renditions of real life.

At its core, Could Futurism is in the business of selling ideas rather than truly exploring possibilities. At its worst, Could Futurism represents little more than the creation of juicy content designed to elicit some sort of irresistible engagement, and it knows what works. The images that pop up when we search Google for "the future" look so homogenous because those images have proved to be the most enticing, engaging, and clickable. Those soaring glass skyscrapers, glossy robots, and fabulous gadgets act as little pleasure bombs that detonate endorphins in our brains and pull us toward them with their exotic allure and perhaps remind us of those exciting things we saw in all those movies.

The keen-eyed reader will no doubt have picked up the disdain I have for this type of work. It typically represents an overbearing, overexcited, yet ultimately vacuous form of futurism that feels ill-equipped to deliver anything beyond jaw-dropping wonder and that crumbles with even the humblest requests for rigor or detail. Worse than that, it actively hinders any semblance of meaningful discussion or exploration by filling popular discourse with its noisy, flashy, and fantasist imaginings. Could Futurism markets itself incredibly well, and has found a way to appeal to our most lustful urges, but in so doing it actively erases us from the conversation by replacing us with unattainable, heroic characters, products, and situations. Whenever you encounter Could Futurism of this sort, it's worth resisting the urge to gorge on its empty calories. Instead, you might try asking where you fit in it, and what impact your exclusion might be having.

•

Aside from its well-documented class system, Britain also divides its population between the North and the South. My hometown of Derby lies almost exactly in the center of England, equidistant from the sea in all directions, in a region noncommittally named the Midlands. It's neither here nor there, neither hardworking, tough-minded Northern, nor wealthy, cosmopolitan Southern. Growing up, I never knew which faction I was supposed to represent—my friends in the North thought I was a soft Southerner, and my friends in the South thought I was a rough Northerner. Even with its declining industrial fortunes, Derby was neither particularly rich nor poor, and the median income in Derby today remains almost exactly equivalent to the median income for the entire UK. It's truly a middling city, in every sense of the word, and this all-encompassing sense of averageness has been at my core since birth, ultimately defining how I see my position in the grand scheme of things.

I vividly remember lying on my belly on the floor of my grandma's house at some point in the 1980s. If I close my eyes and concentrate, I can almost feel the heat from the gas fire and see the crumbs from my toast on the plate in front of me. It was well beyond my bedtime, but Nana and I had an agreement that I could stay up to watch a certain renegade arts program, which that night happened to feature an interview with Morrissey and the Smiths. I don't know why this sticks so firmly in my memory—and I certainly can't recall the full context of the interview—but hearing this group of lads tell stories in local accents against a backdrop of wet Manchester streets made me feel like a system was breaking in front of me. Up to this point my media diet had been dominated by well-groomed BBC presenters with plummy Southeastern accents, which seemed to thematically center everything on London and the middle class. Even the children's TV presenters sat up straight in neatly pressed slacks and knitwear, with tidy hair and politely clipped accents, but suddenly I was made aware of a whole different media universe, a different set of cultures, other worlds to discover and other stories to hear. I remember being genuinely shocked that these people were even *allowed* on television, using slang and speaking in accents I'd typically hear on a local bus. Perhaps this simply coincided with a yearning to find my own form of youthful rebellion, but it tickled me somehow. It felt like the rules were being broken. It felt like the music they were producing was somehow intended *for me*, and it felt like my experience of the world was also suddenly valid. As I grew older, I discovered more of these "everyday" voices through bands like The Wedding Present, The Cribs, and Minor Threat, the movies of Ken Loach, Steve McQueen, and Shane Meadows, and the photography of Martin Parr, Wolfgang Tillmans, Tracey Emin, Richard Billingham, and many more.

Later in life I moved to London and began working for a design consulting firm, contributing to a wide variety of projects for automotive, technology, and consumer product design clients. Very quickly, I found myself drawn toward the future-oriented projects that came through the studio. There was something alluring about helping clients think about their long-term future, discussing how they might use a new technology, or exploring how they might define entirely new products, behaviors, or lifestyles. During this early phase of my career, if I'm being truly honest, I produced a lot of Could Futurism. Glossy renderings of exotic products, enticing vision videos, and ambitious expressions of emerging newness filled my sketchbooks and hard drives. The designers I admired all seemed to produce this kind of thing, and the images in the magazines I bought all looked like this. I thought that's what being a futures designer consisted of, I thought that's what I was *supposed to do*, and for a while that assumption seemed to be right. Clients appeared to be enamored of my work and genuinely excited by what I'd produced, which I found incredibly flattering. They would include my contributions in their slideshows, my images would find their way into annual reports, and the vision videos I produced were uploaded to company websites—but beyond that it felt largely ineffectual. The work never really went anywhere; it didn't seem to shift anything of note, and nothing really came from these propositions. Over time, it became clear that the function of this work was not to drive new thinking but to fulfill some other agenda, perhaps a means to reposition a brand or reassure employees and investors that the company was focused on the future, even if it wasn't.

The work I produced wasn't truthful, honest, or sincere. It ignored pragmatic realities in favor of heroic, ambitious, escapist storytelling. I began to realize that portraying the future as an abstract place populated with impossible people, impossible products, and impossible lives rarely led anywhere productive because it didn't embrace reality, and that feeling began to eat away at me.

There's a specific term in the movie industry used to describe the type of people who lurk behind the main characters as the story plays out, those roles such as "tall man in supermarket" or "angry old lady" that lurk way down at the bottom of movie credits. These people are generally referred to as "background talent." You might be more familiar with the theatrical term "extras"; in video games they're called "nonplayable characters," and in the opera they're "supernumeraries," but in recent years, I've found huge value in thinking about the future through their eyes. What might the future be like for them, or more pointedly, what might the future be like for *us*? How might we *actually* experience gene editing, artificial intelligence, or quantum computing? When delivery drones fill the sky, what will that *actually* feel like for people living in the suburbs of Leeds? We might initially encounter these things beamed from our TVs, conference stages, and futures exhibits as whizzbang objects of wonder, but how will they look when they've been value engineered, when they've become part of a supply chain, when they're covered by our home insurance or part of a shrink-wrapped meal deal at the 24-hour supermarket?

The vast majority of us aren't comfortable with where we sit in a given demographic hierarchy. We want to be richer, more successful, prettier, taller, stronger, slimmer, funnier, smarter, or more popular. Advertising knows this, and it uses all the tools at its disposal to exploit these desires—and create entirely new ones—which can make some people incredibly unhappy. Could Futurism also works this way, keeping the future just out of reach, a distant fantasy of unattainable purity, incredible performance, and impossible achievement, and for that reason its utility is limited. It can be powerful to free oneself from the clutches of pragmatism and to truly dream beyond the limits of reality—indeed, this should occasionally be encouraged—but due to the addictive, escapist nature of this kind of work, we all start to crave it, and it begins to dominate and overshadow more grounded conversations about the future. In science fiction literature and cinema, Could Futurism has found the perfect partners to shape, inspire, and authenticate its perspectives, and as science fiction has grown, so has the dominance of this way of thinking.

Once you become aware of this type of work, and once you've been around it for some time, the gloss quickly wears away and you begin to notice an air of irritating repetition and uninspired orthodoxy in its output. Could Futurism actually represents an act of intellectual cowardice. It offers us the space to dream, but then what? It talks of distant possibilities but rarely illustrates the actionable steps to get us there. Could Futurism pitches us brand-new worlds populated by heroic characters living dreamlike lives but fails to take a look outside the window. It treats the future as an emotional fantasyland, but once the spotlights have been turned off, the applause has died down, and the credits have rolled, what a client, an investor, or a customer needs is a decision. They need some sort of a plan, some statement of what to do next. They need to know much more than what they *could* do. They need to know what they *should* do.

SHOULD

THE SHOULD FUTURISTS

Theirs is the realm of certainty and assuredness.

They're driven by decision and are action oriented.

They believe the future is theirs to define.

They know what better looks like, and they want you to think the same.

They evangelize their position and ridicule naysayers.

They wear their ideology proudly and defend it vehemently.

They have conviction.

They believe in their data or their dogma.

They are singular and focused.

They wouldn't want you to call them a futurist.

They trust the dotted line.

"BETTER"

Every one of us tries to shape our life to fit a future we have envisioned for ourselves. We peer out into the distance and build an image of the world as we'd like to see it, which acts as a powerful magnet in the present, telling us what we should do, how we should act, and what we should prioritize. Once defined, this end point tells us to save money, to recycle, to make wise investments, and to cast our votes with purpose. It tells us what issues to prioritize, what causes to champion, and what to care about. It encourages us to focus on key issues, to build toward defined goals, and to make hard choices. This guiding light shapes our decisions through a directional mindset that I call "Should Futurism," whose core function is to clearly define a future state of the world and then nudge us toward it.

So, what *should* we do in the future?

Should we clean up our oceans? Free our seas from rotting plastic, poisonous chemicals, and industrial waste? Create expansive oceans of pure, blue waters filled with vibrant biodiversity, endless shoals of frolicking dolphins, and singing whales? That'd be good, wouldn't it? Or how about addressing our future energy needs? Should we put all our efforts behind the creation of wind farms and solar furnaces, bringing clean, limitless electricity to our homes and businesses? Isn't that the most pressing issue of the day? How about the acceptance of all forms of love around the world? Should we work toward that? A world where gay, trans, and queer people can travel anywhere without fear of suppression, persecution, or segregation? Should we increase the size of our nation's military? What about doubling the congregation of the Catholic Church? Is that what we should do? Or maybe we should find a way to even out the wealth between nations? Should we limit how much water we use or ban cell phones in schools? Should we push for a transition to vegetarianism or veganism? How about free education for all, a downtown filled with bicycles, or a universal basic income? In 1909, Marinetti thought Italians should knock down all their museums. In the 1950s, Americans thought they should eat margarine rather than butter. In 1982, the Chinese government thought that couples should limit themselves to one child. In the 1990s, Coca-Cola thought we should use plastic bottles rather than glass. Today Elon Musk thinks we should become a multiplanetary species, the Instagram algorithm thinks I should buy a knife-sharpening kit, T-Mobile thinks I should switch to a $50 cell phone plan, and my mate Jo thinks I should watch more football.

When we think of the future, it can often feel like a vast open landscape stretching out ahead of us, a nothingness that could feel emancipatory and freeing if it weren't so overwhelming. As a means to cope with this nothingness, we often insert some sort of target or goal in the distance that helpfully narrows this expanse and prevents life in the present from feeling rudderless. If we want a future where there's a certain figure in our bank account, we can make sense of some of the things we're wrangling with in the present, we can prioritize our actions and make decisions based on that defined ambition. If our company wants to double its customers over the next three years, we can make that a priority and turn the resources we have toward that target. If a country wants to increase its GDP by 10 percent before the next election, then it can adjust its strategies, policies, and priorities accordingly. Should Futurism represents the outcome of this mindset: a type of futurism that offers guidance on the actions we should take today based on where we want to end up. A strong-willed, opinionated, and cocksure confection that dominates almost every decision we make in the present and wheedles its way deep into our subconscious. Should Futurism is immensely powerful and resilient, and is by far the most self-assured form of futurism we have. It thrives mostly because of the reassuring clarity it offers, preventing the unknowable vacuum of the future from becoming paralyzing.

Typically speaking, we place targets in our future that correlate to some notion we have of an improved situation, some notion of progress or something we consider to be "better." This is where things get a little wobbly, as the meaning of "better" is far from universal; it's a comparative adjective that requires some level of mutual agreement, not only on the destination, but also in its assessment of the present. Countless books fill our shelves with titles confidently brandishing the term "better": a better life, a better you, better living through yoga. A better diet, a better workweek, how to be a better traveler, how to sleep better, a guide to better parenting, better garden management, better colon health. But how are we measuring this improvement? Who is this better for? Do we agree on what "better" means, and who is the "we" here, exactly? "Better" could mean cleaner air in our cities, free schooling for our kids, or an affordable cure for cancer. Likewise, it could mean crushing the competition, doubling profits, or increasing factory automation. Throughout history, for some people "better" has also meant the rapid extraction of the world's oil, the stockpiling of nuclear weapons, and the eradication of the Jews. "Better" is such a potent force in each of us that we rarely question it. It becomes so culturally, institutionally, and socially ingrained in us that when we use the term "better," we assume our neighbors, colleagues, and countrymen feel the same way. "Better" is a political word that expresses desires rather than truths. Basic ambitions such as clean air to breathe, respect for others, and opportunity for all would surely fall into anyone's definition of a better world, yet they have all been ignored or actively suppressed for generations by countless individuals, corporations, and nations. We all want a better future, but when the meaning of better isn't universally shared, the sentiment becomes all but meaningless.

I've used the term "utopia" a few times already. It's a helpful word to express the ultimate version of "better"—perhaps even the "best": a place where the things you care about are fixed and the things you dislike are eradicated. You're likely familiar with utopia's oppositional, apocalyptic sibling, "dystopia," where the things you care the most about are significantly "worse" or utterly broken. These diametrically opposed states offer two end points to any discussion, but are largely poor representations of reality, dragging us toward extremes that feel more like fantasy and nightmare than true ambitions or credible outcomes. For this reason, Kevin Kelly—the chin-bearded polymath and founder of *Wired* magazine—coined the term "protopia" to define "a state that is better today than yesterday" in order to prioritize a more rational, incremental, and approachable version of the future. While I'm hugely supportive of almost any initiative that pulls us away from extremes and toward a more collective, general middle, the challenge I face with this term is the barely concealed philosophical qualifier "better" at its core. For Kelly, this likely represents his own underlying beliefs, which are centered on technological advancement and liberal Bay Area values. For Monika Bielskyte, founder of the Protopia Futures collective, a "better" world is one focused on LGBTQ, Indigenous, and disability justice. For Micha Narberhaus, founder of the nonprofit Protopia Lab, "better" represents a focus on social and environmental matters. "Better" means different things to different people, and reflects their own emotional position or belief structure. In this regard the term "protopia" doesn't really help push us forward in any meaningful way, but it does offer us a cool new word to describe how we'd like things to be.

It's an important question to ask oneself from time to time: What does "better" really look like, and why do I feel that way? It might feel obvious, rational, and straightforward to you, but if you agnostically interrogate what you're articulating, what you'll find is a reflection of your own personal, organizational, or cultural *preferences*. When someone proposes any concept, idea, or vision, they're hoping that you both share their definition of "better" before they even begin their pitch. Whenever I hear the word "better" in a presentation, I've found that continually asking "Why?" (just as an annoying toddler might do) quickly drills past lofty propositions and corporate gibberish to reveal the naked ambitions that lie beneath. I worked for almost a decade for a company that had the phrase "to make the world a radically better place" in its mission statement, without ever really describing what "better" meant. When I pushed our senior leaders on this point it became abundantly clear that everyone's idea of "better" was different in some way—some even took oppositional stances—which rendered the term largely useless.

It feels good to say out loud, but "better" is a truly problematic word. It defines what we see as "problems" and begins to shape what we see as "solutions," driving us toward a very particular version of the future. Should Futurism ultimately represents a raw reflection of this truth, revealing what lies at its core: a manifestation of our own beliefs, preferences, dogmas, philosophies, and ideologies.

BELIEF

The term "ideology" was coined in 1796 by the aristocratic French philosopher Antoine Destutt de Tracy while he was imprisoned during the French Revolution. He and his fellow well-dressed intellectuals (whom he referred to as "ideologues") wanted to reflect the emergence of a new science built around rationalism, in stark opposition to what they saw as the distinctly irrational impulses of the French revolutionary mob. Researchers and sociologists wrangle with a contemporary definition for "ideology" (and the term has undoubtedly developed a somewhat negative bent), but generally speaking every ideology is formed from two parts: an interpretation and a prescription. The former offers a lens through which to observe the world and make sense of it; the latter offers a recommendation for a course of action. In this manner, ideologies are futurist tools, as they each aim to reach their preferred version of the future through the changing of the present.

Let's take a simple example. I have a preference for how cakes should look and taste. As I see it, cakes should be golden brown with a loose crumb structure, not pale and soggy or dry and chewy—for this exercise we'll call this my "cake ideology." So let's imagine I'm baking a cake at home. I take a look in the oven and it seems like the cake is just about the right color—that's my interpretation. My prescription, therefore, is that we should take the cake out of the oven now, as failure to do so would lead the cake to become darker and drier in the future, which is an outcome that contravenes my cake ideology. (Are you still with me?) In this example "the future" is relatively close and the ideology is relatively simple, but it illustrates how our future desires shape our decisions in the present—and this relationship forms the core of Should Futurism. When we are thinking about cakes this all feels rather logical and sensible, but when we stretch the timeline further, or attempt to tackle more complex topics than baking, this simplicity begins to break down. When we are working with multivalent issues like employment strategy, fiscal frameworks, mass manufacturing, gender politics, or international relations things get significantly thornier. Disagreements over the interpretation of the current state of affairs dominate proceedings before we even get to prescriptions or recommendations for the future. These disagreements begin to open up into schisms and disputes, with each position endlessly debated and defended, before oppositional visions for the future become targets for skepticism and mockery.

Ideologies are essentially representations of beliefs about the future, and for these beliefs to gain momentum they need support, which often comes through the creation and distribution of a manifesto. Manifestos typically originate from a place of discontent, an articulation of something "wrong" or "broken," and offer an idea of how the situation may be improved somehow. They are often deliberately incendiary, polemical, disruptive, or rousing; indeed, the most successful manifestos tend to offer some sort of radical shift in the status quo or something confrontational to shake the reader into a new frame of reference. Throughout history, manifestos have acted as rallying cries to gather people together under an ideology, declaring a particular perspective on what's "broken" in the present and how the future would be significantly "better" if we approached the issue in a different way.

Manifestos seek to rewire society, culture, or industry, to adjust it or remake it, and to grab the steering wheel of the future and yank it in a different direction. They can exist as standalone documents—such as the countless manifestos that Marinetti produced—but occasionally manifestos are carefully nestled within stories, which can be a powerful and persuasive way to illustrate how a new world might work. The spooky-eyed capitalist philosopher Ayn Rand used this technique to great effect in her mid-century novels *The Fountainhead* and *Atlas Shrugged*, whose narrative arcs helped to illustrate her ideological objectivist fantasies. These books allowed her ideas to reach a broader audience, and many of the world's biggest names from Silicon Valley and Wall Street continue to reference Rand's ideas on technology and laissez-faire economics to this day.

Manifestos can be incredibly useful, helpfully narrowing the scope of decision-making for a target community around a shared set of values and allowing them to move forward with some clearer notion of purpose, which can be as dangerous as it is powerful. Once enough people share a particular perspective—or when it becomes sufficiently well defined—society typically assigns it a name:

a helpful bucket into which the idea can be poured, or a shorthand identifier to contain a complex idea. Capitalism, socialism, communism, Catholicism, nationalism, conservatism, Keynesianism, collectivism, Nazism, anarchism, nihilism, and countless other labeled ideologies exist alongside one another, each representing the philosophical, political, or moral doctrine at their core. The only thing they share is an articulation of the future they're trying to create and a belief in its deliverance of something "better."

Ideologies can act as phenomenally useful social constructs, spanning generations and allowing people to unite under a series of shared desires. Karl Marx, author of perhaps the world's most famous manifesto, described ideologies as "instruments of social reproduction," a means to build continuity and social structure beyond individual lives and human timescales, and to create multigenerational change. Many of the world's most impressive feats are the result of dedication to an ideology, a desire to make the world anew, or a drive to accelerate change. People devote huge amounts of their free time to push their community toward an ideological goal. They work eighty-hour weeks to build a company they believe will yield a preferable transformation in the world. They volunteer, they create, and they campaign, driven by their belief in positive change, and while it's undoubtedly true that ideologies allow us to create incredible things, they are also typically found at the heart of conflicts. Ideologies are often separatist, seeking to exclude or actively denigrate other positions or counterperspectives, and they can be incredibly persuasive. Throughout history, ideologies have led people to commit countless horrific acts of selfishness, appalling cruelty, and oppression, which are so numerous and notorious we need not list them here.

Ideologies may war with one another (sometimes literally), but they also have a habit of warring with themselves. Let's take capitalism as an example, the dominant economic and political mindset of the developed world, in which a country's trade and industry are controlled by private owners for profit. The overwhelming majority of the world operates under this general model, but we don't need to dig very far before we identify a fragmentation of this core belief. We find the ordoliberalists, the monopolists, the objectivists, the anarcho-capitalists, the oligarchic capitalists, the state-driven capitalists, and the entrepreneurial capitalists, each of whom apparently agrees on the big picture, but vehemently opposes the others on the details. Before long we find ourselves in tricky territory, arguing about the minute differences between factions and sounding like the bickering Judean clans in *The Life of Brian*. Rather than acting as monolithic truths, most major ideologies may be considered fractal, gradually breaking down into factions, subideologies, and coalitions with slightly differing takes on the core tenets of their belief system. They all see a different ideal future and want to work toward that while destroying, derailing, or deriding their opponents.

Ideologies are also frequently presented as singular propositions, but people aren't singular in nature. Every individual represents a kaleidoscopic, intermingled mesh of overlapping beliefs, and while people may claim to hold a flagship ideology such as socialism, republicanism, or environmentalism, these terms unhelpfully simplify our own strangely interlinked network of beliefs that can evolve, distort, and even contradict one another. In reality, every one of us represents an endless Venn diagram of overlaps, subsets, and contextual exceptions that constantly fight with one another to create a dizzying internal turbulence.

It might seem odd, for example, that American Christians broadly support a man like Donald Trump. Without diving too deeply into the murky waters of United States politics, it's curious that a combative capitalist with criminal convictions, an indisputably dubious ethical record, and a conspicuous lack of church attendance is embraced by this demographic. Churchgoers are typically focused on values like humility, charity, and moral rectitude, but Trump has proved popular with Christians of all denominations, which is due to the complex, compound nature of ideologies. Donald Trump may contravene many Christians' beliefs on decorum, decency, and ethics, but these may be of lower significance to another ideological issue that they feel is more heavily weighted, or that represents a different if seemingly contradictory aspect of their ideological stack.

I've lived and worked in Silicon Valley for over a decade and have observed its own curious interplay of ideologies in close proximity. This part of the world is dominated by emergent technologies (most notably computer-related technologies), which are seen as a trigger for change by the overwhelming majority of technocrats who live and work here. The region has long been a magnet for the world's best computer scientists and software engineers, who have developed some of the most transformative products of our time. Apple, Google, HP, Facebook, Oracle, and Intel were all born in this small corner of California, but the San Francisco Bay Area was also home to the counterculture movement of the 1960s, a freewheeling period of sexual exploration, experimental drug use, radical politics, and societal change. It gave us the Black Panthers, Harvey Milk, Charles Manson, Burning Man, and the hippies, and the region leads the world in explorations of self-expression and civic protest to this day. It's also one of the richest parts of the world, with immense wealth concentrated into a relatively small area. Venture capitalists in branded fleeces fill the city's coffee shops, and San Francisco is home to many of capitalism's heroes, with companies here frequently valued in the trillions of dollars. These cultures collide in incredibly odd and often contradictory ways. I've been present in rooms where eccentric, bearded computer engineers, radical, countercultural idealists, straight-laced lawyers, and thirty-year-old millionaires are all trying to create a single thing. When someone here says "better," it's incredibly difficult to know what they actually mean, as multiple ideologies jostle and fight for their position in every document, presentation, pitch, and project.

We all like the words "better" and "should," and they feel so clear and obvious, but these words are simply a result of the accumulation of lessons and cultural nudges we receive throughout our lives. Many of the beliefs we hold are squeezed into our infant brains and continually reinforced through our early years, ossifying into immovable, immutable truths as we grow into adults. It's no surprise, therefore, that even in a famously individualistic culture such as the United States over 80 percent of children share the same religion and political orientation as their parents. We all know (or feel that we know) what we should do for any given social situation. It feels obvious how we should behave, what we should focus on, what we should build toward, and what we should consider important, but in truth, this represents a swirling maelstrom of political, social, epistemological, and ethical directionality that shapes the ways in which we move through our lives.

The future we should aim for might feel self-evident to you. It might feel abundantly clear what we should prioritize, what's right and wrong, what needs fixing, and what our priorities should be in the years to come, but unpicking the origins of these apparent certainties can be incredibly difficult. Should Futurism represents the ideologies embedded within every individual, community, company, and government, ideologies which often act silently and unquestioned in the background, and actively shut out other possibilities or perspectives. Every decision we make about the future is inextricably tied to these frameworks of belief, and every assertion of what "should" happen reflects a particular ideological stance. Should Futurism is absolutely dependent on a mutually agreed-upon form of "better"; otherwise it has nothing.

ON PREDICTION

You may not know anything about the issue, but I bet you "reckon" something. So why not tell us what you "reckon"? Let us enjoy the full majesty of your uninformed, ad-hoc "reckon."
—DAVID MITCHELL

One of the prevailing players in any conversation about the future is the prediction—a statement of confident clarity pitched far off in the mists of the unknown, glowing through the gloom and drawing us toward it like moths to a flame. Whenever people find out what I do for a living, they almost always ask me for some sort of prediction. You see predictions in business reports, you hear them on sports channels, and you read them in the news. They sit at the top of magazine articles, their staggering numerals blown up to 200-point bold type, and they're projected in the slideshows of politicians, investors, analysts, and futurists. "The Methodist Church will disappear by 2045." "38% of today's jobs will be automated by 2050." "In ten years' time, half of all passenger vehicles will be electric." Predictions are assertions that attempt to use some form of insight to make assured statements about the future, typically with the intention of guiding some decisions in the present. Predictions feel like soothing tethers in the future, giving us unequivocal feedback on what we should do in the present, and we've developed something of an addiction to their reassuring solidity.

Since the beginning of recorded history, humans have used anything at hand to seek insights about what might lie ahead. The patterns of fungus growing under a tree, the passage of the stars across the night sky, and the unique shapes of spilled animal guts have all been used to carve nuggets of truth from the unknowable void of the future. Likewise, the dreams and visions of shamans, oracles, seers, and prophets have all been used to define apparent truths somewhere out there in the distance, to give us something to point at or to avoid. The ancient Greeks used a technique known as hydromancy, wherein a piece of bread was thrown into a fountain in the city of Epidaurus and a question was asked of the goddess Ino. If the bread sank in the water, this was taken to be a positive response, but a piece of floating bread indicated the opposite. The Romans often employed eggs in divination, in a practice referred to as oomancy. Soothsaying through eggs took many forms, with one prevalent method involving the submersion of egg whites in boiling water to discern predictions from the resulting shapes. A flawlessly circular shape signified an impending wedding, while an irregular, serpent-like form was construed as an ominous harbinger of impending peril.

As a child I became acutely aware of the sixteenth-century French astrologer Nostradamus, who would perhaps have been an unlikely target for my interest, were it not for the fact that he seemed to be absolutely everywhere in the 1980s. His name frequently featured in those fun little palate-cleanser segments at the end of local news bulletins, focusing on whatever disaster he predicted would be coming next. "Hopefully this weekend's cheese festival won't be disrupted by the deadly shower of fireballs over Nottingham," followed by polite laughter, that sort of thing. In total, it appears Nostradamus made at least 6,338 prophecies (obviously abiding by the "quantity over quality" adage), but he's perhaps most well-known for his 1555 book *Les prophéties*, which contained 942 poetic quatrains predicting future events, occasionally pegged to specific dates. He was viewed as a bit of a crank by many but managed to build a significant following of devotees, including Catherine de' Medici, the wife of King Henry II of France, who summoned him to explain his predictions that the royal family were under some sort of nonspecific threat. Following their meeting, Nostradamus was asked to produce horoscopes for Catherine's children and became Counselor and Physician-in-Ordinary to her son, King Charles IX, such is the undeniable attraction of a clearly articulated idea about the future.

Today, we use the term "the occult" to define and broadly dismiss these sorts of practices. It's easy to scoff at historical predictions of this kind, but a significant level of occultism still persists in most modern societies. In February 2023, *Fortune* magazine ran an article with the headline "Many of the World's Billionaires Share a Zodiac Sign" (my condolences to all the Capricorns out there—you're apparently least likely to become megarich). In 2022, in the United States, 37 percent of adults under thirty said they believed in the power of astrology, and in 2021, the global astrology market was valued at $12.8 billion. Every social media platform features occult content, from the tips, tarot readings, and elemental predictions of practitioners on WitchTok to the crowds of psychic mediums plying their wares on YouTube. It seems that we have an almost insatiable appetite for prediction and will readily grasp at anything—no matter how seemingly absurd—to feed our craving.

Purveyors of predictions typically achieve sustained success through three core techniques. First, they integrate huge margins of error and leave plenty of space for interpretation, an approach typically used by palmists and astrologers in a process known as "shotgunning," which involves dwelling on hits and rapidly accelerating past misses. These deliberately loose descriptions of future events allow the recipient to fill in the blanks and add their own embellishments, which leads to a heightened perception of accuracy and an increased level of belief in those making the predictions. Second, they produce a great quantity of predictions, increasing their chances of success and hoping that the good guesses mask all of the duds. This is the Nostradamus gambit, where a thousand arrows may miss the target but one might hit the bullseye, blinding us to all the previous errors. Their final tactic is to push a prediction far off into the distance, allowing plenty of time to dine out on the statement in the meantime. This is the tactic often used by a number of Could Futurists when promising technological miracles "at some point" in our collective future, but it's broadly used by the most overt and persuasive prediction machine of our time—organized religion.

To me, the persistence, prevalence, and power of religious belief in contemporary society is something of an uncomfortable curiosity, a remnant of our occult past when much more was unknown than known. I am not a religious man. I'll happily sing along to a carol or exchange presents at Christmas, but I find the belief in gods to be highly problematic on a number of fronts. I've built my life around notions of evidence and proof, and that leaves very little room for faith, but this way of thinking clearly puts me in the global minority. The Pew Research Center estimates that over 84 percent of people on Earth affiliate with a religion, the largest of which are Christianity, Islam, Hinduism, and Buddhism. Thirty percent of the world's countries insist their leader is a member of a specified religious group, and 67 percent of Americans believe the United States is a "Christian nation." While around 1.2 billion humans currently identify as secular, nonreligious, agnostic, or atheist, the number of countries where the unaffiliated face harassment was much higher in 2020 than in 2012, and religion and daily life still go hand in hand in the vast majority of communities on Earth. Religion forms a central pillar in the lives of the majority of humans, offering them cultural identity, an ethical framework, a social community, and a slew of answers for their own spiritual questions. It also offers comforting structure, helpful goals, and desired end points that neatly fill the otherwise daunting expanse of the future.

We often view religious writing as immovable and fixed, but in truth, religions have proved to be surprisingly pliable. Just as national constitutions have undergone amendments and adjustments, the world's major religions have also changed their ideas over time, albeit a little more slowly than most cultural and legal frameworks have. The Catholic Church has undergone numerous doctrinal reforms, adjusting their interpretation of the scriptures to reassess their position on everything from capital punishment to slavery. Likewise, Islamic doctrine has evolved to both embrace and deny scientific inquiry, and has developed numerous interpretive legal constructs based on its own holy scriptures. In spite of this drift in values and evolving interpretation of these texts, religions deploy Shouldism with alarming regularity, dictating the timing, location, and frequency of prayer, how individuals ought to dress, what they should eat, when they should eat it, how they should style their hair, and even how their genitals should look. In theology, predictions are relatively commonplace, from the Old Testament prophecies of Isaiah and the Book of Revelation in the Bible to the verses of Surah Ar-Rum and Surah Ad-Dukhan in the Quran.

Many of these predictions are latter-day interpretations of fairly vague historical verses announcing the arrival of an important individual or event (a prophet or a military defeat, for example), but where these predictions get more defined and strident is when they describe the end of humankind.

In almost all organized theology, there exists some form of eschatology, a notion of our collective destiny, marked by a catastrophic, redemptive, apocalyptic, or cosmic event. Almost all religions go to great lengths to describe these moments and then work backward from that point, filling in the blanks and creating a dogma that dictates the behavior required to survive this prescribed future. The most successful religions push their predictions far off into the future (or refuse to specify a date at all), perhaps learning their lesson from the American Baptist William Miller, who in 1843 made the first of several proclamations that the world would end in only a few months. As his predictions failed to come to fruition (a moment somewhat amusingly known as the Great Disappointment), followers of Miller lost faith in him and his premonitions and created a handful of new churches of their own, including the Seventh-day Adventists.

Even today, many people are quick to point at contemporary events as a means to validate ancient prophecies laid down in scripture. On April 26, 1986, the number 4 reactor at the Chernobyl Nuclear Power Plant in Ukraine exploded during a routine cooling exercise. The initial blast claimed the lives of two engineers and severely burned two others, but subsequent exposure to nuclear material led to the deaths of an estimated nine thousand employees, rescue workers, and members of the local population in nearby Pripyat. Soon after the event, numerous theologians began pointing at a biblical reference in the Book of Revelation which stated that "a great star, blazing like a torch, fell from the sky" and "the name of the star is Wormwood." As it happens, wormwood belongs to the *Artemisia* genus of plants, the Ukrainian name for which is *chornobyl*, and it doesn't take much imagination to link a nuclear explosion with something akin to a "great star." Whether this connection represents a mere coincidence or true divine foreshadowing, the linking of modern tragedies to references within ancient texts reflects our enduring need to find patterns in the chaos of life, and when those links appear, they further reinforce our collective belief in the power of prediction. While prophecies don't represent the entirety of religious dogma, most religions appear to be working toward some sort of confident assertion about the ultimate end point and purpose for humankind. These predictions act as powerfully bright targets in the future, pulling followers toward them and showering the present in Should. In many regards, religion negates the notion of individual agency in the future, instead defining the present as part of a much broader plan, to which followers must be submissive, deferential, and obedient.

The secular world is not afraid of prediction either, and many people—indeed, many futurists—are fond of pointing at things from the past (particularly works of science fiction) and drawing a causal line to the present. Many armchair theorists and science fiction acolytes will loudly proclaim that science fiction predicted everything from laptops and cell phones to vapes and hovercrafts, but this misses two very important facts. The first is that science fiction has introduced us to perhaps millions of ideas over the years, the overwhelming majority of which are nowhere close to reality. People will happily gloss over concepts such as lightsabers, teleportation, time travel, gravitational shielding, force fields, hoverboards, human miniaturization, and faster-than-light travel for that one scene where somebody is holding a glass rectangle, which they'll claim is evidence that this movie predicted the iPad. The Nostradamus gambit applies here too—the chances of a science fiction idea having a close contemporary parallel increase in relation to the number of ideas generated (which is incredibly high). The second important factor is that science fiction predicts the future only if one is extremely generous with the definition of "predict."

There were conversation screens in *The Jetsons*, but did that *predict* video telephony? People ride in driverless cars in *Minority Report*, but did that *predict* driverless cars? There are replicators in *Star Trek*, but did that *predict* 3D printers?

There's a deeply embedded prediction story within science fiction lore which involves the Motorola StarTAC phone, a clamshell device launched in 1996 that many believe was the world's first flip phone (it wasn't, not by many years). The phone was wildly popular, selling approximately 60 million units thanks to its small size and the satisfying gesture of snapping it open and closed at the beginning and end of a call. Back in 1966, the TV series *Star Trek* introduced a small black device that allowed Starfleet crew members to talk to one another. The communicator (as it was known) was a simple black device with a golden folding lid, one of many props developed for the show by Wah Ming Chang, a designer who also created *Star Trek* classics such as the phaser, the tricorder, and the first Romulan starship. When one is speaking to a sci-fi fan, it's not unusual to hear them declare that *Star Trek* predicted the cell phone, because of the apparent similarity between the StarTAC phone and the communicator in both form and function. It's perhaps easy to see why people believe this, as the two perform broadly similar jobs, have broadly similar appearances, and feature the same unique gesture, but this asssertion is far from true. When *Star Trek* debuted in 1966, cellular technology had already been in existence for almost a decade. A team at Motorola led by Martin Cooper was already well underway with the development of a mobile phone, and they made the first cellular call in October 1973. Earlier still, the

Canadian inventor Donald Hings had created a portable radio signaling system for his employer CM&S way back in 1937, and his model C-58 Handie-Talkie was in broad military service as early as 1942. The handheld communicator device was not a new idea in 1966, not by a long shot. The *Star Trek* production team simply made an extrapolation of broadly available contemporary technologies. There's sketchy evidence that the Motorola team took inspiration from the TV show (not least for the product name), but retrospective inspiration is a very different proposition from ancient prediction. As the multiple Hugo Award–winning sci-fi author Charles Stross said, "We are not trying to accurately predict possible futures but to earn a living: any foresight is strictly coincidental."

Within the commercial world, there also exists a very specific type of prediction that purports to identify weak signals or thematic groundswells in an industry in order to inform an audience about a more significant impending change: the loosely defined and somewhat questionable practice of identifying "trends." This work is less about specifying a singular end point or ambition, and more about identifying general directionality. Trends practitioners exist in every industry from fashion to finance, and countless futurists pride themselves on their ability to spot these drifts and pivots before anyone else. It's seen as something of a superpower, and it represents a marketable, sellable skill for many who graft titles such as "tastemaker" or "superforecaster" onto their online profiles. Trends work involves digesting massive amounts of input material and identifying the common links and threads that run through it, in the belief that these signals act like foreshocks to a major earthquake. A trend can emerge from something quite small, like recognizing an emerging teenage habit, recording an uptick in bicycle sales, or identifying the increasing popularity of sourdough bread. It takes a particularly observant kind of person to notice such things, and identifying these shifts sufficiently early can be quite useful in planning for the future.

But of course, where there's something useful, there will always be an army of people keen to blow it out of proportion. In 1982, John Naisbitt published *Megatrends: Ten New Directions Transforming Our Lives*, in which he introduced a list of major cultural, social, economic, and political changes that he claimed would define the world in years to come. The book was a mega-bestseller, but, in truth, the majority of the trends within it were simply well-defined summaries of fairly obvious shifts that were currently underway. When big, complicated ideas are summarized into pithy, digestible concepts and given a simply remembered name, they can be seen as more insightful or prophetic than they actually are. What the publication of this book did more broadly was encourage us all to use single phrases to define massive, multimodal shifts in the world, often sacrificing a great deal of detail and nuance in the process. It's become a popular pastime of opinion columnists, business analysts, and onstage futurists to seek out these shifts and give them brand names, and in the process develop their reputations for being somehow able to "see around corners."

I'm most familiar with trends work in the field of design, where it's frequently used to focus a conversation, define a direction, or identify a potential future opportunity. For example, if one is attempting to identify the overarching trajectory of the interior design industry, it's common practice to travel to the design fairs and festivals held around the world—such as the Salone del Mobile in Milan or Maison&Objet in Paris—to see the latest offerings and prototypes from the world's most respected furniture makers. Photographs are taken by the thousand, and notes are made on the fabrics, materials, formal languages, colors, and construction techniques on show. Back in the office, this body of work is endlessly shuffled around on walls and gathered together under collective headings, and in this way "trends" emerge—but it's hard to discern whether these patterns actually exist or are merely the product of our subconscious predilections. The mind is a remarkably pliable thing, and humans are pattern-seeking primates who can very quickly be encouraged to see connections that might not actually exist. Collecting even a few similar images or data points together (and actively excluding outliers) can create the illusion of some sort of collective momentum, and it's incredibly simple to convince an audience of an undeniable future trajectory based on what appears to be overwhelming evidence. I know this because I've done it.

The validity of any observed trend is also tightly linked to the person or organization making the observation. If an authority figure such as Anna Wintour of *Vogue* magazine writes that sleeveless knitwear will be popular next year, clothing designers and manufacturers all over the world prick up their ears. Derivative brands and fast fashion houses rush to create new garments that follow this steer, and in this manner trends can often be self-fulfilling. Next year, all the stores are filled with sleeveless knitwear, it seems as if Anna was right, and the cycle moves on. When Warren Buffett declares that he thinks shifts in urbanization will affect the price of automobiles, thousands of investors adjust their portfolios accordingly, nudging his hunch a few steps closer to reality. With enough industrial clout, what originated as little more than an aggregated observation becomes a subtle directive, muddying the waters and leading all the relevant players to quickly follow suit. Being able to accurately spot a trend is a difficult skill, and the ability to summarize, define, and segment an industry can be very useful, but again, calling this "prediction" is misleading at best. Powerful players in every industry have an audience who hang on their every word, and as such they have a "thumb on the scale" when it comes to their observations about the direction of the future.

Every so often, trends appear that seem to have incredible momentum, convincing us of their imminent domination and sweeping us all up in the hullabaloo before collapsing under the weight of their own hype. In 2014, I attended CES (the Consumer Electronics Show) in Las Vegas, and the big news of the year was the launch of curved televisions. Thanks to the emergence of cutting-edge technologies such as OLEDs (organic light-emitting diodes), manufacturers including Samsung, Sony, and LG were now liberated from the formal constraints of flat slabs of glass. Prototype televisions with gently curving screens sat at the front of their booths, surrounded by enthusiastic marketing material extolling the virtues of these new designs. The screens would feel more cinematic, we were told, more engaging and engrossing; they would enhance the televisual experience, so they said, and thoroughly reignite the stagnating TV industry. Technology journalists and pundits also jumped on the story, declaring curved TVs to be the "next big thing," parroting long lists of purported benefits and predicting massive market interest. If you're going to invest in a TV, you should invest in a curved TV. If you're a company that makes TVs, you should start making curved TVs. The future looked set, and it wasn't long before other manufacturers began announcing their own models, but the hype proved no match for reality. In truth, curved televisions looked decidedly odd. Their screens were dogged by strange reflections, and the curve didn't enhance the viewing experience much, if at all. Undeterred, manufacturers pushed ahead and proudly mounted their curved televisions on plinths at the front of their stores, but customers weren't interested and sales languished. By the time I returned to CES in 2017, they were nowhere to be seen and had become something of an industry joke. Today, curved TVs are still available for sale, but we rarely see them, and when we do, we're reminded of just how daft they look sagging limply on the wall of a bar or in the waiting room of a doctor's office.

When presented with sufficient authority and gusto, predictions and trends can feel like inescapable on-ramps to the future, but unfortunately that doesn't necessarily make them true. Futurists of all ilk frequently frame their hopes, wishes, and musings as predictions, because confidence in the future can be alluring. Apparent truths in the distance can be soothing and placatory, giving us a clear destination, defining where to place our bets, and supplying us with a bearing for our compass. Organized religions and occult practices might easily be dismissed as irrational, superstitious quackery, but they still play a remarkably significant role in our projection of the future and associated decisions in the present. While we no longer appear to trust eggs and entrails to describe our future, ancient folkloric beliefs still define the structures undergirding a great many of our organizations, institutions, and nations, and an arresting number of decisions appear to be defined by these mythical end points. Even so, this kind of blind faith and belief in the unwavering trajectory of the future regularly comes up short. For more tactical or nearer-term decisions, we typically demand significantly more reassurance. We need something more robust and reliable than ancient prophecies or tarot card readings, a need we've collectively responded to with the creation of an incredibly persuasive tool: data.

EMPIRICAL FUTURES

I grew up copying Garfield cartoons, tinkering with Lego, and building whatever I could from whatever I found, ultimately developing a way of seeing the world through drawing and making, or what we might loosely term "design." It's proved to be a remarkably effective set of skills in my working life, and I've been able to help people see, experience, and ultimately understand any number of complex ideas just by making things. It's often enjoyable and engaging work, and I find immense joy in the process, but beyond design there's an altogether different group of people who play a major role in exploring and shaping our collective future. They have strident opinions about what we should do and why, but the work undertaken by this group is not really considered futurism, particularly by other futurists. In fact, it's unlikely that these people would refer to themselves as futurists either. It just doesn't fit their brand; it's too whimsical, vague, loose, and speculative. Their form of futurism has its own language, it wears different shoes and eats at different restaurants, but it's futurism, make no bones about it. These people are responsible for helping companies figure out what their futures might hold—just like me—but they don't use my tools, they use *numbers*.

Numbers emerged as a result of the human need to agree on quantity, distance, and time, as loose, relativistic notions like "many," "far," and "early" don't allow for comparison or arithmetic, and significantly hinder any attempts at long-distance trade, large-scale engineering, or repeatable science. As a result, successive civilizations have developed an increasingly numeric gaze on the world. Prior to the nineteenth century, countless forms of measurement were in use concurrently, forming a patchwork of Anglo-Saxon, Roman, and Asian unitary schemes, many of which dated back hundreds of years and only applied in specific industries or trades. This included units with wonderful names such as shaftment, perch, twip, Gunter's chain, skein, spindle, and barleycorn (which we oddly still use today to measure our shoes). When I was a child, my grandmother would occasionally use the numbers "yan, tan, tether, mether, pip" in place of "one, two, three, four, five," a relic of the ancient Cumbric language her husband used when counting his sheep, and which can still be heard in pockets of the North of England today.

The Weights and Measures Act of 1824 sought to repeal all these existing methods of measurement, replacing them with a single "imperial" system for use across the expansive British Empire. A few years earlier, the French Academy of Sciences was tasked with addressing their country's own chaotic system of weights and measures, and by 1795 the French government officially adopted a new system of measurement based on the distance from the North Pole to the equator. In major French cities, standard meters made from brass or marble, from which the public could take their own measurements or copies, were installed in the façades of government buildings. If you're lucky enough to find yourself in Paris, you can still see one of these standard meters on a wall across the street from the Senate at the Palais du Luxembourg, one of only sixteen still in existence. In 1875, the Conférence générale des poids et mesures (General Conference on Weights and Measures) was founded in Paris to tackle a number of emerging variations in this system. What resulted was a standardized record of seven base units: seconds for time, meters for distance, kilograms for mass, amperes for electrical current, kelvins for thermodynamic temperature, moles for quantity, and candelas for luminous intensity. The adoption of this international standard by almost every country on Earth means people can work remotely from one another, safe in the knowledge that everyone is talking about the same thing. For almost a hundred years the International Bureau of Weights and Measures maintained physical masters for these references, including a lump of platinum-iridium alloy affectionately named Big K, from which all other kilograms were measured. Today, these standard measurements are no longer referenced by physical objects (which can fall prey to variables such as heat, light, and humidity) but are instead tied to the mathematically reliable Planck constant, nudging us one step closer to global numeric consistency (if only Myanmar, Liberia, and the United States would play the metric game).

As humanity developed more reliable forms of measurement, we began to attribute units to ever more diverse aspects of our lives. This began with straightforward natural phenomena such as time, temperature, distance, and weight, before we moved on to more complex things like weather, chemical reactions, and cellular biology. In time, we've explored the measurement of more ephemeral phenomena like depression, trust, and creativity, developing new means of empiricism to help us understand our world. Of course, once we can measure something accurately, we can record it. If we collect a data point repeatedly, we can create a dataset from which a table may be created and a graph may be drawn. With just two data points, we can create a trend line projecting out into the unwritten future space ahead. If we recorded a value of "10" last Monday and this Monday's recorded number is "20," then a dotted line naturally emerges that points at "30" by next Monday, if things continue in a similar vein. With three data points, we can get a better idea of that trend, with four points a better idea still. With even more data points over a longer period of time, we can start to observe patterns beyond linear projections. If something has dipped for the last three summers, then it stands to reason that this is likely to happen again next summer. Cyclical movements begin to reveal themselves, allowing us to project forward through extrapolation and helping us to make informed decisions. If a farmer has harvested his corn for the last five years and noticed that the corn harvested later in the season has been more durable or more profitable, then he's more likely to leave next year's crop in the ground a little longer. This is empirically minded Should Futurism in action.

These techniques can become even more powerful once we combine datasets, allowing us to explore how one thing might relate to another. If we can measure the temperature and the amount of rain every day, we can plot these values on the same chart, which might help our farmer see corollaries, dependencies, and relationships in his cornfield. With enough data and measurement, we can even discover relationships that step beyond the obvious; the challenge then becomes one of attributing causation. How can we be sure that a shift in one dataset has directly caused a change elsewhere? Is it just a coincidence, or are they actually linked? Occasionally, two disconnected datasets exhibit spooky levels of connectivity in an often-humorous phenomenon known as "spurious correlation." For example, between 2000 and 2009 there is a 99.26 percent correlation between the divorce rates in Maine and the consumption of margarine in the United States. It's hard to see how the two might be related, but the pattern exists nonetheless. As even more datasets are collected, any statistician worth their salt can begin to map the interconnections and relationships between huge quantities of variables. In order for our farmer's corn to grow, we need the soil to have the correct balance of nutrients and acidity, there needs to be an appropriate mix of sunshine and rain, pests need to be managed, and pollinators need to be encouraged. In the observable world, a single event is almost always the result of a host of influencing factors, and adjustments in their relative weights and relationships can significantly affect the overall outcome.

The emergence of unitary consistency and the development of statistical analysis have undoubtedly resulted in significant advances in our world, many of which we now take for granted. Our ability to record data, recognize patterns, create models, and project those models forward has unlocked a great many of life's mysteries, making commonplace what would feel like absolute magic to our predecessors. Today, I can open a free app on my phone and see that next Wednesday the temperature will be around twenty-six degrees with a little cloud in the morning, and sure enough when Wednesday rolls around, it's about twenty-six degrees and a little cloudy. This kind of predictive ability has naturally proved incredibly useful to our species. Statistical techniques, probability, modeling, and numeric representation have allowed us to project forward with remarkable accuracy, across everything from medicine and finance to social sciences, engineering, and sports.

Almost every industry of sufficient maturity uses some form of modeling approach to help them pry open the future and make bets in the present, but as with any technology, the intoxicating nature of these techniques can frequently blind us to their pitfalls. When we are considering any complex arrangement of things, there's a tendency to see the interconnections between the variables as a mechanical system. As one thing goes up and another goes down, our minds begin to create fixed linkages between the two. This metaphorical parallelization has led to a mechanistic representation of countless aspects of our lives, and a belief in connected cycles of cause and effect that operate with singular, predictable, and reliable outcomes.

The English botanist Arthur Tansley became fascinated with this mechanistic mental model and the desire to understand the relationships between individual elements in nature. In 1935, he published "The Use and Abuse of Vegetational Concepts and Terms," in which he first used the term "ecosystem" to describe the vast complexity of nature as a series of connected inputs, outputs, and feedback loops. This approach led to an explosion in the numeric, mechanistic representation of complex structures and the emergence of an interdisciplinary practice known as systems theory. This posits that every arrangement—no matter how complex—may be understood in measurable terms. It can be mapped out with each variable linked to its neighbors in a system diagram resembling an electrical circuit or city-scale sewer system. As one thing increases, the adjoining parts of the system need to cope with that increase. As one thing reduces, it might require more from those things connected to it; if one thing fails catastrophically, then connected parts of the system may also fail. It's a clean, rational, and fundamentally logical way to look at the world. Once a system is measured, mapped, and understood, we can start playing with these variables, tweaking the knobs and dials to see what might happen and converting recorded data into a means for simulation or prediction. There's an underlying attitude here, stemming from the Enlightenment era, which proposes that the more empirical evidence we can gather, the more we can understand, and this drive to extract more data from the world around us has been at the heart of much of our thinking for at least half a century.

As computer systems evolved and allowed larger and more numerous data streams to be compared and correlated, we began tying more and more sources of data together into complex webs of cause and effect, creating systems that reached beyond the abilities of individual human calculation. Immensely intricate networks and interdependencies became subsections of even larger systems, and people began to off-load their decisions to models which many didn't truly understand, and which even fewer could fully interrogate. Many of our most vital systems are now built atop this kind of complexity, running incredibly detailed mathematical models to try to isolate underlying patterns, and generating algorithms to allow us to move from recorded data into simulations about the future. Nowhere is this more evident than with money, perhaps the most important numbers in many of our lives. Our economic systems have become tightly interlinked, exceptionally rapid and essentially unmappable, regularly working well beyond the general cognitive abilities of humans. Pricing strategies, credit ratings, risk profiles, and arbitrage decisions are all built upon immensely complicated, sprawling, and interlinked systems whose real edges are all but impossible to discern. For example, in the US stock market, around 75 percent of overall trading volume is now generated through algorithmically defined deals—computers are making deals with other computers, and it's increasingly difficult for us to follow their reasoning.

This empirically minded branch of Should Futurism looks backward through recorded history, observing our essentially chaotic world and seeking to represent it numerically, systematically, and algorithmically. It has a voracious appetite for data and uses numbers to interpret what it sees, aiming to reduce even the most multifaceted, nuanced relationships into graphable systems or codes to be broken. Once a system is mapped, Should Futurists use this data to develop a position, building ever more impenetrable walls of logic around their ideas and making singular, unemotional, and assertedly rational statements about the future. This type of work has no time for hopes, wishes, superstitions, or beliefs, and has no interest in the shape of fallen entrails, the outcomes of Ouija boards, or the prognostications of palmistry. It bases its ideas about the future on the trajectory of measured data and finds its roots deep within our adoption of the scientific method, an approach that has become so ingrained in us that we trust it perhaps more than we should.

NUMERIC FICTION

ROMAN ROY: *Where did those fun little numbers, where did that come from?*
KENDALL ROY: *Hey, projections . . . right?*

We began this section on Should Futurism by discussing the thorny concept of "better," a slippery comparative adjective that develops throughout our lives, sits deep within us all, and underpins every one of our decisions. There are topics on which the vast majority of people agree, and where the word "better" is more easily deployed, but for every proposition there's undoubtedly a counterperspective. In order to convince people that we have a more robust or more viable destination in mind, we find ourselves instinctively searching for ways to bolster our arguments, to make them feel more rational or reasonable, and for that it's hard to beat a compelling stack of numbers.

With a bit of skill, numbers can be deployed to add heft and believability to any argument—I've done that numerous times already in this book—and when we're talking about the future, a prediction with numbers attached is much more effective than one without. The entire business of venture capital (and, indeed, all investing) has been built on our comfort with projected figures. Huge bets of people, resources, and capital are regularly made based on the trajectory of a trend line. Numbers are an incredibly persuasive tool for futurists. There's just something about them. They feel so reliable, so solid, and so real. If you say "six," I see six. There's no ambiguity and no uncertainty there. You say "a 50 percent reduction," and I see half of what was there just a moment ago. You show me a dotted line that reaches 50,000 by 2030, and it feels like we'll be at 50,000 by 2030. While it's probably not wise to head too far down the path of philosophy, objectivity, and scientific realism, it feels like numbers hold the upper hand in almost any debate about the future; however, this sense of surety conceals a myth. Economists, strategists, and analysts create mathematical models with lofty titles like "dynamic stochastic general equilibrium" and "autoregressive integrated moving averages," but—like all models—they're based on historical data. Once the line on a chart changes from solid to dotted and we step beyond the present into the future, these numbers cease to be data. These dotted lines don't *know* the future; they're projections, hunches, or stories that are created from what's happened in the past. So let's call them what they are. They're "numeric fiction."

Over time—and with sufficient experience—most futurists stop making predictions. Bombastic, confident, singular declarations about the future are easily mocked, as their visionary certainty feels silly and is likely to be disproved over time. However, in numeric fiction, this culture of confident certainty appears to be alive and well. While margins of error and elements of uncertainty are integrated into some of this work, we've become accustomed to seeing figures firmly pinned to dates, dotted lines striding boldly toward the future, and the confident use of numbers to define the shape of tomorrow. A dotted line on a chart can be alluring—particularly if it's headed in a direction you approve of—but make no mistake: *it's a story.*

Take a look at the following chart, for example, produced by the US Energy Information Administration in 2018. The three dotted lines show the growth predictions for total primary energy use in the United States from 2000, 2002, and 2004, and the solid line shows the actual recorded figures.

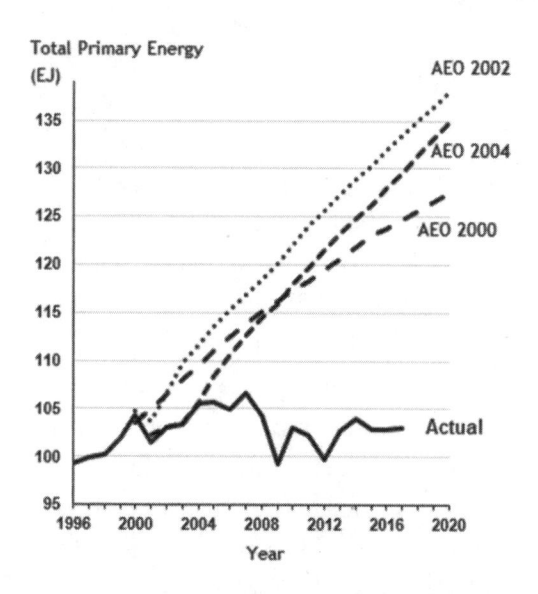

Total primary energy use projected in *Annual Energy Outlook* (AEO) (Peter D. Saundry, *Energy, Sustainability and Society,* Springer Nature, Jan 25, 2019)

With the benefit of hindsight you can see that those dotted lines were hilariously incorrect, year after year after year. Many people and businesses pride themselves on being able to make projections of this kind, and indeed we all strive to be somehow "ahead of the curve," but inaccuracies and predictive gaffes such as these are surprisingly common in the world of numeric fiction. The renowned economist Irving Fisher declared that US stock prices had reached "a permanently high plateau" in 1929, just days before the stock market crashed. Many financial experts failed to see the risks associated with subprime mortgages in the US housing market shortly before that bubble burst, leading to the global financial crisis of 2008. In the early 2000s many analysts projected that oil prices would remain low due to abundant supply and weak demand, yet oil prices subsequently surged to record highs within a decade. Following this spike, the Goldman Sachs analyst Arjun Murti—who was dubbed the "oracle of oil" by *The New York Times*—predicted in May 2008 that prices would increase to over $200 per barrel, before they promptly plummeted back down to around $32 by December. In 2011, Gartner predicted that the Android operating system would command less than 50 percent market share by 2015, but in reality, it gobbled up 84 percent of the world's cell phone users.

I could go on, yet despite this well-documented history of wild inaccuracy, somehow a spreadsheet, figure, or chart still carries incredible heft. These things feel more rational, less whimsical, and more objective than other types of futurism, which makes them incredibly alluring to corporate leadership, investors, and the general public. A definitive statistic adds a tantalizing level of certainty to the future, but certainty is the enemy of doubt, and all too often the suppressor of curiosity. Should Futurists regularly quote the Canadian ice hockey legend Wayne Gretzky, who allegedly said, "I skate to where the puck is going to be, not where it has been." They adore this quote, as it reflects their view on the world, but their belief in it is misplaced. A hockey puck is an inert object moving in a linear fashion over an essentially frictionless surface, but in the vast majority of situations outside of ice hockey, knowing where the "puck" is going to be is, as I've mentioned, a story.

We're beginning to realize, albeit slowly, that the world doesn't really work like one of Arthur Tansley's neatly calibrated interlinked systems. While mechanical metaphors can be useful at a macro scale, once we begin to dive deeper into a system, we find even more variables, each of which has the ability to dramatically skew the system's performance and outputs. Not only that, but in recent years, the world of numbers has become increasingly volatile and capricious. Half a century of progress in sensing, monitoring, and cataloguing the intricacies of our world has led us to believe that we can start to see the little green digits lurking beneath the skin of the Matrix, but we're also beginning to realize that our ability to accurately forecast important numbers isn't perhaps as good as we thought. As the drumbeat of change has quickened, previously reliable norms have become changeable, stochastic, and precipitous, which means that spotting patterns and relationships is becoming even more complex. Despite this, numeric fiction (in the forms of projections, estimates, and predictions) sits at the heart of almost all decision-making in industry, and it's often presented more like synthetic fact than speculation. It shapes our world in every possible regard, and despite frequently being flawed, it's characterized by an air of abundant, effortless superiority and still remains the most trusted futures technique for governments, businesses, financiers, and economists.

This kind of Should Futurism finds its way into business primarily in the form of "corporate strategy," a deliberately nebulous description for what is little more than intuition backed by data. Many companies employ full-time strategists to help chart a path into the future, but this work is frequently supplemented by external management consulting firms, a world dominated by the "Big Three": Bain & Company, McKinsey & Company, and Boston Consulting Group. These firms collectively employ around 80,000 employees in over 250 offices worldwide, and they exist to help large organizations with a great number of services, typically focused on optimization, performance improvement, and advice to aid in decision-making. In order to do this, they build huge dossiers of information, casebooks full of interviews, recorded data, and observed trends, which they use to make their recommendations. It's easy to pick holes in this work—and people regularly do—but these consultants offer a valuable service. All businesses need to make decisions about their future, and those decisions feel significantly better when backed by some level of numeric reassurance. Given the world as it is, the work of these external consultants is valid, and in many cases vital, but there is little acknowledgment of the significant levels of intuition that sit at its core. Implicit in the partnership with these consultants is a level of trust—something that seems at odds with the core proposition of the scientific mindset. The data on any given question is available to all who seek it, but the future described by this data is interpretive. When you hire these companies, you're paying for their perspective on the future, not an absolute, empirical truth.

The greatest trick this type of futurism ever played was convincing the world it doesn't exist. We rarely—if ever—think of this type of work as futurism. It disappears deep into our collective consciousness, a backbeat of ideas playing constantly in the distance yet affecting everything around it. It spills out in political manifestos, investment predictions, and strategy documents. It dances across our screens in business news chyrons, in stock market punditry, and in the proclamations of market analysts. We see it in the pages of investment prospectuses, in pitch decks, and in projected sales data. It slides underneath yield outlooks, consumer targets, inflation estimates, traffic forecasts, user-adoption metrics, government policy, house-price trajectories, and sports predictions. We're so convinced by its logic that when it breaks—and it regularly breaks—we feel somehow cheated. It builds confidence in its guesses with data in an attempt to domesticate the future, but such is our bias toward a logistic, numeric assessment of the world that we place an inappropriate level of trust in these guesses. The work of our economists and data scientists feels at odds with the whimsical, emotional work of most other futurists, but I'm convinced the two worlds share significantly more than they might claim. Where a futurist might say "research," a strategist might say "analysis." Where a futurist might say "pattern," a strategist might say "model," and where a futurist might use the term "visions," a strategist might use "projections." Their work is essentially the same, but the predominantly numeric presentation medium of corporate strategy affords it a significant level of hierarchical supremacy—and a warm seat at the top table.

While we're here, we should touch on a peculiar quirk of data-driven Should Futurism, one which perhaps represents the ultimate expression of the steadfast rationalism that sits at its core. Should Futurism typically focuses on incremental change toward a defined goal, gradually nudging us toward some desired end point through small, daily adjustments. For this reason, it could be accused of having a limited imagination, but that couldn't be further from the truth. Occasionally, this kind of numeric, empirical disposition can lead to a strident, audacious form of vision, which would feel outlandish and fantastical were it not for the reassuring numbers expressed alongside it.

The English polymath Sir Francis Galton (a half cousin of Charles Darwin) was a highly regarded member of the Victorian scientific community, known for his work in statistics, meteorology, and psychology, but he's perhaps most notorious for his other, less wholesome work. The practice of animal husbandry to create more humanly desirable offspring has been a well-known and widely deployed agricultural practice for centuries, but following the publication of Darwin's book *On the Origin of Species* in 1859, the concept of intentional breeding became significantly more formalized. If one is trying to produce sturdy cattle with thick fat deposits for tastier beef, it makes sense to breed two animals with those characteristics, and thus gradually move the herd toward this intentional goal. Francis Galton became enamored of Darwin's work and attempted to transpose these ideas onto humans, suggesting that families with "good marks" should be financially incentivized to interbreed. In order to help him define what he considered to be preferential characteristics, Galton set about measuring human subjects with specifically designed apparatus to collect their height, weight, head circumference, and other body proportions to create a huge database of human physiological data. In parallel, he assessed their family histories, intelligence, and cognitive functions and created countless statistical models to build further evidence around his case, leading to a numerically based rating system for each individual, in an approach he termed "eugenics." Eugenics offered a seemingly rational and logical framing to what was actually an abhorrent underlying idea—that of numerically justified racism. Galton's approach was so compelling that the core tenets of eugenics were later adopted by the Third Reich in Germany to justify its segregation policies and the ultimate destruction of countless groups it viewed as "undesirable" for the future it sought. Even following the abject horror of the Second World War, the principles of eugenics remained in use in the United States until as late as the 1970s as part of its immigration, racial segregation, and compulsory sterilization programs. Similar practices persisted in Denmark, Finland, Iceland, and Norway, leading to as many as 170,000 forced sterilizations, the overwhelming majority of which were performed on women. Numbers have an ability to feel incredibly rational and trustworthy when one is talking about the future, even when the things they're measuring are not.

In the modern world, the numerically driven radical position is perhaps best exemplified by Elon Musk. Despite his seemingly impulsive decisions, Musk is a science buff at heart who relies heavily on data and numeric projections to validate his visions for radical change. His quest to turn humans into a multiplanetary species originates from an assertion that life on Earth is simply too precarious (particularly in the face of asteroid strikes) and his projections of all the available data lead to only one logical outcome, however absurd or extreme that might sound. Musk tells us that it's not simply that he *wants* a colony on Mars—his data *proves that we need one.* Silicon Valley is a curious place in this regard. It's a region utterly dominated by data and populated by those who can play comfortably in its presence. This often leads to mechanistic mindsets and an associated lack of imagination, but can occasionally lead to outlandish propositions and outrageous conclusions, such is the compelling nature of data and the soothing certainty of projected logic.

THE FUTURE IS ACCRETIVE

Put simply, Should Futurism seeks to precisely describe the future (either the one it wants to create or the one it believes will occur), and then report that vision back to the present in order to shape our decisions and priorities. This type of clear-cut focus can be extremely helpful, and it's what makes this mindset so prevalent and so popular, but it also represents a considerable and underappreciated weakness. Thinking about the future as a declarative statistic, a dot on a graph, or a well-defined, singular prediction can be reassuring, but this way of thinking about the future is deliberately exclusive. It creates an environment of artificial certainty and encourages us to think of the future as a singular, quantifiable destination when in reality, it's anything but.

When envisioning the future, we tend to think about it as some sort of "different" place, an abstract location that exists separated from the world we now inhabit. I realize that it's stating the obvious, but the future is simply an evolution of the present. Each moment ticks along, days gradually become weeks, and months become years. We take trips, we celebrate birthdays, we change jobs and move homes, and before we can gather our thoughts, a decade has passed. In the 1980s, I would've struggled to picture the year 2025, a full ten years beyond the Hill Valley of *Back to the Future Part II*. My imagination would have spiraled out of control if I was asked to think about it, but when I look around today it doesn't really *feel* like the future. It's just crept up on me, bit by bit, little by little, and here we are. Ford Cortinas, floppy disks, and telephone directories have all but disappeared, while cell phones, electric scooters, search engines, and Zero Sugar Wild Cherry Pepsi have all slid into view. This is how change happens. Not in some big sweep, but as a series of sparks and splutters, gradually changing the average over time. It's also important to remember that since the 1980s our cutlery, pavements, tea towels, pencils, carpets, socks, and tennis balls have stayed largely the same, remaining relatively unchanged by the passage of the decades. As the science fiction writer Bruce Sterling commented so eloquently in 2004: "The future isn't a noun, it's a verb." The future isn't a destination or a single figure on a chart, *it's a process.*

Once we come to terms with this reality, we can begin to construct a more thoughtful vision of what the future might hold, and perhaps reconsider the language we use to discuss it. Over the last twenty years of working on future-oriented projects I've been frequently reminded that the future builds up like sedimentary rock. New things pile upon the past and create layers that evolve and erode at different speeds. Some things appear with a great flourish, shine brightly for a brief moment, and quickly disappear (NFTs, for example), while other things evolve slowly and hang around for decades (such as telephones), but, importantly, these things never exist in isolation. They overlap, nestle together, interact, intertwine, interlace, converge, collide, and complement one another in ways that are as complex as they are numerous.

Let's imagine you've just purchased a genuinely modern device, a VR headset for example. It represents the tip of our technological spear and is crammed full of the very latest chips, drivers, optical units, and sensors. It's so new you aren't even sure what to do with it yet. On one side of the box is a beautiful CGI representation of the thing, on the other side are images of people wearing the headset with mouths agape in wonder. When it arrives in your home, you remove it from the box and plug it into a games console that is two years old. The console is plugged into an extension cord that also powers the TV and your phone charger, and it sits on a table that you inherited from your sister when she left for university. The table leg was fixed a couple of years ago with screws you found in the garage, and everything sits on a rug you bought from Ikea in 2004, in the living room of a house that was built in 1948. The electricity supply for this device runs on a utility frequency protocol developed in the early 1900s that oscillates at either 50 or 60 Hz depending on where you live. Your VR headset features a double insulation icon in accordance with IEC 60335–1 and is assembled to comply with Federal Communications Commission guidelines, which regulate the electromagnetic emissions of electronic devices to prevent interference with other devices and systems. The software running on the games console is connected to a Wi-Fi router in the upstairs bedroom, which connects via ethernet to the telecommunications network, which is licensed and maintained by an internet service provider. In truth, I've only just begun to describe this immense web of interconnected systems and artifacts—and we should probably stop here—but all contemporary life works in this way. Seemingly simple devices, services, or ideas are infinitely tethered to one another in vast, interdependent networks whose edges are almost impossible to define. In a fleeting moment of interaction, complex arrangements of systems are invoked, building off one another in a tightly interlinked series of relationships, all working at different speeds, with different motivations, hierarchies, and priorities.

We're all surrounded by countless layers of paint, plaster, brick, metal, plastic, and wood held together in something we call "the present," which meshes with third-party systems, is managed by layers of government oversight and legal policies, and is threaded through a complex web of societal, cultural, and behavioral norms. It all just piles together over the decades, or, to use a more academic word, our world is "accretive." But this is rarely how we think about the future, nor how we represent it. We produce artists' impressions of future objects floating magically in infinite white environments. Our charts feature single dotted lines projecting forward to *X*s drawn in free space, unbothered by anything surrounding them. We illustrate the future with individual statistics representing the one factor we care the most about. We make predictions with certainty and gusto, reassured by our dogmas or our huge collections of data. We've become accustomed to thinking about the future in this manner: as a noncontextual space with a singular thing in it to admire, an idea on a plinth in an infinitely bright gallery over which we have total control.

As is so often the case, there's a lovely German word that is useful here—*Gesamtkunstwerk*, which loosely translated means "a total work of art." The term was first made popular by Richard Wagner in an 1849 essay where he advocated for a harmonious reconciliation of art, opera, and drama in a unified and cohesive setting. More broadly, the term is used today in the fields of design and architecture to describe works wherein a single hand defines all aspects of a project. Frank Lloyd Wright had a penchant for specifying everything in his buildings, from the exterior, interior, and furniture to the wall coverings, door hinges, paint colors, fabric patterns, and cutlery. In theory, a *Gesamtkunstwerk* is an expression of unity, but in reality, it's also a manifestation of control, a desire to impose a creative will on every aspect of a project. It's introverted, self-admiring, and isolationist, or—to go even further—it's *selfish*, because that's just not how the world works. Any future intervention will naturally reach into the existing landscape, sending out shock waves of impact in all directions, and the existing landscape will do likewise in return. Ideas about the future don't have hard edges; they're fuzzy, imprecise, and unpredictable. Yet these monolithic, singular, all-encompassing visions of the future continue to dominate our imagination.

Perhaps nowhere is this singular, self-centered approach to the future more accurately illustrated than by a gargantuan project that is currently rising from the sands along the Red Sea. In Tabuk Province of northwestern

Saudi Arabia, a breathtaking venture is underway which may prove to be a defining example (positive or otherwise) of our generation's mark on the planet, an audacious architectural plan to build a new city at a scale which utterly dwarfs the urban planning ambitions of Georges-Eugène Haussmann, Ebenezer Howard, or Walt Disney. As part of Crown Prince Mohammed bin Salman's vision to diversify the Saudi economy—and reduce its dependence on oil revenues—The Line forms the centerpiece of the region's Neom project and consists of a perfectly straight building 170 kilometers long, 200 meters wide, and 500 meters tall. The renderings of the project are so extreme and arresting that they feel like absurd fantasies, or modern versions of the unrestrained ideas from the Vkhutemas students, but this is not simply a concept: the project has already broken ground. The Line is an almost perfect example of a *Gesamtkunstwerk*, enforcing its own will on anything external and ignoring any local context—a huge, reflective monolith reaching out across the barren desert as far as the eye can see. But of course the desert's not barren, is it? We often use deserts as a metaphor for nothingness (indeed, I did that earlier), but in reality, The Line cuts right across acres of landscape that have been occupied by the Huwaitat tribe for centuries. Animals, plants, and other living species also call this place their home, or pass through it on daily or seasonal migrations. The Line will also exert its own force on the local climate and make huge demands on the region's natural resources. During construction, global supply chains will be reconfigured, new commerce routes will emerge, and labor forces will be drawn into the area. Economic norms will be altered, new addresses will be created, and wealth will be redistributed. The Line may appear to be a singular, assertive statement, but it's actually attempting to dovetail into the existing world in a billion ways, many of which may yet be invisible.

At a more local scale, you're no doubt familiar with the renderings of future buildings that architectural firms often paste on the temporary walls that surround construction sites. One thing you'll notice in these images is that it's almost always sunny. There's never any rain, hot dog carts, or queues of traffic in these worlds—which is perhaps understandable given that they're attempting to attract new tenants—but what's less forgivable is that the surrounding neighborhoods are often entirely excluded from these images. If the neighborhood *is* included, it's often merely hinted at in the background haze, or represented by simplified, gray rectangular blocks, lest they steal attention from the majesty of the central proposition. In truth—as we're all well aware—the surrounding neighborhood will play an absolutely integral role in how this new building will function, dictating flows of people, the passage of light, complex interplays of wildlife and traffic, socioeconomic relationships, noise, pollution, parking, and more. While we're here, we should acknowledge that the tools we use to explore, visualize, and present the future might also be contributing to this singular way of thinking. When opening a new document, Photoshop file, CAD drawing, or spreadsheet, we're always greeted by an empty page, an infinite open space where our idea can be brought to life without any reference to anything else. It's hardly surprising that what results is often a representation of isolated, noncontextual futures, which don't acknowledge their role in broader ongoing events or the effects they might have on the things around them. Should Futurism regularly falls into the *Gesamtkunstwerk* trap, making singular, self-assured statements and unconsciously expressing levels of control on variables over which it has very little agency. I firmly believe that all futures work would be significantly improved if we embraced the notion that any new idea has to integrate into the ongoing flow of life—that is, we have to write our new character into the play *as it's being performed*. We have to understand the other players, identify the spaces for change, and draft behind the ongoing storylines. We have to understand the plots currently underway, the tone of the dialogue, and the overall act structure of the work; otherwise our addition will arrive with a thud, stand out awkwardly, or derail the production entirely. If we're thinking about the world as a Tansleyesque interconnected system, we have to acknowledge that the web of interconnected elements is perhaps more expansive than we could ever imagine.

If you're a person who likes models and metaphors, there's a way of thinking about the world that might be useful here. The concept of Pace Layers was proposed by the American polymath Stewart Brand to describe how different global systems move at different speeds, itself a modification of the Shearing Layers concept introduced by the British architect Frank Duffy in the 1970s. In Brand's 1994 book *How Buildings Learn*, he describes a lamination of multiple layers, each of which moves at a different speed and represents a functionally different aspect of life on Earth. At the bottom of the stack is nature, the slowest-moving of all the layers, above which follow culture, governance, infrastructure, and commerce, before we reach the fastest-moving layer: fashion. This represents a diagrammatic simplification, of course, but it helps us think about what might be happening when we introduce anything new into the world and how it needs to find its place within these layers, each of which has different priorities and different operating methods. When we think about the future, a conscious effort to consider these spheres of influence always makes a proposition markedly richer, certainly more so than a single statistic, a dot on a chart, a pithy prediction, or an isolated image of Shangri-La.

Of course, an important aspect of the Pace Layers model is the different speeds at which the layers change, and being aware of this difference in pacing can help in the development of more rigorous propositions for the future. But this is becoming increasingly complex, as we have to acknowledge that the layers in Brand's model might be shuffling somewhat. Nature used to be the most stable layer in this model, moving and evolving so slowly that it appeared almost static, but thanks primarily to the behavior of humans over the last couple of centuries, many aspects of our natural world are now changing at previously unseen rates. Likewise, culture often feels like it's moving significantly faster than governance, driven by the ubiquity of communications technologies that have allowed ideas and beliefs to spread at incredible speeds and radically changed the ways in which communities think and behave. Whatever the order of these layers (and whatever this order might become in the future), what's important is to understand that they exist, and that ignoring how an idea, prediction, or proposition might nestle within them introduces a huge number of blind spots and significant associated risk.

I've been somewhat strong in my criticism of the use of science fiction in futures work so far, but works of science fiction can occasionally embrace this notion of accretion and Pace Layers remarkably well. Ridley Scott's 1982 masterpiece *Blade Runner* features some significant technological leaps in its world-building—flying vehicles, city-height screens, and replicant robots, to name but three—but the reason these changes feel so real and so engaging is the careful inclusion of elements that feel like they've endured the change. Seedy noodle bars, scruffy leather jackets, heavy rainstorms, and urban congestion make this future world feel like an evolution of the present rather than a completely new proposition. The world of *Blade Runner* feels a little bit like the world I recognize, and this helps the new things settle into my imagination a little more comfortably. A contemporary master of this technique is Charlie Brooker, whose Netflix anthology series *Black Mirror* explores—and frequently satirizes—emerging technologies, often with great subtlety. These episodes succeed in their storytelling ambitions because they're accretive. The worlds portrayed in *Black Mirror* still have awkward dinner parties, petty arguments, foul language, and comfortable sweaters. The characters live lives that feel broadly familiar, which makes the introduction of new technologies or ideas much more relatable. Any compelling story about the future needs this kind of grounding; otherwise everything starts to feel abstract. Brooker also appears to understand that "technology" becomes "stuff" incredibly rapidly. When visualizing the future, we need to acknowledge that the stories we're telling are happening to the characters as normal, ordinary, everyday occurrences. They're accustomed to using this new thing, this new service, or this new office building; it's simply become a part of their everyday life. Future storytelling succeeds when new ideas feel normalized, embedded, and enmeshed with the forward momentum of everything around them. The future isn't a single thing, it's accretive. The future isn't a noun, it's a verb.

Whenever we find ourselves feeling overly confident about the future, it's likely we've strayed into Should territory. Before we get to that point, it would probably make sense to have spent significant time looking into the infinitely dense network of complexity on either side of our idea, full of conditions we might have missed, potential variables we might have ignored, and countless other things our new idea might bump into. The ideologies that sit within us all do a good job of blinkering us to this process of lateral curiosity, offering simplified and confident perspectives to frame our actions and convenient ways to ignore other possibilities. "Should" can be a dangerous word. It's self-assured, confident, and secure, and actively deletes other avenues of thought. In order to bolster this veil of surety, it can be tempting to lean on historical data to defend our version of the future, but data often isn't as good as we think it is—and in many fields may actually be getting worse. Where no data exists, we point at irrefutable predictions or projections from our trusted experts, expensive analysts, or sacred scriptures. In this way, we build layers of artificial truth around the future, reassuring scaffolds of conviction that can be blown away by the lightest breeze of reality, a missed implication, an unpredicted force.

I've been lucky to have worked for some brilliant people in my career, many of whom have fundamentally shaped the ways in which I think about the future. When I was a part of Nokia's Advanced Design team, I'd often get strident about my beliefs regarding the direction of a project. I was confident that I'd identified the right thing to do, why it was inconceivable to do anything else, and why this was what we absolutely *should do*. My boss would often respond in his quiet, friendly Welsh voice: "Are you sure?"

A confident singularity of vision can be reassuring, and compelling when thinking about the future, but such conviction can frequently underestimate the levels of uncertainty under which we all operate, and how that vision might sit in the broader landscape of our incredibly complex world. Even so, singular, simplified, confident beacons in the future remain enduringly popular. Any politician knows that a slogan reaches more minds than a manifesto, and any business leader knows that a single, bold statistic reaches more investors than a thoughtful, open-minded debate. But complexity doesn't go away; it just hides in the shadows, waiting to surprise us at a later date. In order to counter this challenge, we've developed a series of approaches that are more circumspect, more pluralistic, and more uncertain than Should Futurism. A world where every probability has a counterpossibility. A world with an infinite number of potential outcomes, possible routes, or plausible impacts. A world where an almost infinite number of futures are fair game for discussion.

Welcome to the world of the Might Futurists.

MIGHT

THE MIGHT FUTURISTS

Theirs is the realm of sprawling discussion.

They are agnostic, analytic, and thoughtful.

They have a counter for every idea.

They think broadly.

They revel in the discovery of overlooked but important details.

They explore beyond the subject at hand.

They believe in their methods, models, and frameworks.

They're comfortable holding many things in tension.

They embrace uncertainty, discuss plurality, and constantly reassess.

They overflow with opinions and relish debate.

They can be indecisive, uncertain, and apprehensive.

FUTURES PLURAL

It is impossible to forecast the future, and it is foolish to try to do so.
—PIERRE WACK

Over the last few decades, the commercial world has grown a little tired of the wide-eyed fantasies of Could Futurism, and, while still dominant, the certainty and confidence of Should Futurism's pronouncements seem increasingly unreliable in today's volatile and interconnected world. Into the space between these two factions has stepped Might Futurism, which now occupies a significant segment of the professional futures landscape. It's pragmatic, pluralistic, and methodological, which also makes it perhaps the least glamorous member of the futures scene. You may have noticed that I've regularly used the term "futures" rather than "future" throughout this book. This very trendy affectation represents the central conceit of Might Futurism: that we cannot know exactly what the future will be, so it's essential to consider multiple possible outcomes. Essentially, Might Futurism engages with probability; it's an exercise in likelihood that continually stack-ranks all imaginable scenarios based on the currently available information. This way of thinking reflects the ways in which many of us subconsciously approach what lies ahead. We build strategies, plans, and contingencies into our decisions and try to think of everything that might happen and what we might do if it does. If we're planning a birthday party for a kid, for example, we might book a bouncy castle and clear the backyard, but we might also make a plan for what to do if it rains. We should also get a number of different snacks in case there are some kids who have special dietary requirements or others who just don't like ice cream, and we should probably make sure there's fuel in the car to drop everyone home afterward. This type of strategic thinking underpins how we all approach the future and influences us in ways we rarely notice.

Ideas of strategy and contingency run deep in all cultures, but they become more formalized when the stakes are particularly high—most notably in times of war. The ability to see multiple steps ahead and preempt what your opponent might do becomes a vital skill in any situation when lives, liberty, or land are at stake. There's a clear benefit in being able to lay out all possible permutations, think through their likelihoods, and use that exercise to identify your next move, and we've countless examples of where it's been done well. In 216 BCE during the Second Punic War, though significantly outnumbered by the Romans, the Carthaginian general Hannibal employed a clever double-envelopment tactic, surrounding and encircling the Roman army and leading to a crushing victory for Carthage. In 1415 King Henry V's forces used the range advantage of his longbowmen to devastating effect against a much larger French army in the fields around Agincourt. In 1942, Soviet forces used a combination of urban warfare, fortifications, and attrition techniques to withstand the German siege, eventually turning the tide and leading to the encirclement and surrender of the German 6th Army at Stalingrad. The ability to explore all options and outthink opponents is revered in all cultures. We respect the complexity of this kind of thought and erect statues and monuments to those who use this ability to good effect.

While the overwhelming majority of us are not in a position to plan wars, this strategic, tactical mindset also acts as the origin for board games such as chess, go, shogi, and xiangqi, all of which are all based on the principles of probability, planning, and an agreed-upon definition of "winning." If the opposition makes a certain move, what's our best counter? What will leave us in the best position to make an attack? What are the best ways to build our defense? Unfortunately, this kind of cumulative decision-making can quickly become unwieldy. If we're playing chess, our first move is fairly simple, a selection from only 20 possible options. Our opponent then responds, resulting in 400 possible board setups. After the second pair of turns, there are 197,742 possible arrangements of pieces, and after three moves, 121 million. Most of us can think a couple of moves ahead before this complexity becomes unwieldy; a chess grandmaster is able to think around fifteen moves ahead, in an astounding feat of mental computation beyond the reach of almost all of us. Over the last century this complex interplay of action, probability, and strategy—learned from decades of real and theoretical combat—has evolved to become the preeminent way in which the world's industries, militaries, and governments approach the future. A consulting industry worth billions of dollars has sprung up around a heady mix of methodological techniques, algorithmic simulations, and large-scale computation efforts, largely building on the work of the Hungarian American math prodigy John von Neumann.

We bandy the term "prodigy" around fairly loosely these days, pinning it on kids who can juggle or play piano scales, but von Neumann truly earned this title. By the age of six he could divide two eight-digit numbers in his head; by eight, he was working on differential and integral calculus. So it's no surprise that he played a major role in defining the mathematical landscape of the developed world throughout his life. In 1928, aged just twenty-five, von Neumann published what he called his Minimax Theorem in the German journal *Mathematische Annalen*, asserting that in a zero-sum game where both sides are fully aware of every move of the opposition, there exists a perfect strategy that minimizes their losses. His work was a revelation, introducing structure to the concept of competition, converting what was considered an instinctual skill into an algebraic expression and birthing the mathematical discipline of game theory. In subsequent years, he extended the Minimax Theorem to include models with imperfect information and more than two players, eventually coauthoring a book on the subject, *Theory of Games and Economic Behavior*, in 1944 with Oskar Morgenstern. The book was a hit with intellectuals across the world, and *The New York Times* covered von Neumann's work on its front page, sparking the emergence of a new discipline of computational economics and strategic analysis.

Four years later, in Santa Monica, California, a small research team left the Douglas Aircraft Company and created an independent organization to provide objective and unbiased analysis of the complex societal and economic challenges following the Second World War. The group named itself RAND (a somewhat lazy contraction of "Research and Development"), and it was to play a major role in American military and political strategy in the coming decades. Building on the game theory work of von Neumann and the systems-thinking approaches of Arthur Tansley, RAND developed mathematical models and analytic techniques to create what the historian David Jardini calls "a science of war through systems analysis." The precursors of these approaches were originally developed by Allied mathematicians during the Second World War, but their limits quickly became apparent, as they focused on static systems that couldn't handle dynamic variables. In many of the complex questions RAND wished to tackle, similar issues quickly arose, and the variables soon became too numerous and too complex for these traditional methods, so the team sought ways to increase their computational and mathematical capability. They initially acquired a Reeves Electronic Analog Computer, a modified electric accounting machine that was capable of simple arithmetic but was hampered by its primitive punched-card interface and had an average run time for a single problem of around a minute. In late 1953, RAND installed an IBM 701 machine, one of only nineteen on Earth, that was capable of undertaking more complex mathematical problems and generating significantly more detail in its outputs. The era of large-scale computation was now well underway, followed closely by the industry of scenario planning and algorithmic simulation.

Meanwhile, on the other side of the world, the United States' primary adversary was making significant technical strides of its own. On October 4, 1957, the USSR launched the world's first satellite from Baikonur Cosmodrome in Kazakhstan. The small, spherical device known as *Sputnik 1* circled the planet every ninety-six minutes, sending a radio signal back to Earth for three weeks before its silver-zinc batteries finally expired. Tensions across the United States spiked immediately. If the Soviet government was able to launch missiles into space, it seemed logical that these missiles could be equipped with warheads and rain terror on the United States at will. The questions of how this could happen, what might happen next, and what the United States could do in response proved to be the perfect challenge for RAND, and the team began to focus most of their thinking on this complex emerging puzzle. They believed that if they could gather huge amounts of information about Russian activity and feed it into immensely complex mathematical models, they could use their computer systems and bespoke software to run through endless cycles of action and reaction to establish a series of strategies, responses, and escalations. Their premise involved looking into the future and outlining countless potential narratives, each branching and dividing with possible responses and retaliations, and filling the unknown future space with an endlessly forking decision tree stretching far off into the distance.

One of the major proponents of these new methods was Herman J. Kahn, a portly chap described by one journalist as being built "like a prize-winning pear" (judging by the evidence of numerous biographies, it seems impossible or at least untoward to introduce him without mentioning his weight, so I have followed suit). Kahn had joined RAND in 1947 and rapidly become a leading figure in the team, combining mathematics, systems theory, and game theory to analyze the likely consequences of a nuclear war. Kahn's core strategy was built around the notion of an overwhelming "second strike" capability, which would lead the Russians to believe that even with a highly coordinated initial attack, the American response would lead to their total destruction. In order to reach this conclusion, the RAND team completed thousands of if-this-then-that scenarios, running data through their analytical models, assigning values to every city and potential missile target, and calculating the likelihood of every possible provocation and retaliation. Kahn's prowess lay in broadening the scope of probability away from the norm, or, as *Scientific American* magazine described it, "thinking the unthinkable"—a characterization Kahn gleefully embraced. By expanding the scope of imagination and projecting multiple possible outcomes forward, Kahn and RAND were able to build ever more potential moves into their calculations, running through what-if and then-what scenarios in an almost infinite cycle of war game simulations. Kahn would regularly make confident proclamations about the outputs of these scenario planning exercises, reassured by the rational numeric bedrock upon which they were built. This analytical mindset also encouraged Kahn to reduce every outcome—no matter how horrific—to a percentage, duration, or dollar amount.

This unwavering dedication to logic came to broad public knowledge with the release of his 1960 book *On Thermonuclear War*, which proposed the idea of a "winnable" nuclear exchange and included numerous breathtaking passages such as "It might well turn out that U.S. decision makers would be willing, among other things, to accept the high risk of an additional one percent of our children being born deformed if that meant not giving up Europe to Soviet Russia." This cold devotion to numeric rationalism would come to define Kahn in the popular press and provided inspiration for the eponymous lead character in Stanley Kubrick's 1964 satire, *Dr. Strangelove*.

The methods and approaches developed by Kahn and RAND originated as tools for large-scale military problems, but it wasn't long before the private sector began to take notice. In the late 1960s, petrochemical giant Royal Dutch/Shell began exploring scenario-planning practices themselves, led by the visionary French executive Pierre Wack (who is quoted at the top of this chapter). In 1965, the company was using a rational financial forecasting tool that it referred to by the less-than-inspiring title of "Unified Planning Machinery" (UPM). This approach was built upon a "business as usual" projection mindset, which made executives anxious and was, to quote Wack, "perceived as a dangerous substitute for real thinking in times of uncertainty and potential discontinuity."

In 1971, Shell ran an experiment with scenario-planning methods as an alternative approach to thinking about the future. Wack and his team set about building four scenarios to explore the potential future of the organization, hoping to push their thinking into unusual but plausible territories. The first scenario was a future lifted almost wholesale from the Unified Planning Machinery forecasts, free from significant surprises and disruptions. The second projected high taxation, low economic growth, and a depressed oil market. The third explored another low-growth model, with a slowdown in international trade, increased economic nationalism, and the introduction of protective tariffs. The final scenario explored increasing demands for coal and nuclear energy at the expense of oil. Once these four scenarios were in place, Wack's team began to examine how each player in the oil industry might behave in each case, and what became clear was that their interests differed, sometimes significantly. Under each circumstance every player would behave in a different way, which was also curiously reflected in their present-day decisions and actions. These what-if scenarios allowed Shell's leadership not only to explore new potentials but also to better understand the present-day behaviors, motivations, and threats within their industry, which proved incredibly useful. In 1972, the scenario-planning approach was extended to Shell's central offices and larger business units before it was finally recommended throughout the group in 1973, replacing the UPM process company-wide. Advocates of these techniques claim that their adoption helped Shell "predict" everything from the 1973 energy crisis to the collapse of the oil market in 1986, the fall of the Soviet Union, and the rise of Muslim radicalism, but that's missing the point. Scenario work isn't really about prediction at all—it's about *plurality*. It's about stretching the imagination further, casting the net wider, and developing multiple perspectives on what might lie ahead.

THINK TANKS

I'd like to take a moment here to talk about think tanks, a peculiar and somewhat distorted offshoot of the pioneering work of early scenario futurists such as Wack and Kahn. Following the incendiary publication of *On Thermonuclear War*, relations soured between Herman Kahn and RAND, and he departed to form a new organization that better suited his ideological stance and satisfied his desire for greater independence. Along with Max Singer (a young government lawyer and former RAND colleague) and the New York attorney Oscar M. Ruebhausen, he founded the Hudson Institute in New York in 1961, with a mission to "think about the future in unconventional ways." In parallel with his Cold War work, Kahn hoped to apply his knowledge of military strategy and scenario planning to other fields of study, including geopolitics, economics, demography, anthropology, science, and technology. He set about hiring experts and advisors from increasingly diverse backgrounds, including philosophers, novelists, political scientists, and conceptual artists, and used scenario-planning techniques to forecast long-term developments well beyond defense, gradually evolving the Hudson Institute into a full-fledged think tank.

Think tanks are strange beasts, not typically associated with futurism in any meaningful way, but they play a remarkably powerful role in exploring, projecting, and shaping the world ahead of us. Their outputs aren't sexy images of sleek hovering vehicles or enticing magical devices; their work most frequently results in proposals for government policy, lobbying materials, or research reports. Before the Second World War, the term "think tank" was primarily used to describe a person's brain—an almost poetic metaphor for a reservoir of ideas. It was only in the 1950s that the term became synonymous with a safe place for the discussion of plans and strategies, yet throughout history, various groups have performed remarkably similar functions.

The first institution we might identify as a precursor to the modern think tank was the grandly titled Royal United Services Institute for Defence and Security Studies, founded in London in 1831 by the Duke of Wellington to formalize the science of British defense. The descendant of this institution, RUSI, is still in existence today, over 190 years later, albeit with a slightly modified (and intentionally more wholesome) ambition to "inform, influence, and enhance public debate to help build a safer and more stable world." In the early 1900s, the wealthy philanthropist Andrew Carnegie founded the Carnegie Endowment for International Peace with a donation of $10 million; it now has centers in Washington, DC, Moscow, Beirut, Beijing, Brussels, and New Delhi. In 1916, the eminent businessman Robert S. Brookings founded the Brookings Institution with ambitions to "strengthen American democracy; foster the economic and social welfare, security, and opportunity of all

Americans; and secure a more open, safe, prosperous, and cooperative international system." (There appears to be some sort of competition within the think-tank community for the longest and most pompous mission statement.) Three years later, Herbert Hoover founded the Hoover War Library, which would later become the Hoover Institution, dedicated to "making and preserving peace, and sustaining for America the safeguards of the American way of life." Since the inception of these pioneering organizations, the growth in the prevalence, scope, and influence of think tanks has been remarkable. Over 90 percent of the world's think tanks were created after 1951, and the *Global Think Tank Index Report* now ranks more than 8,000 of them across eighty-five countries. Think tanks exist to form a bridge between academia and government; they undertake research on a particular topic or domain and are often described as "universities without students," building teams of experts and analysts to create scenarios that might meaningfully inform policy.

In an ideal world, the research and projections of think tanks would be independent and agnostic, comprising multistranded scenario work based on information gathered from primary research. There are think tanks that proudly proclaim their independent, nonpartisan positions, but the majority of them have morphed into barely veiled bastions of "Should Futurism," representing and promoting particular worldviews, political positions, or ideologies. Over the last fifty years, many of these organizations have shifted their pitches, rebranding themselves from "think tanks" to "policy institutes" and adjusting their missions from "research" to "advocacy." Most think tanks are nongovernmental organizations, but some act as semi-autonomous agencies within governments, which further deepens their partisan perspectives. Think tanks are also typically funded by individual donations or government grants, which has the potential to deepen their biases and define their priorities even further. The result is a futures machine driven not by possibility but by desire and the selective use of data to bolster a predetermined ambition.

Think tanks have become peculiar and shadowy players in the process of thinking about the future and running our countries. They have developed remarkably quickly, and they play a disproportionately large role in government strategy and planning, taking up the slack where governments don't want to look (or lack the resources to do so) and driving agendas based on their faction's agreed-upon version of "better." Nowhere is their presence more tangible than in the United States, which is home to nearly a third of the world's think tanks (followed by China and the UK). The gap between think tanks and lobbyists has become razor-thin, and the two are now largely indistinguishable from each other on both the left and right sides of politics. Researchers within think tanks regularly and simultaneously work as lobbyists, as members of corporate boards, or as outside consultants in litigation and regulatory disputes, and many of these positions remain undisclosed. Long-term thinking and deep futures work has been replaced by a focus on nearer-term goals to fit more closely with the fast-paced rhythms and tempos of politics. It's therefore hardly surprising that even though American politics is dominated by think tanks, a recent study found that only 20 percent of Americans trust these organizations.

The original RAND corporation has also been bitten by the think-tank bug; it now positions itself as "a research organization that develops solutions to public policy challenges to help make communities throughout the world safer and more secure, healthier and more prosperous." It still has a bias toward defense, but it also studies elements of education, labor, healthcare, and social well-being. As for the Hudson Institute, following Herman Kahn's death in 1983 it emerged as one of the most prominent conservative think tanks in the world. In 2011, it moved its headquarters to Washington, DC, to be closer to its clients, and it has accepted donations from both Exxon Mobil and the Koch family foundations. It donates to the political campaigns of prominent conservatives and plays a role in defining and advocating right-wing values, bestowing awards upon such stars as Mike Pence, Paul Ryan, Rupert Murdoch, Dick Cheney, and Benjamin Netanyahu. Far from exploring the full expanse of what might happen in the future, think tanks have become powerful assets in the creation of biased future narratives, while hiding behind a smoke screen of seemingly thorough methodologies and academic rigor.

STRATEGIC FORESIGHT

Beyond think tanks, government agencies, and corporate strategy teams, the pluralistic futures mindsets created by RAND, Kahn, Wack, and others have led to the emergence of another branch of futures work with which you may be unfamiliar. As we've established, Could Futurism represents the magniloquent, escapist branch of futurism that dominates our press, product, exhibition, and conference cultures. It's loud, brash, simplistic, and energetic, full of bold hubris, vibrant images, and confrontational confidence, but lurking in the shadows behind this hullabaloo sits an army of entirely different future-focused characters. They're calm, considered, reflective, rigorous, and process-oriented. They're exasperated by grandiose approaches to the future, and they roll their eyes and sigh (quietly and politely) at this irrational and ostentatious work. Debate and discussion sit at the center of their approach, a trait that even extends to how this type of futurism defines itself as a practice. Countless hours of vigorous debate have been dedicated to arguing the differences between strategic foresight, futures research, innovation strategy, futures design, futuristics, futures thinking, futuring, and futurology. (We'll put a pin in this and call this work "strategic foresight" from here, just to keep things moving.) This work is most comfortable around models, frameworks, and processes—or what the futurist Stuart Candy brilliantly describes as "intellectual prostheses"—and consistently aims to add a level of considered methodology and analytical rigor to its brand. Within this world you'll find backcasting, EmTech horizon scanning, morphological analysis, cross-impact analysis, and causal layered analysis, each with its own matrix, framework, or pyramid to be covered in swathes of sticky notes during endless workshop sessions. In spite of these differences and nuances, all strategic foresight work essentially focuses on the exploration of scenarios and likelihoods, a mindset helpfully illustrated by the rather ominously titled "cone of uncertainty."

You may not be familiar with the cone of uncertainty per se, but you're probably familiar with the underlying principle. Let's imagine a tropical storm pops up somewhere over the Caribbean and threatens to make landfall. The graphic design team at the National Weather Service springs into action, printing oversized maps that are hurriedly propped up on an easel in the Oval Office for an impromptu press conference. These infographics usually show the current position of the storm with a dotted line pointing eastward, defining its assumed direction of travel. But as this line projects out over the coming days, the meteorologists become less certain about what might happen—the storm could veer north over Florida by Wednesday or fizzle out in the deep Atlantic by Thursday. What results is a widening region that describes the decreasing certainty we all feel as time reaches out into the future. These possibilities mark out the boundaries of the cone of uncertainty—a potential territory of future events.

In the field of strategic foresight, this model has been developed into a variant more broadly known as the futures cone (or the Voros cone, after Joseph Voros, a vocal proponent of the method). This model projects a consistently broadening region out into the future along the same axis as we're currently traveling, which is named the "probable" cone, and indicates what we think is *most likely* to happen. Outside this sits another concentric cone flaring a little wider than the first. This is the "plausible" cone, and it's home to the things that are a little less likely to happen. Beyond that cone is a third, which is wider still—this is the "possible" cone, and it defines every potential outcome that we can imagine. This is the opposite of an *X* on a map or a single dotted line on a chart that clearly defines the projected

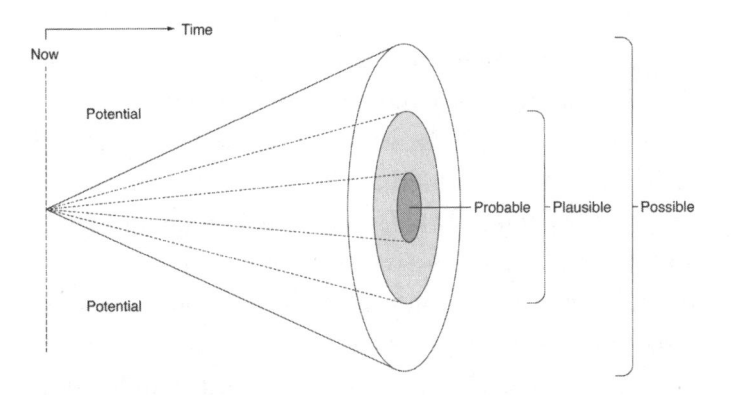

The futures cone (Adapted from Joseph Voros, 2000)

future. Abusing the famous Wayne Gretzky quote again for a moment, this is less about skating to where the puck will be, and more about mapping out *all the places the puck might go.*

This is simply a model—and we'll talk about its pitfalls later—but it's a useful proxy for the pluralistic mode of thinking at the heart of strategic foresight. Having a structure like the Voros cone allows a group of individuals to propose lots of different ideas, and then discuss how far out they are (their time horizon) and how far they deviate from the center line (their probability). Keeping a spread of ideas across this territory allows room for all ideas and offers a framework for debate; the challenge then becomes selecting which path to take. This model formally represents a mindset that many of us may find highly relatable—a method frequently used subconsciously when approaching the planning of anything from the kid's party I mentioned earlier to a commercial takeover. We lay out the options ahead of us, assess their relative likelihoods, and then make our choice, reassured that we've considered a broad spectrum of options. It's such an ingrained behavior in all of us that it occurs daily in organizations in mostly instinctive ways.

Strategic foresight is perhaps the most stealthy of all forms of commercial futures work, hiding underneath other projects, building frameworks for thinking, hosting workshops, and steering creative sessions. It typically offers very little publicly, preferring to support the work of others through discussions, analysis, provocation, and facilitation. It also straddles the worlds of academia and industry, and numerous university courses in this field have appeared in recent years, creating a seemingly boundless source of books, papers, case studies, and frameworks for the community to argue about. In spite of this overwhelming diversity of content, the prevailing mindset behind this kind of work builds on the foundational scenario-planning approaches of Herman Kahn and RAND, taking an "outside in" approach—looking at a question objectively and aiming to understand all its possible outcomes. Somewhat unfortunately, the urge to use strategic foresight methodologies to "predict" the future still runs deep (as we've seen from the postrationalized assessments of Pierre Wack's scenarios for Shell). As such, it can sometimes be difficult to introduce this kind of work into large organizations, particularly those focused on near-term goals and rapid decision-making. In my experience these approaches are initially welcomed, then tolerated, before exasperation ultimately sets in. When involved in these (sometimes lengthy) exercises, impatient leaders can rapidly become itchy for direction and decision rather than more discussion, endless analysis, or the introduction of more research. When done poorly, strategic foresight runs the risk of never deciding anything, clutching its pearls while bringing yet more ideas, thoughts, and questions to the table, or dropping some pithy insights and what-ifs before strolling off to its next client.

In order to give some sort of structure to their work, strategic foresight practitioners often rely on structured methods and techniques that help to formalize things, but this can often oversimplify or proceduralize an essentially unbounded activity. The creation of any model, matrix, or template is the result of a willful act of simplification, a process of reduction in the quest to create generalizable, repeatable routines, but these procedural ways of thinking can quickly become self-destructive. Slavishly adhering to a particular matrix or five-step plan can be as self-defeating as it is emancipatory, yet there exists a belief—and, indeed, a trust—in these models, methods, and techniques that is often misplaced.

The jargon-filled, diagrammatic nature of this work can make it feel self-assured, technical, and systematic, but in reality, Might Futurism relies on a significant amount of intuition and gut-feel. In generating future scenarios for any question, how significant might any single influence be? Is the weather a factor? International trade tariffs? The purchasing power of European teens? The growth of 3D printing in India or the Asian skin-whitening industry? One person might consider a data point to be a deeply influential factor, but the same data may be dismissed by another party as irrelevant. In order to create an appropriate number of scenarios with sufficient depth and diversity, strategic foresight has developed yet more frameworks that aim to insure against this type of preferential bias. One popular technique is named STEEP, where a team generates a list of driving forces spread across social, technical, economic, environmental, and political categories. While this can help generate a better spread of influences than random, I've witnessed productive discussions derailed for hours by participants overstressing or diminishing the potential weight of an influencing factor based on their pet peeves, personal ideologies, or opinions on any specific challenge. In the 1950s, many futurists felt confident introducing mass space travel into such discussions but failed to imagine the impact of ubiquitous personal computing, streaming television, or consumer recycling. Likewise, the creators of *The Jetsons* had no problem imagining domestic robots, hovering cars, and jetpacks, but couldn't conceive of a world where a mother would do anything other than shopping for clothes or cooking the family dinners.

Another key challenge in any scenario-based work lies in the acquisition of high-quality information. Even within the closed system of a single business, this kind of scenario work is often met with unreliable, unsynchronized, or incomplete data sources. When we consider the future more broadly, this challenge becomes increasingly complex. The data we require from competitors or other influential players either isn't available or is actively hidden from view. In military strategy, one power's strength in building complex probability models is often matched by its opponent's skill in concealing the very data on which those models rely. Control of information—and an active deployment of misinformation—is now a strong tactical thrust in the world's military and industrial powers, and derailing predictive strategies is an increasingly commonplace affair. The scenarios developed by Kahn, RAND, Wack, and Shell were hugely influential, but they were essentially exquisitely crafted pieces of numeric fiction. Their wonderfully complex processes appeared to be algorithmically and empirically provable chains of objective and rational information, but they were regularly hamstrung by incorrect, unreliable, or missing data. For example, in 1957 the CIA claimed that the Soviet Union had erected functioning missile silos across the entirety of Russia and that by 1961 it would be significantly ahead of the United States in its long-range missile capability. When 1961 arrived, a new reconnaissance satellite discovered that the Russians didn't have several hundred missiles as the Americans thought: they had four. This gargantuan mistake was somewhat ludicrously referred to as the "missile gap," and even though it represented a total fabrication, this huge figure remained embedded within popular and military culture for many years, affecting opinions and algorithms alike. As with any system based on data and computation, the same adage is as true today as it was back then: GIGO—garbage in, garbage out. This level of error, guesswork, and interpretation in seemingly scientific methods hasn't gone unnoticed in military circles. In 1987, shortly before the fall of the Berlin Wall, the United States Army began broadly using the term "VUCA"—an acronym adopted from the leadership theories of Warren Bennis and Burt Nanus—to represent the strange, multilateral, unknowable world they found themselves in, a world that was volatile, uncertain, complex, and ambiguous.

Even when we feel that we've managed to generate a sufficient number of well-researched and diverse scenarios, we add yet another layer of interpretation to the mix when considering which are probable, possible, or plausible. In truth, probability rarely works how we think it does. We regularly assign chance with all sorts of mystical powers, and we assume levels of likelihood that aren't mathematically accurate. The roulette ball doesn't land in any preordained cycle; your number isn't "due" anytime soon. When a flipped coin lands on heads six times in a row, we tend to think the seventh is more likely to be heads rather than the statistically accurate 50/50 chance. Our understanding of exponential growth (when the rate of change with respect to time is proportional to the quantity itself) is also notoriously bad, so we dramatically underestimate the shape of this kind of evolution, or, as the futurist Ray Kurzweil said, "Our intuition about the future is linear." In almost all situations, "probable," "possible," and "plausible" are subjective opinions rather than empirical truths. These problems occur even in well-controlled mathematical systems like those found in casinos, but when considering the multivalent wider world, any question of probability becomes infinitely more complex.

When constructing a futures cone around any question, we all struggle to see beyond the bounds of our own experience, industry, or problem space. If we take a moment to zoom out far enough, it becomes clear that every situation, evolution, or conundrum that challenges every business, industry, and economy is playing out concurrently, but companies have a habit of thinking about their future in company terms. You may have noticed that the scenarios generated by Pierre Wack and his team at Shell were all focused on energy and the energy industry. This perhaps made sense at the time, as Shell was in an utterly dominant position, controlling everything from the extraction and sale of oil to the political and economic structures that encircled the industry. But as we've observed more recently, the futures facing companies like Shell are now as likely to be external environmental and cultural pressures as industrial or economic issues, factors which may have seemed largely irrelevant in the 1970s. If you've spent a career developing pharmaceuticals, you're more likely to view the world's problems through a pharmacological gaze and attempt to solve what you see as its problems with the development or distribution of more drugs. This mistake has tripped up a long list of organizations, from Nokia to Kodak and Blockbuster, each of which incrementally narrowed their cone of probability only to be upended by a disruption that they placed well out into the "unlikely" zone, or didn't see coming at all.

Even if you're able to integrate a high level of peripheral vision into your thinking, the path of any scenario never runs true. Every future concept, strategy, or plan undergoes untold buffeting, being permanently pelted with external forces, unseen pitfalls, and erratic influences. A competitor could collapse, LeBron James could say something damning about your CEO, a container ship could overturn in the Suez Canal, or Oprah could be photographed using your product. The progress of any idea through its future is more akin to Brownian motion than to a neatly planned rocket trajectory, bouncing and ricocheting its way through the days, weeks, and months and leaving an average trend line in its wake. As Shell's head of group planning Jimmy Davidson stated, "You can never identify all the forces at play. If you could, and see their interactions, then real prediction of the future would be simple. This is never likely to be possible, and furthermore, there are some situations that balance on a hair's breadth." Scenarios are not fixed lines into the future—quite the opposite, they change by the hour, minute, and second. Strategic foresight work is often sold as a neatly bound consulting package, with a beginning, a middle, and an end. In truth, it's almost all middle.

When engaging with this type of work, one should think about it more like insurance than advice, as an exercise in illuminating unknown territories or trying to spot trouble rather than setting out to discover El Dorado. When done well, these methods create the conditions for more detailed and more expansive conversations about the future to occur. They provoke groups to have uncomfortable debates and develop scenarios that can act as props to point at and to argue around, to think deeply and rehearse their potential responses. It's worth remembering that it's the process of *doing the thinking* that matters, not necessarily the outcomes. Despite its many shortcomings, strategic foresight is grown-up, serious, and analytical, and it likely represents a collection of the "best-in-class" commercial futures techniques we have today because it broadly reflects how most of us think. These approaches are used by everyone from the World Bank to the UN, but this level of highbrow, methodological rationalism conceals a few uncomfortable truths. It's incredibly simple to disregard the impacts of seemingly irrelevant external forces in these exercises. Probability doesn't work like we think it does (or wish that it did). Our models only help us think rather than show us the answer, and our data is almost always unreliable or incomplete. In truth, any question about the future is bound by our ability to create and manage rich scenarios, which is itself bound by the limits of our imagination.

THE LIMITS OF IMAGINATION

There's a great exercise in lateral thinking and creativity that I remember from a class I attended in the mid-1990s. We were split into a few small teams and asked to write down a hundred answers to the question "How might we get to the top of a tree?" At first our answers were fairly straightforward: use a ladder, climb the tree, or use a rope, that sort of thing, but in time these simple ideas began to dry up and our teams started to think in more unorthodox ways. What if we find a very short tree? Maybe we could Photoshop a picture of me at the top of the tree? Perhaps we could cut the tree down and stand where the top falls? With even more time our ideas became incredibly creative: Could we develop and distribute a new language where "top" means "any part of a tree"? What if we stood on a seed and waited for fifty years? Could we turn my body into a mist and allow me to evaporate upward through the branches? Given enough time, enough pressure, and enough incentive, people can become immensely imaginative, but without this kind of forced environment—or the time and space to train themselves—people's imagination about the full scope of what *might* happen is notoriously poor. A great many things in life proceed with metronomic reliability: the sun rises and falls, the seasons pass, and debts inevitably come due. This sort of stuff falls right on the central axis of the cone of uncertainty—the closest things we have to future truths—but when we try to fully map what's likely, unlikely, outlandish, or impossible, it's easy to be blinded, nudged, and manipulated by our own experiences.

I recently spent some time talking about this with a remarkably calm, affable man with a ponytail. Joseph Kable is a neurobiologist and researcher at the University of Pennsylvania who has dedicated his career to figuring out what actually goes on inside our bodies and brains when we think about the future. By recent estimations, the human brain is built from over 80 billion neurons, and in truth we're just at the beginning of our journey to understand what all of them do and how they work with one another. When it comes to thinking about the future, humans are not alone. Other animals with brains think about the future too, but they do so only in a very specific manner. During a chase, a deer might think a few moments ahead to plan an escape route. A chaffinch might build a nest to raise its young, squirrels might hoard food for winter, and whales might set off on long migrations in preparation for more suitable weather conditions. In some cases, animals such as ravens, apes, elephants, and octopuses might even figure out puzzles or use tools to get food; however, as impressive as these feats are, they often simply reflect adaptations shaped by evolutionary pressures rather than anything we might recognize as "imagination." The sophisticated, broad-reaching, abstract contemplation of future scenarios—something that we engage in effortlessly every day—appears to be somewhat unique to humans, which feels like quite a privilege.

In 2001, a research team led by the American neurologist Marcus Raichle uncovered a series of physically distinct regions within the brain that they referred to collectively as the "default mode network." Within this expansive collection of neurons lie two recently discovered subnetworks: one focused on envisioning and forecasting future scenarios (known as the generative network), and the other focused on deciding whether those scenarios will yield positive or negative outcomes (known as the evaluative network). In studying this relationship, Joe and his team have discovered that the hippocampus—which has long been associated with memory—also plays a role in the generation of new ideas and imagination. On a neurological scale, when we ask someone to imagine the future, it appears that the same parts of the brain spark into life as when we ask them about the past. Scientists are beginning to believe that the function of our memory is not to act as a factual storage facility for past events, but to *help us to shape our ideas about the future.*

This is one of the reasons why stage magic and illusions can be so compelling. When we watch David Copperfield ride a Harley-Davidson out of a previously empty box, we're caught unawares. The sense of wonder we feel comes from the breaking of our own internal probability model—we struggle to imagine a motorcycle appearing from thin air because we haven't seen it happen before. If an experienced illusionist watched the same show, they would have a clearer sense of how such a feat was achieved. With their knowledge and experience of the magician's craft, they would be attuned to subtle "tells" in the performance, allowing them to anticipate more accurately what might happen next. For the rest of us, a lack of appropriate experience affects our ability to imagine such a thing, a factor that includes not only the things we've seen, but where we've been and what we've encountered.

So far in this book we've taken a largely Western, technocratic swing at the future, which is undoubtedly a reflection of my own personal experiences and perspectives. We all like to think that we're reasonably good at imagining life from a different point of view, but in reality, nothing could be further from the truth. Over decades of sitting in lengthy observation sessions, workshops, ethnography studies, and interviews, I've come to realize that real empathy is incredibly difficult. We're all programmed through every moment of every day to see the world from our own point of view, and attempts to break free from this often result in little more than clichéd, caricatured, or clumsy role-play. Truly seeing the world from a different perspective takes immense training, and I've rarely seen *anyone* do it well.

In the early 2000s, Nokia was a powerhouse of the cell phone world. At its peak, the company was operating in 140 countries and was particularly successful in economically underdeveloped regions such as Africa and India. With its home in Finland (not in Japan, as many people believe), Nokia was a decidedly European company with its own attitudes and priorities, but a major contributor to its success was the significant budget it allocated to ethnographic research. Huge teams of people would be dispatched to all corners of the globe to spend time with Nokia customers. They would observe their daily routines in minute detail, recording their habits, photographing their homes, documenting their schedules, and interviewing them at great length. When I joined Nokia in 2009 this work was still very much underway, the most extreme versions of which were led by a talented and swashbuckling ethnographer whom we affectionately referred to as "Indiana Phones." I attended many such sessions, and while they were incredibly interesting, I found them to be hard work. Unpicking another person's mental models, cultural biases, behavioral patterns, and emotional preferences is remarkably complex, and to do it well requires a level of skill that very few people possess.

Whenever we think about the future, our ability to imagine anything new is restricted, directed, and focused by who we are as people, and there's very little we can do to change that. As such, there are increasing calls in the professional world of futures and foresight to introduce more voices into the field, to cultivate different points of view, to encourage new perspectives, and to bring more diversity to proceedings. Futurists have typically been white, male, and financially privileged, and they have approached questions about the future from primarily technocratic or philosophical backgrounds, which has (broadly speaking) led to the type of future imaginings we see so much of today, with their own traits and predilections. In order to increase any scope of imagination, we need to go beyond empathy and ethnography and truly integrate and promote different perspectives in futures work. Thankfully, this change is happening, though it's happening woefully slowly.

In arts academia, many students are bringing about a major change in the ways in which we explore the future, and who is involved in this type of work. Participatory futures, futures with underrepresented voices, historically ignored or suppressed cultures, alternative societies, and marginalized outlooks are now being welcomed into the discussion. Afrocentric futures, feminist futures, postcolonial futures, and postcapitalist futures are becoming ever more commonplace—and a little more broadly understood. Beyond that, an increasing number of researchers and futurists are taking a pan-species, ecosystemic approach to their work, aiming to redress the anthropocentric bias that exists in almost all of contemporary society. This work can prove difficult to digest for many audiences—and is still largely dismissed as a fringe activity—but its perspectives are shaping a new breed of futurists who are gradually moving into professional research, commercial enterprise, and governmental roles, and they will undoubtedly shape those industries in the coming decades. I think this shift represents more than simply an act of newly cool radical inclusivity. Taking these other perspectives into consideration serves to actively *expand* the cone of uncertainty. It helps shift the starting point of the conversation and can then reframe its possible end points, resulting in a significantly broader portfolio of potential scenarios. When I talk about exploring the future with more rigor, this is one of the things that I mean. Admittedly, this makes the job of deciding what to do much harder, but incorporating these perspectives can drastically increase the opportunity space ahead of us and reduce the potential impact of unseen consequences.

Beyond our personal experiences, another limit to our ability to imagine the future is how we think about time. When we are plotting out what might happen in the future, it's worth thinking about how far into the gloom our flashlight reaches. Is it six weeks, six months, or six decades? Changing this scale can markedly change the types of scenarios we might create and how likely or unlikely something may appear to be. In the cone of uncertainty, the use of a straight axis also implies a model of "linear time." If you're reading this from a Western perspective, you're no doubt familiar with weeks, months, quarters, years, and decades, but many Latin American, African, and Middle Eastern cultures view time through a polychronic lens, with less-rigid ideas about the passage of time and time management. Some Indigenous cultures also embrace notions of "circular" time, where events happen in repeated rhythms, with associated tempos and patterns. Time doesn't mean the same thing to everyone, and our own models of the future are almost always pegged to a heavily biased notion of scale. The passage of time happens to us every moment of every day—and we all feel its effects—yet our mental models of the past and future vary across different cultures. In most Western societies, the past is viewed as something spatially behind us, and the future sits out in front. In Mandarin-speaking countries, the past sits above us and the future is below, and in some Indigenous tribes (such as the Yupno in Papua New Guinea), metaphors for the past are "downhill" whereas the future is "uphill." Each of us is also notoriously unreliable when it comes to our sense of the passing of time and the order in which things happened. The passage of years, decades, and even centuries can shrink, stretch, twist, and distend in our minds. Folktales can become facts. Timelines can warp, and the order of historical events can become shuffled, which affects our ability to imagine when things might happen in the future—sometimes wildly so. By means of example, the sharks in our oceans have been there since before Saturn had its rings, *Ghostbusters* was released closer to the reign of Adolf Hitler than the present day, and ciabatta bread was invented more than thirty years *after* the color television.

In order to poke at our understanding of time—and perhaps to reset our perspectives—a small group of dedicated engineers have set their minds toward building a mechanical clock inside a Nevada mountain that, once completed, will run for the next ten thousand years. The Long Now Foundation was created in 1996 by Danny Hillis and Stewart Brand (hello again!) to encourage what they call "long-term thinking" and to foster more responsibility for the future. This represents a direct response to the world that we currently inhabit, one of rapid change, multitasking, fast-twitch attention spans, and near-term gains, which the foundation refers to as the "Short Now." The creation of structures that take longer than the span of our own lives to complete is something we've grown unfamiliar with since the days of pyramids and grand cathedrals, but the

Long Now Foundation is aiming to see if we've still got what it takes. The project is well underway—thanks, in no small part, to a $42 million donation from Jeff Bezos—but the team has intentionally avoided announcing a completion date. Their clock is a mechanical masterpiece—a huge construction with gears over eight feet in diameter, a polyphonic chime system, and a huge drive weight weighing ten thousand pounds, all housed within a vertical tube bored through solid rock. It's designed to be easily maintained over millennia, and will be made without precious metals or jewels that might attract looters from future civilizations. It's intended to communicate its purpose without being disassembled, and it will calibrate itself by a shaft of light shining through a tiny window at noon. The primary function of the clock is to tell the time, but beyond that it's a means to provoke us to think about our own future, the legacy we might be building, and the challenges we might be creating for generations to come. In order to further pick at our preconceptions of time, the Long Now Foundation adds a zero to the front of every year it quotes, writing 2025 as 02025, for example. As a provocation it's rather subtle, but I find its effects profound.

The most significant issue Might Futurism faces is the potential for a crisis of imagination. When done well, this kind of work is focused on exploring a broad tapestry of possibility, but that's something we're not very good at, and we're certainly not as good at it as we think we are. Every one of us finds it difficult to envisage the full scope of possibility for any question, and we have a habit of diminishing things that feel unlikely or less preferable. We struggle to take other perspectives into consideration and select timescales that make us feel most comfortable, resulting in often-fragile scenarios and unrealistically narrow lists of possibilities, which ultimately leave us ill-prepared for the inevitable onslaught of reality. The ability to generate extreme breadth and vivid depth in our ideas about the future is something that takes real effort. We have to find ways to stretch how we think about the future, to lengthen and widen the cone of uncertainty and avoid regurgitating the same old ideas and tropes, which is something we all clearly struggle to do.

REGURGITATIVE FUTURES

If we hear the same narratives over and over again, and if we see the same visuals over and over again, then that becomes our scope of possibility.
—ANGELA OGUNTALA

In 2021, I was interviewed by the chief technical officer of one of the world's largest companies. The session was intended to be a fairly light discussion about the future, the state of technology and design, and my own journey to Silicon Valley, hopefully resulting in some engaging content for the press team to use internally and share on social media. We both arranged ourselves on those uncomfortable stools that corporations keep for such events, a technician checked our microphones and fiddled with a couple of lights, and soon enough the cameras went live. After a brief introduction and some pleasantries, the CTO's first question to me was "So, where are we at with flying cars, then?"

I began this book by talking about how our ideas of the future tend to fall into well-trod patterns. There appears to be a rhythm to our ideas and obsessions, and the same projections happen so frequently that they become familiar. At any one moment there's a short list of "hot" things that dominate any conversation about the future, from automation and robotics to self-driving vehicles and AI, and each tugs at us like a magnet. No matter how much we like to consider ourselves independent thinkers, we all fall prey to these fashions, fads, obsessions, and trends, absorbing ideas from all around us and repeating them as our own. The interesting thing about these preoccupations is that they can be difficult to see when you're living within them. A trend makes sense at the time, and we typically only recognize its impact or absurdity in retrospect. As an example, we all appear to have become experts at mocking the 1980s. Nightclubs in cities all over the world host '80s nights where people wear neon clothes and dance to Rick Astley, chuckling at the absurdity of it all, and finding it amazing that this was how people lived back then. The same goes for future visions from the '80s—they look exactly like '80s futures, and reflect the technologies, challenges, aspirations, and fears of the day. It's easy to look back on them and smirk at their naivety, but they all made some sort of sense at the time. We also conveniently forget that the next generation will likely do the same to our contemporary ideas, which seem rational, well-reasoned, and intellectually rigorous today. I'm sure that in the near future, provincial nightclubs across the land will host "2020s nights," where partygoers will dance ironically to Taylor Swift and Kendrick Lamar songs wearing Crocs and hoodies, sipping on White Claws and making heart emojis with their fingers.

Every era has its own technological obsessions that fundamentally shape the kinds of things its people are able to imagine. This fact becomes surprisingly clear when we look at how the dominant technologies of every decade are adopted into popular language. In the 1920s modernity meant "radio." Adding "radio" to anything meant it was new, exciting, and high tech, a fact that marketeers jumped on eagerly. In the 1950s the adjective of choice was "atomic," and it was added to everything from kitchen ovens to wristwatches and flasks. The 1960s saw significant interest in robotics, which resulted in a parallel marketing boom for "robo-" and "-matic" domestic products. By the 1970s, our attention had shifted to entertainment technology, with the development of games like Pong, the release of VHS, and the associated rise of the term "video." In the 1980s, our attention turned to "digital," reflecting the growth of the electronics industry and the introduction of microchips in a great number of our products. In the 1990s, we focused on making everything "connected," from doorbells and refrigerators to cameras and thermostats. In the 2000s, everything became "social," focused on bringing people together and creating communities, and in the 2010s, all our data floated off into "the cloud." We're now entering the era of applied artificial intelligence, and every startup, incumbent, government, and technologist is appending their work with appropriately trendy "AI," "generative," and "intelligent" branding, complete with purple sparkles.

These fixations and obsessions feel so natural and appropriate at the time that we barely notice them, but in retrospect these distinct thematic epochs become incredibly obvious. If we were to bring a group of people together today and ask them about the future, it's unlikely that any of them would talk about milk cartons, umbrellas, chocolate bars, printers, carbonated drinks, ballrooms, or supermarkets. Today, those things just don't have a role in our collective conversation about the future, but they undoubtedly did at some point. And they might again. Our ideas, projections, and images of the future move in cycles, peaking and dipping in the collective consciousness and riding the waves of excitement and troughs of boredom as they go. Of course, where there's an observable pattern someone will inevitably create a diagram.

The American research agency Gartner gave shape to this phenomenon in 1995 with the creation of the Gartner Hype Cycle, which is still in broad use today. They observed that any emerging technology appears to follow a similar path of excitement (and associated media hype), and that figuring out where society and industry are in that cycle can help us understand its state of maturity and its place in popular discourse. A Hype Cycle begins with an innovation trigger (some sort of discovery or invention), and then its path moves through four major sections, beginning with the "Peak of Inflated Expectations." The emergence of any new technology typically leads to an explosion of excitement: Could Futurists begin exclaiming the transformative power of this new tool and illustrating all the ways it could fundamentally change our lives for the better. Journalists get swept up in the furor and write energetic articles about this nascent capability, and the extent of its transformative potential. As the technology moves from R&D toward productization, its true shape rapidly becomes apparent, its limits come to the fore, and previously unseen complexities become serious problems. This is when excitement dips significantly and we enter the "Trough of Disillusionment."

Investors lose interest, magazines stop printing articles, and the magic begins to wear off. Over time, a few tenacious souls persevere, gradually working out the kinks in the technology and uncovering the true shape of its power during a phase Gartner calls the "Slope of Enlightenment." Finally, the technology finds its place in the world, the shape of its influence becomes clear, and its products become effective, a period that Gartner refers to as the "Plateau of Productivity," which is when "technology" becomes "products" and eventually "stuff."

Take antilock braking in cars as an example. Antilock braking systems have roots that go back almost a century, but it would take decades of dogged work before Chrysler introduced a computerized system called Sure-Brake to its Imperial model in 1971. When I was growing up in the 1980s, antilock braking systems were still considered a relatively new innovation, and countless vehicles proudly proclaimed this hot new feature by flaunting little chrome "ABS" badges on their rear ends. In time, the technology decreased in price and increased in reliability, making it possible to integrate it into more vehicles, until it became standard in almost every car for sale, and the little chrome ABS badges disappeared. Innovation becomes technology, technology becomes features, and features become norms.

It would be nice if all technologies followed such a simple, singular path, but the world doesn't really work like that. Many ideas fall off this curve entirely, or fail to get going at all, stymied by unseen issues or insurmountable complexities. Sometimes the Trough of Disillusionment can be decades long; sometimes technologies can cycle through countless ups and downs, becoming fashionable and dropping out of favor like hemlines and haircuts. Even wildly successful technologies can tarnish and lose their luster, and presently, we find ourselves in just such a moment. The allure of social networks—which once seemed like the future of media to many people—has dulled somewhat, to put it mildly. The utopian promises made by these networks have failed to materialize, and we've become more aware of the data deals we've made with their parent companies, so much so that in a 2021 *Washington Post* survey, 72 percent of respondents said they didn't trust Facebook "much or at all." This number was 63 percent for TikTok, about the same for Instagram, and today Twitter is estimated to have lost over 80 percent of its brand value since Elon Musk acquired and renamed the company in 2022.

For a while, cryptocurrency and blockchain technologies stepped into the arena before diving deep into the trough of disillusionment as regulations and reality caught up with them. These technologies are now reinventing themselves and starting to emerge in a more serious and well-considered guise, but what's now dominating our conversation about the future is the field of artificial intelligence (AI), and in particular large language models. These cunning and seductive technologies have allowed people to simply create text, computer code, audio, images, and video with an uncanny level of accuracy, which has cracked open a veritable Pandora's box of opportunity. As a result, recent conversations about the future have focused intently on AI, so much so that Google mentioned "AI" over 140 times during a two-hour presentation at its annual developer conference in 2023. While we're currently swamped by excitement and consternation about AI, this is far from a new phenomenon. The Second World War computing hero Alan Turing proposed the concept of a theoretical artificial intelligence in the 1930s, which laid the groundwork for our thinking on the subject, but it wouldn't be until the 1950s that researchers built the first primitive intelligent programs. What followed was a long period where AI theory far exceeded the practical capabilities of available technologies, a period broadly known as the "AI winter," which lasted for decades. In the 1980s, huge, highly specialized computer systems began to appear that showed promise in their ability to handle the complex computation required for AI, but it wasn't until the early 1990s that the tools and theory began to practically realign and productive work could begin once again. In 1997, IBM's Deep Blue beat Garry Kasparov at chess, but it wasn't until 2015 that a Google team triumphed against the world champion Go player Fan Hui. The recent "AI revolution" is, in truth, the latest upswing in a long, long roller coaster of hype, learning, failure, and disappointment, a future idea that kept peeking around the door, waiting for its moment to enter the room.

However, piercing through this bewildering fog of cyclical faddery are ideas that seem to endure through the ages—ideas that somehow feel like permanent fixtures in the future and call us toward them over and over again. Certain ideas just seem to be somehow stickier than others, and society just can't seem to shake them. For example, it appears that humans have always been enchanted by the idea of flight, and from Leonardo da Vinci and the Montgolfier brothers to Orville and Wilbur Wright and NASA, we've devoted hundreds of years of work to achieving that ambition. We've now largely mastered the art of flight, and we have countless well-designed options at our disposal, from planes and balloons to gliders, airships, drones, helicopters, microlights, jetpacks, and parachutes. But even with all these riches, for some reason we keep trying to crowbar flight into the form of a family car. It's a recurrent obsession that seems to appeal to a great many of us, and it clearly sat at the forefront of my curious CTO's mind when asking his "flying car" question. It's hard to know why some ideas just won't quit, but all around us sit these perpetually recurrent themes, repeating over and over again as countless entrepreneurs and inventors fling themselves at these tantalizing totems. After decades of trying, we're drowning in patents, prototypes, and testbeds for flying cars, but the vast majority of these efforts have come to naught. A few auto-aviation projects have made it beyond the drawing board, but in truth they're more like driving planes than flying cars, clumsily tottering around on the roads with folded wings tucked awkwardly under their bellies, and yet in a great number of people the ambition for a flying car apparently still stands.

These kinds of ideas—from bipedal, humanoid robots to 3D-printed foods—continue to stubbornly crop up in our culture, and they pop back into our collective consciousness with alarming regularity. This repetitive recycling unhelpfully narrows the scope of our imagination, closing us off to other possibilities and offering us ready-made replacements for actual thinking. We keep getting stuck in these loops that seem increasingly difficult to escape, repeating the same lines and focusing on the same ideas, and just as with a lot of our thinking about the future, it might have something to do with the movies we're watching.

WAGGING THE DOG

I wouldn't call myself a prophet in any sense of the word. You know there are lots of us making these predictions all the time. Once in a while we get them right, and it's more luck than anything else.
—KEN LIU

Back in the early 2000s I was briefly involved in a peculiar project to explore future ideas for the British Army. The study was part of a much larger "Future Integrated Soldier Technology" initiative, which resulted—intentionally or otherwise—in the hilariously macho acronym FIST. The introductory briefing session was unlike any I'd ever experienced, and took place on the top floor of one of Whitehall's huge bureaucratic buildings. Upon entering we were greeted by the unmistakable aromas of stale tobacco smoke and institutional cleaning products. The carpets were patchy and threadbare from years of vigorous vacuuming, and beneath every window was a rappelling anchor point, as though at any moment the building's inhabitants might need to make a hasty departure. My colleagues and I were shown into a dull boardroom, where we waited patiently under the fluorescent lights until three chaps in full military dress bustled into the room, each followed closely by an attentive dog. After ten minutes of chitchat and pleasantries, the leading officer cut to the chase. He leaned forward and said boldly, "It's simple, really. We want our soldiers to feel like RoboCop."

How does this happen? How does a man with decades of military experience and a responsibility for thinking about the future of his soldiers come to that conclusion? This was a sizable project—with an equally sizable budget—yet when trying to describe the future for his soldiers, his imagination stretched only as far as a pulpy 1980s sci-fi movie. Why?

•

Imagine for a moment that we are making a TV show or a movie set in the 1800s. We would probably expect the production team to hire a number of period consultants for the project. These advisory engagements have become a well-established part of the contemporary film industry, and they play an important role in ensuring everything from set dressing to costume and dialect are period-correct. These experts also help guard against the armies of eagle-eyed armchair historians who are quick to point out anachronistic pistols, wristwatches, or shirt collars, and a great deal of effort is dedicated to ensuring this kind of slipup doesn't happen. Within science fiction literature there has also long been a culture of adherence to factual and scientific rigor. In 1969, Michael Crichton incorporated significant amounts of accurate biological detail into his extraterrestrial novel

The Andromeda Strain. In 1984, William Gibson's *Neuromancer* introduced the concept of cyberspace, following real-world advances in virtual reality technologies. Margaret Atwood's 2003 book *Oryx and Crake* explored the consequences of genetics and bioengineering, in line with real-world concerns about the ethical implications of these emerging techniques.

Science fiction literature can often be escapist and fanciful, but it can equally be immensely thoughtful, dealing with interesting conundrums and detailed extrapolations of real science, technology, and society. In order to delineate this type of work from more outlandish fare, aficionados have developed a habit of grading sci-fi works by co-opting the Mohs scale of mineral hardness to indicate the scientific accuracy of any given tale. Works featuring warp drives, teleportation devices, and anything supernatural are considered "soft science fiction," and more technically astute, linear projections of proven science are considered "hard science fiction." Hard sci-fi wrangles with real questions about the prevailing direction of technology. It understands physics, computer science, biology, and chemistry. It's where you'll find Arthur C. Clarke, Isaac Asimov, and Kim Stanley Robinson, authors who pay meticulous attention to technical accuracy even when describing off-world colonies, space exploration, or galactic empires. It's the kind of stuff that a great many futurists love and refer to often, teetering right on the boundary between fantasy and plausibility. This kind of work is designed to feel tantalizingly believable, if we could just stretch the scientific truth far enough.

In our movie landscape, however, this level of dedication to detail has historically been something of a rarity. The creative freedoms afforded to movies set in the future mean that world-building efforts often leave a lot to be desired, and it's still depressingly common to see familiar futuristic tropes thrown somewhat lazily on the screen. The result is a science fiction landscape where every computer screen is transparent, every space pistol fires laser beams, and every piece of data arrives line by line, accompanied by beeps and blips, as if powered by some sort of wartime teleprinter. That said, there has been something of a shift in some of our stories set in the future, with a more noticeable push toward scientific, technological, and societal realism, which has resulted in a significantly more formal relationship between the worlds of science and fiction.

In 1999, Global Business Network—a scenario planning consulting firm based in Berkeley, California—received a call from a representative of Steven Spielberg. Following his smash hit movie *E.T.*, Spielberg wanted to get more accurate input about the future into his movies, and he reached out to GBN to help him find some appropriate experts. Shortly afterward, a group of fifteen people convened at a hotel in Santa Monica to discuss Spielberg's new project, a movie adaptation of the 1956 Philip K. Dick short story "Minority Report." This panel consisted of leading figures from the worlds of architecture, computer science, and biomedical research, who began to discuss and deconstruct the future world of the movie. The production designer Alex McDowell compiled these discussions into what he called the "2054 bible," an eighty-page guide that listed in extensive detail the architectural, socioeconomic, political, and technological aspects of this future world.

In November 2000, an MIT research student named John Underkoffler was drafted into the production of *Minority Report* to advise on the design of the film's now-famous gestural interfaces, in response to a prompt from Spielberg to make it "feel like conducting an orchestra." At numerous points during the movie, John Anderton (played by Tom Cruise) is required to search through huge quantities of video data produced by the three "precogs" held in a water tank downstairs. He stands in front of a gigantic, curved, transparent screen holding his arms aloft, gesturing at the content, zooming, cutting, swiping, reordering, and rotating the video images. The result is utterly compelling to watch. It feels like Anderton is grabbing *actual* pixels and moving them around in *real* space. It's certainly more engaging than watching him wait for an SD card to upload, or scrolling and clicking through a database with a mouse. Spielberg's inclusion of this battery of experts and advisors in the production of *Minority Report* is likely why its technologies feel so well-rounded and resolved—and why they continue to be referenced to this day.

As science fiction stories have populated and ultimately dominated our cinema and TV landscape, the inclusion of this kind of science advisor has become a little more commonplace. The Nobel Prize winner Kip Thorne acted as an advisor on the Christopher Nolan picture *Interstellar*, the British physicist Brian Cox was hired by Danny Boyle during the production of *Sunshine*, and the USC professor of theoretical physics Clifford Johnson has advised Hollywood studios on everything from the *Avengers* movies to the TV series *Agent Carter*. As a result, science fiction—while still largely escapist and a little free with its interpretations of technology—occasionally feels a little more real. In parallel, the worlds of science and engineering have drifted closer (or more overtly) toward science fiction—a development that concerns me deeply. It's become abundantly clear to me, after having worked in large technology companies for decades, that there's a serious issue within this culture that is affecting our ability to imagine sufficiently broadly, and it's steering our future world toward a narrow and repetitive set of ideas that were never meant to be made real. Historically, science and engineering were focused on their own endeavors, aiming to solve technical problems or develop new primary technologies, but we're now living through a troubling inversion in the relationship between science fiction and fact.

It's worth reminding ourselves that the people working in technology development, those commenting on it, and those developing future-focused language, policy, and products all read and watch the same science fiction that you and I do. It increasingly appears to dominate the ways in which they see themselves and their work, swamping their imagination and defining the cultures they encourage, the products they develop, and the ways they think about the future. At Google X (the overtly future-oriented part of Alphabet where I once worked) the meeting rooms are all named after famous movie robots, such as WALL-E, Talos, and HAL 9000. The robotics program at Google was code-named

"Replicant," after the bioengineered humanoids featured in *Blade Runner*. Elon Musk is an unabashed sci-fi fan, naming his autonomous drone ships after the fictional vehicles from Iain M. Banks novels, and his largest rocket after the *Millennium Falcon* from *Star Wars*. His bipedal robot project is named Optimus after the lead character in the *Transformers* franchise, and he even secured himself a cameo in *Iron Man 2*. Both Apple and Google have hard-programmed "Easter egg" answers into their voice agents that give sci-fi-inflected responses to specific questions. Chip manufacturer Nvidia named its quad-core mobile chip Kal-El, the Kryptonian birth name of Superman. Microsoft's virtual assistant Cortana is named after the artificial intelligence character in the video game series *Halo*. Amazon founder Jeff Bezos named one of his holding companies Zefram LLC after Zefram Cochrane, the *Star Trek* character who invented the warp drive. Bezos also stated that his vision for the voice-assistant product Alexa was for it to "become the *Star Trek* computer," and in 2016 he even played an alien Starfleet officer on the show, after pestering Paramount for years. After being inspired by her vocal performance as "Samantha" in the 2013 Spike Jonze movie *Her*, OpenAI CEO Sam Altman approached Scarlett Johansson to be the voice of the company's AI assistant—in so doing perhaps misreading what is an essentially dystopian movie. In January 2025, OpenAI also joined forces with SoftBank, Oracle, and the investment firm MGX to begin a $500 billion artificial intelligence project, which it named Stargate, after Roland Emerich's 1994 extraterrestrial science fiction movie.

This backbone of science fiction lore shapes and squeezes

countless products during their inception, development, and delivery, which is then reflected onto customers with a wry smile and a wink. This conflation of fact and fiction feels like something we should be taking more seriously—or at least discussing in more detail. Naming meeting rooms after sci-fi robots might seem like a cute, harmless act, but it serves to position the work of an organization. It tells its staff what the company considers important, it nudges culture, and it develops subconscious priorities, not only in the company's goals and ambitions, but also in how it thinks about the future. As a result of this cultural shift, the creators of science fiction assets have also been drawn closer to the world of real product development. Territory Studio is the visual effects company behind on-screen graphics for hit movies including *The Martian*, *Blade Runner*, and *Prometheus*. Such is the appeal of their flashy movie work that vehicle manufacturers including GMC, Audi, Chevrolet, and Cadillac have hired the firm to create real-world interfaces for their vehicles. Likewise, Perception Studio, which made their name developing fictional interfaces for *Black Panther* and *Guardians of the Galaxy*, have been hired by Ford, Intel, and IBM. The *Minority Report* production designer Alex McDowell also consults for Ford and clients including Nike, Boeing, and the American Society of Civil Engineers. In 2017, Intel hired science fiction writers to join their "Intel Tomorrow Project," and the mixed-reality startup Magic Leap hired the science fiction writer Neal Stephenson as their Chief Futurist. It's become abundantly clear over the last couple of decades that there's an immense hunger to "make science fiction a reality" or "convert science fiction into science fact." We hear these terms in everything from startup pitches to CEO presentations, and we take it for granted. The world's leaders—from politicians and investors to military men and entrepreneurs—all seem utterly transfixed by the world of science fiction. It's taken hold of the reins of our imagination and in many ways become a convenient shorthand for "progress."

Conventional wisdom states that science fiction offers a fantastic resource for new ideas and drives new lines of thinking in innovation, yet I've frequently observed the opposite to be true. I've been in hundreds of meetings about nascent technologies during my career, and they often follow a depressingly familiar pattern. When talking about the technology itself, engineers and other technically minded people dive deeply into scientific minutiae and demand empirical evidence for any stated opinion. But when the conversation swings away from present-day technical details to focus on the types of products we might eventually make, these same people frequently reach for a science fiction archetype, a device they saw in *Star Trek*, an idea from an Asimov novel, or yet another flying car. You've also seen this on the news and in documentaries, where the hosts say something like "It will be like living in the Matrix" or "The holodeck might be one step closer to reality." What this actually represents is a crisis of imagination, which might be significantly more damaging than we think. Maybe we're getting trapped in our stories?

Science fiction is a remarkably versatile construct, and it can do many things. It can provoke us to think about ideas (particularly technologies, but also political and sociocultural systems) in novel and challenging ways. It can liberate us from the unhelpful shackles of reality and allow us to frame more interesting what-if questions. It can deploy the power of storytelling to help a group of people get beyond dry science and strategy conversations. But we must remember—and I can feel my door being battered down by a billion people here—the primary function of science fiction is *entertainment*. It has a fundamentally different central purpose from the creation of real-world technologies. Actually imagining the future is incredibly difficult, and to circumvent this difficulty people have become comfortable using ideas from these TV shows, novels, comic books, and movies as stand-ins for truly deep thinking, critical explorations, or well-considered provocations. In truth, the direct translation of science fiction props to real-world products almost always represents little more than clumsy malapropism, because the future technologies featured in science fiction movies are designed to be conduits for the narrative rather than rational propositions. To use Alfred Hitchcock's term, they're simply MacGuffins.

Many years ago, a friend recounted a story that makes this differentiation abundantly clear. He'd enjoyed a solid career as an industrial designer and developed a number of very successful consumer products but had recently made the exciting leap into the world of movie production. His first role was to develop a future vehicle interior for an upcoming sci-fi movie, and he set to work producing interior sketches of the vehicle, drawing it from all angles, exploring the logical positioning of switches, buttons, steering controls, displays, and more, just as he would for a real vehicle interior. He worked long hours, developing his concepts in great detail, and was therefore taken aback when he was scolded by the production manager for wasting time. He was reminded—in no uncertain terms—that if a detail wasn't in the shot, it didn't need designing. This vehicle featured in four scenes in the screenplay, all of which were to be captured from the perspective of the passenger, so designing anything else was unnecessary. Months later, my friend visited the set and observed this brutal reality firsthand: the parts of the central console facing away from the camera were left as bare, unpainted plywood. Production design for science fiction movies is not intended to be a rigorous design exercise, and props aren't well developed because *they don't need to be.* They're MacGuffins. They're wooden blocks painted to look like metal, they're something on a screen to jab a finger at or a gun-ish thing to point at a bad guy. They simply exist as a means to keep the story moving forward.

Following the runaway success of *Minority Report* in 2002, John Underkoffler and his team spent years attempting to convert the fictional gestural interface into a reality. The technology in the movie was based on an idea that had roots in contemporary research, but the technologies were all prototypical or theoretical at the time the movie was being developed. There are perhaps some benefits to this way of interacting with screen graphics (the lack of hardware needed and the ability to work in three dimensions, for example), but the gradient between movie prop and real-world products is incredibly steep, and ruthlessly uncompromising. If we're committed to this idea, first we need to ask ourselves *why* a product like this should exist and try to understand why the prevailing technologies (such as keyboards and mice) may be failing. This is quite a complex argument, and it wasn't something that was necessary to explore for the movie. The technology in the movie had a very different function—it had to be engaging and photogenic, not productive or efficient. Even if we're able to get beyond this question and are able to accurately define a functional benefit, there's still the problem of turning that into a product. There are sensors that need to be developed that allow for (or do better than) the accuracy we've become accustomed to from keyboards and mice. These sensors also have to be able to ignore unwanted gestures such as sneezing and scratching and not accidentally latch onto other people who might be walking by. Any successful product would also need to be competitively priced to go head-to-head with keyboards and mice (a tall order, given their incredibly optimized incumbent supply chains). Even if we were able to get all this in place, there's still the annoying fleshy bit of the problem—the user. During the filming of *Minority Report*, Tom Cruise reportedly had to take regular breaks due to the awkward ergonomic position of holding one's arms out in front of oneself, which can become remarkably painful remarkably quickly. Indeed, this is used as a "stress position" by interrogation teams and torturers throughout the world.

In spite of all this complexity, the world appears undeterred. The compelling visual metaphor of wafting one's arms around to interact with a computer has resulted in immense amounts of investment aimed at dragging the idea from the movie screen to reality. Everyone from megacorporations, including Microsoft, Intel, and Google, to hundreds of smaller startups has spent countless hours and millions of dollars trying to make the gestural interface in *Minority Report* "real." Gestural interface patents appear regularly to this day, but we're still well short of any real technology in broad use. In his keynote speech at World Architecture Festival 2015 in Singapore, Alex McDowell estimated that over a hundred patents have been issued for ideas featured in the movie. My guess is that number is significantly higher, evidenced by the number of times this reference has been wheeled out in meetings by excited executives, all thirsty for a fictional thing to be made real, but unsure as to exactly why. Science fiction ideas are engaging because they're designed to be, but this doesn't necessarily make them appropriate, achievable, or desirable ambitions for the real world.

It's easy to see why people regularly conflate the output of big tech with science fiction, and that's because the two worlds have become unhelpfully conjoined. Science fiction has made efforts to become more scientifically accurate, and, in parallel, the leaders of future-oriented companies have become increasingly enamored of science fiction, which has seeped into their subconscious and shaped the ways they think and talk. The Tesla Cybertruck is a striking example of the sci-fi aesthetic made real, resembling the low-polygon vehicles that featured in early video games. In truth, the Cybertruck looks the way it does because Elon Musk's eldest son, Saxon, reportedly asked him, "Why doesn't the future look like the future?" It's perhaps no surprise, then, that the Cybertruck feels rather adolescent—a blunt, simplistic rendition of the future cobbled together from a bedroom mood board of video games, science fiction movies, and escapist TV shows.

Our population broadly lacks the verbal or visual vocabulary needed to imagine genuinely new things. It's much easier to grab whatever's on top of the great pile of ideas and use it to conveniently cover that shortfall. Those military men didn't actually *want* their soldiers to feel like RoboCop; they just lacked the imagination to create an idea of their own, or the language to accurately describe it. If they'd thought a little more about the film, they'd also surely have realized that they were playing the roles of the men in the boardroom responsible for commissioning the RoboCop, which would be missing the point of the movie somewhat. Contemporary culture has a habit of tangling itself up in these repetitive patterns. Ideas about the future seem to roll like waves, repeating and repeating in endless cycles of hype and hope, lodging in our brains and ultimately hampering our ability to broadly imagine what the future might hold.

•

Ultimately, all acts of Might Futurism involve gazing out into the huge expanse of uncertainty ahead of us and populating it with a broad number of possibilities. These then need to be somehow "graded" based on their likelihood or their potential impact on the things we care about. In order to create sufficiently broad and sufficiently numerous scenarios, we need to gather and process a huge amount of information, much of which we may not have access to, or which may change as the scenarios play out. Every scenario is also at the mercy of other people's decisions, which often act as the ultimate variable, diverting and deflecting our neat little scenarios in often radical, unforeseen, and illogical ways. Decent scenario work also requires imagination, which a great many people struggle with. They fail to think sufficiently expansively, consider the world to be more constant than it is, or reach lazily for placeholders from futuristic media.

In any piece of scenario work there will (indeed, there must) be a large number of outcomes that go against an ideal, preferred, or "better" outcome. More often than not, we undertake acts of Might Futurism with the hope of improving something or shifting an important curve up and to the right. If we're doing our job correctly when thinking about what *might* happen in the future, the conversation will veer away from what we feel is preferable or ideal into a territory of negative outcomes, failure, unfortunate consequence, or terrible disaster. This type of perspective is often ignored or actively avoided, which is perhaps understandable, but attention to such outcomes is a vital and increasingly vibrant practice that represents the fourth and final mindset in our futures quartet: Don't Futurism.

DON'T

THE DON'T FUTURISTS

Theirs is the realm of the uncomfortable perspective.

They strive to reveal the overlooked.

They endlessly discuss effects, pitfalls, and perils.

They're drawn to negative consequences, potential collapses, and dystopian tales.

They're distrustful of power and the status quo.

They're weary of your promises and assurances.

They are mission driven and campaign minded.

They have done their reading and are confidently informed.

They hold global perspectives and inclusive mindsets.

They are willfully contrarian, occasionally polemical, endlessly dubious.

CRITIQUE, CAUTION, AND FEAR

If science fiction is the mythology of modern technology, then its myth is tragic.
—URSULA K. LeGUIN

This book aims to propose some sort of scaffold around the ways in which we think about the future and in so doing to help break down an incredibly complex act into more manageable chunks. So far, that has involved taking a largely action-oriented approach, focused on seeking direction and defining what we could, should, or might do, but from here we'll explore a slightly different tack. We're all reasonably comfortable defining what we want or where we would like to head, but we also have a pretty good idea of where we shouldn't go, what we wouldn't like, or what we hope will stop. Whenever we make a choice about the future, the direction we choose is usually the result of elbowing a billion other options out of the way, and we can therefore become rather protective of our chosen path. In truth, sitting within any proposal or idea about the future are a huge number of potentially detrimental effects or unintended consequences that we tend to minimize or ignore, but the Don't Futurist seeks to actively bring those to the fore. They live to augment and illuminate this kind of issue or possibility, to raise the profile of overlooked or intentionally suppressed negative outcomes in ideas about the future.

Don't Futurism is perhaps something of an outcast in our futures foursome, and as a general consumer of futurism, you're unlikely to have experienced much of it, at least not in a formal manner. That said, there's a long and distinguished history of looking to the future and exploring negative outcomes, disaster scenarios, or uncomfortable side effects, and of describing the future through subtraction rather than addition. Don't Futurism typically sits outside the major seats of power and offers counterpoints. It exists to dispense warnings, highlight issues, and point out consequences, which often makes it an unwelcome guest in communities built on optimism, positivity, and forward momentum.

Delivering critique is important but notoriously difficult, as anyone who has been employed as a manager can attest. Areas for improvement need to be clearly articulated, and accompanied with accurate and well-documented examples. Recommendations for change need to be sensitively presented, and throughout any critique, language has to be careful, precise, and unambiguous. Likewise, talking about the potentially negative outcomes of a future proposal is essential, and doing so early can save time, money, and reputation; but without the right culture in place, it can be incredibly difficult. Knowing when or how to give a critique is far from straightforward, and a poorly timed comment can be crushing to both confidence and progress. In parallel, structures of power and poorly functioning hierarchies can also adversely affect any semblance of open and honest dialogue, occasionally leading to catastrophic outcomes.

At 1:42 a.m. on August 6, 1997, Korean Air Flight 801 began its descent into A. B. Won Pat International Airport in Guam. The forty-two-year-old captain of the aircraft, Park Yong-chul, was an experienced pilot, but a combination of poor weather conditions and outdated flight charts led him to believe he was closer to the airport than he actually was. As the aircraft descended through the rain, subordinate members of the flight crew appear to have recognized his planning error, but only began challenging the captain six seconds before the Boeing 747–300 plowed into Nimitz Hill, killing 228 of the 254 people aboard. Any member of a team might be able to notice potentially damaging outcomes looming in the mists of the future, but if structures exist that suppress these observations, they may not be raised until it's far too late.

Thinking about disaster, despair, undesirable outcomes, or tragic events isn't something many of us enjoy. Given a choice, most people shy away from thinking about these kinds of futures, and only the very worst kinds of people enjoy being the downer in a conversation. Most of us have a habit of smothering such negative thoughts, and we generally prefer to think about the future as a place where things will improve somehow. We want our families, our businesses, and our communities to be successful, and to triumph through ingenuity, tenacity, and grit rather than dwelling too much on what might go wrong. Any budding strategist will no doubt be familiar with the 2×2 matrix, a simple diagrammatic tool used to plot two variables against each other. For example, it's conceivable that corporate board members might want to have a discussion about profit and purpose, and begin by drawing two crossed lines on the meeting-room whiteboard. The leadership team would love to plot themselves somewhere at the top right, with lots of profit to satisfy investors and lots of purpose to satisfy employees and customers. They'd love to spend all their time brainstorming how they might get to that promised land, but huddled down at the bottom left sits a decidedly stinky quadrant, a land of low profits and low purpose where no one's making any money and people don't know why the company exists. The easy thing to do is to say, "Let's avoid this area at all costs," scrawl something like "Here be dragons," and quickly move the conversation on to more exciting topics. However, the smarter thing to do is to flesh out in great detail what this quadrant would entail, what some early signals might be that the organization was headed in that direction, and, ultimately, what they might do if they found themselves there. Trying to figure out how a current run of good fortune may take a turn for the worse is what smart individuals, organizations, governments, and societies do regularly, and this is where the Don't Futurists play.

Fear is an important and incredibly powerful emotion, and fear about what might lurk around the corner has shaped our thinking since humanity's earliest dalliances with the future; indeed, fear forms the thematic backbone to some of our oldest stories. Almost all religions and folkloric traditions exist to encourage desirable behaviors through the portrayal of rewarding, idyllic places where we can languish after we leave our earthly bodies, but they also feature their own version of an "other place," and the portrayal (often in vivid, bloodcurdling detail) of punishment, retribution, and unimaginable suffering in the afterlife. The polytheistic religions of ancient Egypt featured a lake of fire for those convicted of moral unfitness; the Sumerian afterlife, Kur, was depicted as a dark cavern, deep underground, ruled by the goddess Ereshkigal, where punished souls ate nothing but dust; and Greek mythology featured Tartarus, an abyss filled with torment and suffering especially reserved for the wicked. Abrahamic religions also lean heavily on terrifying future predictions to steer their congregations toward righteousness in the present. Both Christianity and Islam feature fiery and painful futures—in the shape of Hell and Jahannam—for those who fail to meet the standards set by their respective doctrines, while Judaism has the Gehinnom, a place of purgatory and torment where one is judged on one's deeds. Religions broadly exist as frameworks for living, which are typically deployed through the sermons and writings of their leaders. While a considerable portion of moral guidance within religious doctrine stems from encouraging followers to emulate the benevolent deeds of their respective deities or messengers, we're all too familiar with religion's vivid portrayals of ominous consequences should one deviate from the prescribed path. Unless you repent, you shall face oblivion; should you lie with another man's wife, the fires of Hell shall engulf you, and if you collect wood on the Sabbath, you shall be stoned to death. Hope, encouragement, and positive reinforcement about the future can be highly effective approaches for adjusting someone's behavior in the present, but these tactics can only go so far before they butt up against indifferent shrugs and apathetic so-whats. There's a good reason why vivid depictions of judgment, retribution, guilt, pain, and punishment play such a strong role in the overwhelming majority of theologies: in order to really get someone to take your idea seriously, *there's nothing quite as potent as fear.*

As children we don't begin to develop future-oriented cognition until we're around three years old. Before this age we're largely unable to conceive of the future, and we struggle to make decisions that will affect how the future unfolds. If you offer a very young child one cookie now or ten cookies tomorrow, studies show that they'll likely choose the former option, but as we develop an ability to think beyond the present, our minds change in meaningful ways. We become more able to project and imagine outcomes, and we learn the essential tools of planning and prediction, particularly for potentially negative or dangerous futures. As a result, the cautionary tale has become a potent tool in childhood development, using projected fear to help children imagine what might happen if they follow their curiosity into dangerous territories. Stories such as "The Boy Who Cried Wolf," "Hansel and Gretel," and "Little Red Riding Hood" all illustrate to developing minds what might happen if they make up stories, wander off, or talk to strangers, hopefully encouraging children to make smart choices in the real world.

This storytelling technique continues on into adulthood, and literature has proved a powerful tool in helping us safely explore the outcomes of particular lines of curiosity. Mary Shelley's *Frankenstein* is regarded by scholars as one of the first works of what would become known as science fiction, but it's interesting in that it represents a decidedly dark reflection on scientific progress. In 1815, while trapped indoors during a wet summer next to Lake Geneva, Shelley was challenged by Lord Byron to write a ghost story. Instead of focusing on ancient rituals, dead specters, or haunted houses, she penned a tale that explored galvanism, the emerging technique of electro-animation that poked questions at the very nature of life itself. Rather than creating a heroic story that marveled at the potential of contemporary scientific advances, Shelley instead chose to explore the challenging aspects of galvanism, creating a terrifying monster who lumbered through the world tortured by its own existence, and ultimately pursuing his creator to the death. Today, science fiction literature regularly points at utopian worlds, idealized models of society, and breakthrough technologies, but it's perhaps when sailing in opposition to the prevailingly positive winds of the day that it finds its true calling. Science fiction has acted as a means for exploring potentially challenging implications of science and society for over two centuries, and many of the all-time sci-fi classics are built around this central theme, from *Nineteen Eighty-Four* and *Brave New World* to *Fahrenheit 451* and *The Hunger Games*.

It's interesting that in the translation to cinema, science fiction also chose to focus its gaze on tragic, terrifying, and undesirable outcomes. Fritz Lang's 1927 film *Metropolis* is perhaps the world's first full-length science fiction movie, and while breathtaking in both scale and scope, the movie is notable for its focus on themes of social inequality and the dehumanizing effects of industrialization. Cinematic history is peppered with blockbuster films such as *The Day the Earth Stood Still*, *Planet of the Apes*, and *The Omega Man* that drew huge audiences by following the tried-and-true recipe of apocalypse, paranoia, societal collapse, and struggles for survival.

Our television programming has also chosen to tell stories of the future not with energetic excitement but through bleak depictions and fretful extrapolations. When I was growing up in the 1970s, the UK was facing a decidedly unappealing future defined by economic downturn, industrial decline, and terrorism, and the entertainment industry reacted accordingly. At the start of the decade, the BBC commissioned the ominously titled *Doomwatch*, which ran for thirty-eight episodes and followed Dr. Spencer Quist as he led a government agency dedicated to protecting the world from the dangers of unfettered scientific research. In 1975, *The Survivors* debuted on British TV. A truly bleak show set in a postapocalyptic world ravaged by a global pandemic, it followed a small group of individuals as they tried to rebuild society amid endless chaos and devastation. Even the BBC's flagship science fiction show, *Doctor Who*, was built upon themes of fear, oppression, authoritarianism, and human extermination. More recently, future-oriented TV series such as *Black Mirror*, *The Handmaid's Tale*, and *Years and Years* have continued to focus on our collective interest in dark outcomes and downturns in our future, bringing satire and counterperspectives to bear on the broadly optimistic future narratives of the day. The function of these pieces of work is essentially the same as that of those cautionary tales from our childhood. They help us to role-play, to think through where things may be headed and how we might respond if faced with similar choices. Fiction can be immensely powerful in this role, offering an immersive way to explore dark avenues in a consequence-free manner. This type of work is perhaps the most complicated branch of future-oriented media, because it requires not only a detailed understanding of emergent technologies, governance, and social structures, but also an ability to imagine the consequences of present-day decisions and a refined appreciation of human behavior. All too frequently, however, these works find themselves overstepping this fragile line, lured by the salacious and enticing narrative territories of total collapse, disaster scenarios, and the end of the world, veering into the moody and depressing space we call "dystopia."

The term "utopia" was coined by the English polymath Sir Thomas More in his 1516 book of the same name, in which he describes a blueprint for an ideal society with minimal crime, violence, and poverty. Utopian themes exist across almost all cultures, societies, and religions, describing places where humans live a rudimentary and uncomplicated existence yet experience a state of unparalleled joy and contentment. Curiously, it wouldn't be until more than three hundred years later that the oppositional term "dystopia" was introduced by the British philosopher and economist John Stuart Mill. Dystopian tales can be enticing, but they often feel extreme and fantastical. Just as utopian tales can feel unattainable and fanciful, dystopian tales can feel unlikely and extreme, and are just as easily dismissed. Of course, dystopian collapse, existential dread, and threats to life and liberty make for excellent tableaus within which heroes can act, which is perhaps why they remain enduringly popular in our culture.

Our entertainment media is clearly comfortable exploring where things might go awry, but they certainly don't hold a monopoly on that perspective. Don't Futurism has also offered its considerable firepower to the worlds of politics, economics, and societal organization. As I mentioned earlier, at the center of the majority of political parties and social movements sits some form of manifesto, which often proposes exciting new directions for society but almost always originates from a position of dissatisfaction with the world as it is. Manifestos are often filled with woeful extrapolations of the prevailing strategies and policies of the day, providing detailed descriptions of how the world will be much worse if we continue along the current path. In a representative democracy, politics typically exists in a power and opposition structure, where debate and dissent are commonplace and actively encouraged. In principle, much of the role of any opposition party might be regarded as Don't Futurism, aiming to point out the flaws and potential traps, pitfalls, and problems in the future ideas proposed by those in power. Likewise, legal systems, codes of conduct, and national and international laws often help us arrive at an agreed-upon set of behaviors not by telling us what we *should* do but by very clearly articulating what we *shouldn't*.

When I was a child, our local swimming pool had an illustrated poster—with which some of you may be familiar—that featured a grid of nine bawdy cartoons to remind us that running, pushing, acrobatics, shouting, ducking, bombing, diving, smoking, and, ahem, "petting" were not allowed in the pool. Policies, guidelines, and laws exist primarily to steer us away from behaviors that would lead to an undesirable future as defined by the current governing body. The severity of each transgression is typically indicated by the size and shape of the associated penalty, be that a fine, a restriction of privileges, imprisonment, or, in some cases, death. Policing doesn't exist to reward us for performing well; it exists to punish us for performing poorly, and defines our future with Don'ts.

ALGORITHMIC ADVERSITY

When one is proposing preventative laws, alternative political trajectories, or engaging future narratives, believability is incredibly important, and just as with all stories about the future, believability can be greatly improved with data. Confident dotted lines marching off into the future are produced by excitable Should Futurists every day, but our history is also filled with examples where data and projections have been used to offer counternarratives, demand urgent action, or argue for meaningful change.

Just before the end of the eighteenth century, the British economist Thomas Robert Malthus began a deep dive into human demographics with his 1798 work *An Essay on the Principle of Population.* His fundamental observation centered on how an increase in a nation's food production initially boosted the well-being of its citizens, but this improvement was only temporary, as it resulted in population growth that ultimately reset the amount of food per person back to its original state. As he explored deeper, he calculated that population size increased geometrically (doubling every twenty-five years, resulting in an exponential J-shaped curve), while food production increased arithmetically (in a straight line). Projecting forward, he calculated that there would inevitably come a moment when the two lines crossed, when the number of people exceeded the available quantity of food, leading to what we now call a Malthusian catastrophe. In truth, such projections proved inaccurate, as the development of artificial fertilizers and mechanized methods of agriculture kept enough food on our tables as populations increased, but these diagrammatic projections were used to develop Malthus's thinking on everything from controlling birth rates to government welfare policy. In 1856, the British economist William Stanley Jevons published *The Coal Question*, becoming one of the first people to delve into the notion of energy efficiency, or to even discuss the idea of "fuel economy." Though Jevons's work was focused on Britain's increasing reliance on coal, his essay marked the beginning of a global conversation between scientists, economists, government commissions, and geologists that continued well into the early twentieth century, leading to predictions that in short order the world's coal supply would be exhausted and we would all face a global energy crisis. With no viable alternatives to coal, this represented a disastrous potential outcome and, according to the curves, was inevitable. Again, the projected crisis didn't actually happen, but as a result of these investigations, new questions were asked and new discussions were had, which brought about new perspectives on resource scarcity and a transition to oil and natural gas in the second half of the century. These historical examples represent moments when Don't Futurism transcended doomsaying purely for the sake of shock and led directly to meaningful shifts in direction.

Perhaps our most consequential tale of data-driven public concern about the future began in 1965. The Italian industrialist Aurelio Peccei delivered a speech about the dramatic scientific and technological changes happening in the world that captured the attention of the British scientist and government advisor Alexander King. United by a shared skepticism of the potential of technology to adequately address lurking global challenges, Peccei and King convened a small group from the fields of academia, industry, civil society, and diplomacy at Villa Farnesina on the banks of the River Tiber, to discuss novel approaches to social and environmental problems. They named this group the Club of Rome, and it grew into a highly influential organization that exists to this day.

Meanwhile, on the other side of the world at the Massachusetts Institute of Technology, a slim, bespectacled computer scientist was working on the development of what he called system dynamics. Jay Wright Forrester had first arrived at MIT in 1939 as an electrical engineering graduate and rapidly developed something of a formidable reputation after building the largest digital computer of the day. In Forrester's eyes, everything on Earth could be interpreted like one of these large computers: as a system with inputs, outputs, feedback loops, and dependencies connected in an intricate web of interaction, and ticking along like a huge Rube Goldberg machine. Just as Arthur Tansley had posited, Forrester believed that, once mapped, any such system could be re-created inside a computer, where it could be adjusted and tweaked to simulate future outcomes. This approach caught the eye of industrialists wrangling with seemingly intractable and interlinked business problems, and in 1956 Forrester began working with a team at General Electric, converting their corporate policies into algorithms and building complex supply-chain models based on the electronic principles of load and feedback. Over subsequent experiments he created DYNAMO, a generalized computer modeling language that represented managerial decisions as a series of tanks, pipelines, and valves, the principles of which he would later use to assist a wide variety of manufacturers, medical researchers, and city governments who had equally complex questions.

In June 1970, Forrester was invited by the Club of Rome to the picturesque city of Bern, Switzerland. The club had recently issued its inaugural vision statement, lightly titled *The Predicament of Mankind*, and was attempting to secure a $400,000 grant from the Volkswagen Foundation. They were seeking the funding to explore responses to emerging global complexities and uncertainties, but their original proposal had been rejected, leaving the sixty members of the club in a quandary and scrambling to devise an alternative pitch. Forrester suggested that his system dynamics approach might offer what they were looking for, and on his way back home, he quickly sketched out a global model that represented the world as a sophisticated web of interconnected nodes, each influencing its neighbors as they grew and evolved together. He named the model WORLD1, a groundbreaking framework that ultimately enabled the Club of Rome to secure funding from the Volkswagen Foundation.

The following year, Forrester's colleague and former student Dennis Meadows assembled a team of sixteen people to create a significantly more detailed diagram. They worked for almost two years, creating an immensely complex, interconnected representation of planet Earth with inputs, outputs, and feedback loops, each nested within subsystems and defined by constants and variables. The illustrations of their model resemble a sprawling circuit diagram or city map, with countless nodes and junctures representing multiple aspects of population, agriculture, industry, finite resources, and pollution, all interlinked in an intricate representation of an interdependent network. In a nod to Forrester's earlier work, the team named this model WORLD3, and subsequently used it to run projections for a period covering 1900 to 2100. While their model was flawed (which the team openly acknowledged), their simulations appeared to reveal an impending Malthusian catastrophe—nonrenewable resources would be exhausted by the middle of the twenty-first century, causing steep declines in growth and food production, resulting in a disastrous drop in human population. The Club of Rome presented several reports and publications that laid out these findings, but it was the production of a straightforward and easily digestible book that brought their insights into the limelight. *The Limits to Growth* was published in 1972 and became a worldwide hit, selling over 30 million copies in more than thirty languages, making it the bestselling environmental book in history.

The Limits to Growth stands as a landmark book for many people, chiefly for its use of data and econometric projections to weave a narrative about the future of our planet and our survival upon it. Following its debut, the book found itself the subject of widespread derision from lobbyists, journalists, industrialists, and analysts alike, as it unabashedly defied the conventional norms of economic models and growth paradigms upon which almost everything was built. Today, many critics point to *The Limits to Growth* as the moment we became catastrophists, with a morbid preoccupation with disaster, collapse, and impending doom. Others point to the book as a clear warning from the past, highlighting just how much we knew and how little we did, drawing attention to the stark cautions embedded within the text, which many now believe are unfolding precisely as written. Whichever of these perspectives is true, what's clear is that we've become just as comfortable using data, projections, and modeling techniques to advocate for restraint and prudence as we have to advocate for investments, acquisitions, and growth, and that this way of representing the world has fundamentally shaped the ways in which many of us now view the future. Al Gore's 2006 cinematic lecture *An Inconvenient Truth* unmistakably inherits the ethos of *The Limits to Growth*, using a compelling mix of data and charts interspersed with engaging movie clips to illustrate the shape of the climate crisis, and to passionately plead for substantial and immediate action. In a particularly striking moment in the film, Gore steps onto an industrial scissor lift to reach the top of a graph of atmospheric carbon dioxide concentration, as the line climbs almost vertically upward and extends beyond the projection screen.

Our enchantment with data—and particularly its portrayal within interconnected systems—has granted us the ability to discern intricate relationships between an ever-expanding array of variables. From global weather patterns to interest rates, disease transmission, and the flow of traffic, a staggering amount of our daily decisions and priorities are made directly through the analysis of incoming data. Data is intoxicating, but as I mentioned previously, projections of recorded data can quickly become problematic, whether encouraging an audience to start something or stop something. Data is raw, brutal, flawed, and always incomplete, and even when we have the data we seek, it only becomes a useful tool for futurism once it's interpreted. When it comes to the future, data can nudge, hint, propose, and suggest, but it doesn't actually *tell* us anything.

When Thomas Malthus was writing his *Essay on the Principle of Population* in 1798, there were estimated to be around a billion people alive on Earth. A hundred years later this number had swollen to around 1.6 billion. When I was born there were around 4 billion people alive, and this number has more than doubled in my lifetime and continues to rise by around 75 million people every year. That seems like a lot of change in a short amount of time, and when plotted against history, the curve looks incredibly steep. But is it cause for concern? Should we do something about it? Will this line continue into a steepening curve or flatten out? Should we step in and try to change it somehow, or try to get the line to trend downward (ignoring for a second the complexity involved in actually attempting such a thing)? The prevailing belief among the world's population experts is that this astonishing growth isn't inherently problematic, and that population numbers will plateau if we continue to focus on education, reproductive healthcare, and the emancipation of women—but how confident are we of that? Might there be something the analysts are missing? What nuances, variables, or contributing factors might have been omitted, ignored, or diminished in their models? Are there unimagined innovations around the corner (such as the invention of fertilizers that Malthus didn't imagine) that could neutralize any detrimental effects of this growth? Could these experts be under any commercial, industrial, societal, or political pressure to generate particular conclusions? Will this change evolve into a global disaster or become a comfortable norm? Should we be taking drastic action to address population change or not? Only time will tell. The demographic data we have is incredibly dense—and I don't doubt its accuracy—but where it will go in the future is an educated guess, at best.

•

Whenever any of us encounters a future proposition, it's natural to compare it with our own ideals, and where we disagree with what we see, negative feelings can gather momentum remarkably quickly. In the face of this kind of gap, our opinions can rapidly become strident and vehement, focusing intently on the potentially detrimental aspects of the proposition and ignoring even the slightest hint of anything beneficial. We make arguments against the plan, hoping to illustrate our points with images, examples, and stories. We reach for data to prove the opposition wrong. We post our thoughts on social media, join like-minded groups, and seek out others with similarly negative opinions on the projected future. In this way, Don't Futurism can often form the origin point of protests, blockades, acts of civil disobedience, direct action, and—in some extreme cases—war.

Throughout history, when ideas have emerged that contravene some established ideology, many people have committed themselves to incredible acts of devotion, dogged determination, immense bravery, and self-sacrifice, but we must also acknowledge that not every future projection warrants such an extreme, oppositional stance. When poorly deployed, a strong-willed attitude can quickly unravel into dogmatism, pulling populations apart into simplistic, pugnacious factions of "goodies" and "baddies" and leading to emphatically oppositional politics, ideological extremism, and the perils of all-or-nothing bigotry. In discussions about the future, dystopian portrayals can often act like catnip for an audience, but they can also harm the credibility of an argument, making it easier to dismiss valid concerns as hyperbole or overly dramatic pessimism.

The future of anything sufficiently complex is inherently ambiguous, convoluted, and interdependent, and such things often respond better to suggestions, gradual changes, or small nudges. There's a way of thinking about the future that is more attuned to these nuances, one that emphasizes caution, care, and attention rather than simply jamming on the brakes. It encourages longer time horizons, broader perspectives, and persistently asking "Then what?" over and over (and over) again. It's concerned with which *parts* of a problem to address, to what extent those parts might need changing, and in which order. Dramatic gestures like shouting "Burn it all down!" or flipping the table might be useful to grab someone's attention (and in many cases may represent a last resort), but more often, conversation, education, and guidance can prove much more powerful tools in driving meaningful course correction, or encouraging someone to slow down, pivot, or stop.

This mindset represents a growing and increasingly potent force in contemporary futures work, a more sophisticated form of Don't Futurism that looks at the world and tries to uncover its complexity, highlight implications, and surface the ignored or suppressed symptoms of change. This seems like a sensible thing to do—after all, preparedness and an openness to the unknown are traits drilled into us from an early age—but this level of rigor feels surprisingly limited in today's conversations about the future. Awkward discussions about implications and potentially negative outcomes seem to have been ousted in favor of punchy headlines, podium promises, or resolutely positive rhetoric. Selling an idea as somehow inherently beneficial, obvious, or straightforward has become the norm in everything from politics to retailing. Sharp points need to be smoothed off and bumps in the road need to be downplayed in favor of more simplistic, idealized versions of the future, and it's become incredibly rare to acknowledge any level of uncertainty or complexity in our future propositions. This may be changing a little at the fringes, but how did we end up here?

TOXIC POSITIVITY AND SOLUTIONISM

There's always more to discover if you pay more attention.
—JAMES BRIDLE

At its core, design is an inherently positive act that focuses on the reduction of challenging or problematic experiences. That's a lovely thing to be involved in, and designers like me revel in the removal of roadblocks, making things simpler, more efficient, or more joyful. It can be a wonderfully fulfilling profession, and designers routinely dedicate months of tenacious work to chasing small improvements and tiny moments of pleasure for their customers. When my iPhone remembers a loyalty number for an airline I haven't used in months, that feels like good design. The pull tab that stays attached to the soda can, preventing it from being discarded in the street and finding its way into the throat of a local mammal, is almost certainly good design too. In any object or service, changing a small detail can make all the difference, and a little bit of thought can transform an average product into a favorite product. This attention to the creation of positive experiences can be hugely satisfying, but it can also be good for business. Reducing friction in a digital checkout means people are likely to do it more often. Making products a pleasure to use means a customer is more likely to return. Creating consistency across a line of products means people can more easily experiment across a brand. This is the often unspoken (and rather icky) role of contemporary design—it is a means to gather customers together, create desire in their minds, and harvest the silver in their pockets.

As a result of this underlying ambition to create simplicity and joy, our culture tends to focus somewhat myopically on the positive aspects of innovation, which ultimately shape the ways in which we explore and talk about our future. Pitches for new products typically tout exciting features, improved experiences, and better performance, as it seems that's what customers want—and investors want customers. Talking about potential issues, unsolved problems, or, indeed, any level of complexity in an idea just doesn't feel like good business. Any crack of doubt needs to be minimized, filled in, or painted over in favor of a good story or an enticing proposition, which results in an environment defined by what psychologists refer to as "toxic positivity." We see this kind of toxic positivity everywhere, from the kitchen cleaner ads on TV to the breathy pitches of entrepreneurs on *Shark Tank*—we only hear the good things. Our use of language also reflects this shift. Ideas about the future have gradually morphed from propositions or theories into "solutions," and we've become accustomed to hearing the word "solutions" as a metaphor for progress almost everywhere. We use it to name our companies, launch our products, and describe their features. It's such a lovely, well-rounded word too. "Solutions" reeks of closure and finality. A solution feels good, it feels complete, it feels *done*.

The fact that we've arrived at this point is perhaps understandable, no doubt a symptom of the overwhelming volume of ideas clamoring for attention and the pervasive, persuasive attitudes of advertising, but unfortunately, this mindset has made its way beyond marketing and advertising into the very heart of industry. Large companies are responsible for most of the products and services that fill our lives, from computers and phones to cars, food, and clothing, and within these large companies there's often a constant battle for budget, a great many ideas, and a great many teams bickering and bidding for a larger slice of the pie. It's become an uncomfortable truth that in any company of a reasonable size, *everybody works in advertising*. Every individual, team, product manager, vice president, and executive wants their work to be the star. They're always pitching. They want to secure the biggest possible budget, the most resources, and the headline presentation slot at the annual company meeting. The best way to achieve this is to talk only about why an idea is transformative, beneficial, and exciting, to focus on the positive, to build a head of steam around an idea and give the impression of oodles of forward momentum. In an environment like this, there's no time for nuance, doubt, complexity, or concerns when talking about the future, which results in a culture of energetic promotion and the suppression of complexity in order to maintain the illusion of productivity. If you're spending all your time trying to create a clean pitch designed to make a sale, then surprise, surprise—you work in advertising.

This drive toward simplicity and tidy solutions extends beyond the ideas themselves and into the processes by which innovation actually happens. Figuring out the type of products a new technology might enable, or how people will actually experience them, is at the core of most new breakthroughs, and design plays a vital role in this work. But contrary to what some people might think, the process of getting to a new product or creative solution is incredibly messy, nonlinear, and complex. I've worked on many hundreds of future-oriented projects over the years, and each one has been different in some way. The path of innovation is full of dead ends, mistakes, false starts, uncertainty, and experimentation. Timelines can stretch indefinitely, breakthroughs can remain perpetually just out of reach, and there's a freewheeling hope-and-pray attitude at the core of this kind of work, all of which results in a rather difficult activity to sell as a service. When embarking on an innovation project, clients typically want something clean and tidy. They want some process through which a group of people can pass and emerge with a neat, well-rounded "deliverable" on a predetermined deadline for a predetermined price. It's therefore perhaps unsurprising that one of the world's largest innovation consultancies sought to create just such a process and deploy it at scale: the simplified, sequential innovation approach known as Design Thinking.

The roots of this ambition extend back to before the Second World War, and Design Thinking actually represents the latest in a string of attempts to systematize and formalize innovation and design. The process was brought into being by the San Francisco–based consulting firm IDEO (which achieved its prominence by designing the first Apple mouse), and it was pitched as a means to rapidly move from problem to solution by passing a team through five sequential phases: Empathize, Define, Ideate, Prototype, and Test. You might not be familiar with the Design Thinking method itself, but it's a reasonably simple construct that you can probably picture—five steps joined together into a diagram that flows from left to right, with a couple of dotted arrows to indicate repeated steps.

In effect, the Design Thinking process itself was an innovation product, the outcome of an exercise to wrap design up into a digestible framework, and in so doing create a simple, reproducible format. This packaged simplicity made Design Thinking incredibly popular with corporations, and for over a decade countless articles, essays, books, and conferences emerged that effused over the approach. Non-designers warmly embraced its simplicity, signed up for Design Thinking training sessions, and tried to integrate the method into their daily work. IDEO thrived. They hired more people and attracted new clients to their studios, and their leadership team appeared in countless press articles, claiming that they had unlocked the process of innovation and, in so doing, secured designers a seat at the top table.

But many designers remained unconvinced. Over time, Design Thinking came under significant criticism for ignoring, minimizing, and skipping over huge swathes of important work, and for underrepresenting the real-world complexities of design to a sometimes grotesque degree. As the realities of *actual* innovation revealed themselves to

Design Thinkers, many tied themselves in knots, adding more stages, more feedback loops, and more layers to their diagrammatic models, often to the point of absurdity. As I write this, IDEO is reeling following the termination of almost a third of its staff. Design Thinking appears to have failed to deliver on their ambition to transpose a complex, nonlinear act into a sequence of repeatable dance steps, and this may well become the epitaph for this once-great titan of the design world. Framing the inherent complexities of innovation as a "problem" only served to encourage the creation of a "solution," which Design Thinking seemed well placed to offer. Simplicity is alluring, but when simplicity ignores or suppresses important (if annoying) truths, those truths don't disappear; they just return later in often uglier and more pernicious ways. The momentum generated by positivity and simplicity can be incredibly attractive and overwhelming, pushing aside calls for caution or discussions about negative outcomes, and dismissing concerns and complexities as unhelpful distractions to progress.

Over many years of undertaking future-oriented work, it's become clear to me that there's an attitudinal problem at the heart of innovation and future storytelling that fails to acknowledge the complexities in all human behavior and the systems within which we operate—or, worse still, a culture that actively tries to conceal them. Let's think back to those vision videos and product pitches I mentioned earlier, where we follow a fictional user through a future experience with a new piece of technology.

First, the characters in these vision videos are only ever taking part in utterly wholesome activities. They're trying to order a cake for Nana's birthday, book a table for an anniversary dinner, or buy new shoes for their angelic child. It's a sea of perfectly pearly smiles, well-tucked shirts, and appropriately neutral politics, which is clearly not a reflection of the world in which we all live—and it's certainly not a representation of how people *actually use technology*. All across the world people use technology to hook up with partners, buy drugs, gossip with one another, and share memes. They use it to play games while on the toilet, order dog food, check sales receipts, and grab screenshots of an ex-girlfriend's bikini pics. They use it to watch reality TV brawls, spy on their neighbors, diagnose their pimples, order dumplings, figure out how to fix tire punctures, and watch Doja Cat videos while brushing their teeth. They drive their cars too fast, they download illegal copies of movies, they share passwords, they lie about where they are and pretend to be people they're not. Take, for example, one glaring, unspoken truth about contemporary technology—pornography. While it's obviously difficult to gather accurate figures, research suggests that every day humans make around 68 million search queries related to pornography, and porn websites account for around one in ten of all the planet's websites. Thirty-five percent of all internet downloads are related to adult material, and in 2023 OnlyFans users spent over $6.5 billion on content. Yet when talking about the future we all seem to ignore this truth, pretend it doesn't exist, or whitewash it out of our imagination.

Second, in product pitches everything works perfectly. It's best-case scenarios all round. Logins are seamless, friends pick up the call, the products are in stock, and everything unfurls like a finely choreographed ballet. The pleasant ukulele music tinkles along in the background, and the story ends with high fives, smiling grandparents, and couples cuddling on couches with fresh popcorn. These sickly-sweet clips feel like advertisements—and that's entirely intentional—but over years of watching future product pitches, videos, and demos like this I've become frustrated by their disingenuous nature. Nothing on Earth works the way they pretend it does, nowhere even close. Credit cards expire, the Wi-Fi in the kitchen isn't strong enough to stream the movie, your husband used the iPad yesterday and closed all the tabs, there's tape holding the bathroom door together, the dog keeps scratching the wooden floor, the takeout place messed up your order, and damn it, the charger is in your *other* bag.

Let's take another trip back to *Minority Report*. As we've discussed, this movie is a Could Futurist's dream, filled with incredible, eye-popping devices, gestural interfaces, autonomous vehicles, microrobotics, and any number of extreme renditions of transformative technologies. For a big-budget science fiction movie, the level of care that Spielberg and his crew took in the creation of this world is impressive, and it's rightly stood the test of time. That said, while the majority of futurists salivate over these headline-grabbing technologies, there's one moment that sticks in my mind more than any of the flying machines, corneal implants, or transparent screens. Our hero, John Anderton, is in his apartment, sitting at a computer terminal reminiscing over old holographic home movies. He reaches for a box of Pine and Oats cereal sitting nearby, and as he lifts it off the table the animated characters on the box spring into life, dancing and singing along to a cute jingle. This is a clever piece of production design, and it feels almost achievable (some sort of motion sensor and a cheaply produced e-ink screen, perhaps), but what happens next is where things get interesting. When John places the box back down, the characters keep dancing and the jingle keeps playing. Something's gone wrong: the sensor has failed, and the box still thinks it's in the air. John picks it up again and replaces it on the table, aiming to reset the sensor or reboot the animation, but the jingle continues, the characters dance, and the carton won't shut up. In frustration, John grabs the box and slings it across the kitchen, where it crashes into a shelf of glassware. The entire scene lasts less than ten seconds—and is entirely inconsequential to the narrative—but in that moment the *Minority Report* world feels incredibly real. The lead character is surrounded by new technologies, but they don't quite work properly. The future is a little bit broken.

Breakage, decay, misuse, errors, workarounds, consequences, and implications are an important part of everyday life. We know this to be true. Governments invest billions of dollars in fire departments, hospital emergency rooms, police forces, rapid response teams, and emergency preparedness, because of the immutable truth that at some point, everything breaks. We insure against damage, fire, theft, bankruptcy, and any number of unseen but evident threats to the tune of $9.8 trillion globally per year. We all expect things to go wrong, but when talking about the future in terms of innovation or invention, we assume everything will be just fine, somehow. It's understandable, of course, why a budding startup, tech giant, politician, or futurist wouldn't want to talk about this kind of ugly grittiness and would much prefer to squirrel it away under rich, delicious scoops of excited energy, but this kind of toxic positivity is symptomatic of a broader futures culture that I find deeply problematic. These shiny, happy representations of the future feel glib, vacuous, and silly, like something a glamorous candidate might clumsily blurt out onstage at a pageant. They don't feel rigorous. They lack any footing in reality and fail to acknowledge the obvious and evident complexity of our lives. The ways in which we *actually* live are barely ever reflected in the ways in which we talk about our future, through a desire to sell an idea rather than communicate its true impact, and I can't help thinking that's a problem. We appear to have succumbed to our own obsession with heroic storytelling and escapist aspiration rather than embracing the inescapable truths of our existence, in all its wonky, broken, dysfunctional, and complicated glory.

DEPENDENCIES, IMPLICATIONS, AND ENDS

When you invent the ship, you also invent the shipwreck.
—PAUL VIRILIO

Whenever we're confronted with a new technology, it's tempting to think about what we might do with it or what we might make, but we rarely think about what it might *mean*. As we discussed earlier, the future is accretive: it piles upon the past, and every idea interleaves with its neighbors. Yet the vast majority of ideas about the future rarely try to wrap their arms around this web of complexity. In his 2010 book *The Ecological Thought*, the philosopher Timothy Morton coined the term "hyperobject" to define things that are so distributed that they "transcend spatiotemporal specificity." That's a complicated academic way of saying that some things are so interconnected (either to other physical objects, to systems, or to ideas) that their edges become impossible to define. Ideas such as climate change, macroeconomic capitalism, and nuclear waste are hyperobjects, and simplistic calls to "stop" them fail to acknowledge the complexity of their arrangement or of the process of stopping itself. This is an important idea to hold close when thinking about anything new in our future—everything we create or stop is a connected thing that will define (and be defined by) countless other things. Not everything should be considered a hyperobject, but it's an important consideration in thinking about the implications of any change in the future. Ripples, echoes, and fallout result from any intervention, and every new idea has to integrate into the ongoing flow of the world. When done well, Don't Futurism embraces this: it runs toward this kind of complexity and encourages debates about symptoms, outcomes, then-whats, dependencies, implications, and bumps in the road.

The self-driving car feels like a thoroughly modern invention that has captured the contemporary imagination and might point at some interesting futures, but like most things we consider to be new, the idea has been around for a fairly long time. The earliest experiments in driving assistance took place in the 1920s, but it wasn't until 1977 that the first semiautonomous car was developed by Japan's Tsukuba Mechanical Engineering Laboratory. Over the last fifteen years we've seen a spike in performance in this field, accelerated by technologies such as spatial sensing, robotics, image recognition, and raw computing power, not to mention the detailed mapping of our cities and road networks. The technical problems of navigation, speed control, and automation are now largely solved, but we're yet to see large-scale self-driving car adoption as the technology struggles to integrate into the existing infrastructure that surrounds it. We can't simply get rid of other vehicles, pedestrians, road signs, and potholes. We can't ignore adverse weather conditions, jaywalkers, cyclists, parked cars, food trucks, DoorDash scooters, or construction work. We can't skip past existing policy, wave off the government, or ignore the insurance industry. We can't rebuild the city to suit our new idea; our new idea has to integrate into what's already there. It's understandable that people are excited about the technological advances we've seen in this field, but that's just the start. Now the real work begins.

In all futures work, there's a recurrent tendency to overlook this kind of truth or downplay the complexities associated with the introduction of any new thing. A solution only exists as far as we're willing to look. It's easy to become so blinded by an innovation that we fail to see anything that surrounds it or the unhelpful consequences that it might bring about. Even if we're able to identify a negative implication in what we're proposing, it's incredibly tempting to punt it deep into the distance and leave it to another team, company, government, or generation to rectify. While we may feel as though the present-day world belongs to us, the reality is that we're all inhabitants of a giant time capsule that was accidentally planted by our ancestors, and it's now our job to address the implications of their decisions. Many of the challenges we face today were not initiated by our generation but by grainy people from blurry photographs, the majority of whom are long dead.

In the nineteenth century, cities like New York and London grew incredibly quickly. People and products needed to be moved around in ever-greater numbers, and the prevailing solution of the day was horses. By the 1880s, there were around 150,000 horses in New York, dragging buggies, carriages, people, and freight around the city's bustling streets, day and night. The system worked pretty well, and horses offered a reliable, somewhat affordable solution to the city's locomotion challenges, but with one major drawback—manure. A healthy horse can generate about thirty pounds of solid waste every day, which, in the 1880s, totaled around 800,000 tons of manure deposited on Manhattan every year—the equivalent mass of eight aircraft carriers. The streets also ran deep with millions of gallons of urine, and bloated, rotting horse carcasses littered the streets as the unfortunate beasts expired. The result was a city drowning in waste, bathed in swarms of flies, and facing an impending public health crisis. Into this environment rolled the motorcar, which seemed like a clean, reliable, and efficient solution to New York's equine dependency. So compelling was the proposition that the adoption of internal combustion engines was remarkably swift. By 1912 there were more cars than horses in the city, and in 1917 the last horse-drawn streetcar was taken out of public commission. New Yorkers no longer had to contend with mountains of manure and rivers of urine, and motorcars seemed to be the perfect technological solution to a mucky, obnoxious problem. Two thumbs up. Five stars. Great job. Next slide, please.

I'm guessing you're ahead of me here, but that wasn't the end of the story. Cars continued to develop, becoming larger and faster and changing the landscape of the city as the tempos of pedestrians and vehicles became incompatible. Single travelers in cars now took up more room than a person on horseback, so congestion became a considerable issue. To travel the length of Central Park by car today (a distance of around two and a half miles) takes around thirty minutes on an average day—which is considerably slower than traveling the same distance by horse—but the ultimate negative consequence of vehicular adoption in New York City is, without doubt, air pollution. Internal combustion engines generate carbon monoxide, nitrogen oxide, and various forms of particulate matter which bathe the city of New York in a choking cloud, leading to 2,400 deaths per year and thousands of emergency department visits and hospitalizations for asthma and cardiopulmonary problems. In order to tackle the growing burden of vehicles in New York City, plans aimed at dissuading drivers from bringing their vehicles into midtown Manhattan have been repeatedly proposed for almost a century. In March 2024, the Metropolitan Transportation Authority board—following the example of cities such as London, Milan, Stockholm, and Singapore—introduced a $15 congestion fee to drive a car in midtown Manhattan, which was withdrawn before being activated, then reduced to $9 and reinstated in January 2025; as I write this, the plan faces a distinctly uncertain future.

Of course, the adoption of motor vehicles in the last century wasn't restricted solely to New York; at their peak in 2017, 86 million vehicles with internal combustion engines were sold globally. In parallel to its impact on the human respiratory system, the combustion of fossil fuels is also a major source of carbon dioxide, a primary greenhouse gas that is a significant contributor to climate change. If this weren't complicated enough, gasoline is a product derived from crude oil, a diminishing resource that is increasingly difficult to find. The search for enough fuel to feed our vehicular demand has driven mining companies deep into rainforests, beneath the Arctic, and into our deserts, causing major disruption to fragile ecosystems and the displacement of Indigenous communities. Oil reserves are also increasingly restricted to locations with complicated political situations, forcing uncomfortable alliances, unbalanced deals, and distorted dependencies between nations and corporations.

So, should New York have changed to the automobile or continued to use horses? The motorcar represented a seemingly ideal solution to a very pressing problem, but has subsequently yielded a great number of implications and secondary issues of its own and has fundamentally changed the shape of the city. In the 1880s, the idea of sticking with horses seemed preposterous, but if New York had asked more questions, slowed down a little, and thought longer or harder about the future implications of the automobile, would that have meaningfully changed this decision? Were they even in a position to do so? Could they have foreseen any of the subsequent issues and done anything to adjust their course, and who is "they" in this question, exactly? Could there have been a way for horses, pedestrians, and cars to work well together, or could a third option, neither horse nor car, have emerged? To understand the full impact of any new technology, especially one as transformative and pervasive as the motorcar, takes an incredibly dedicated and patient culture. It's work which is full of nuance, responsibility, uncomfortable truths, and difficult perspectives—which are tricky things to cram onto a billboard or fit into a presentation.

What usually results in situations such as this is an ongoing parade of partial fixes, do-overs, patches, and adjustments. As the adoption of the motor vehicle proceeded across the globe, numerous efforts were made by governments, pressure groups, and manufacturers to address the issues brought about by the change. In 1896, the British government introduced the Red Flag Act, which required a person to walk ahead of every motorcar waving a flag as a warning to others. In the 1920s, campaigners in Detroit organized "safety parades" to highlight the potential dangers of the automobile, towing wrecked cars down the street with mannequin drivers dressed as Satan and bloody corpses as passengers. In the 1960s, anger about freeways running through downtown areas reached a peak in many American cities, resulting in sit-ins and protests against the "concrete monsters" coursing through neighborhoods.

Today, the focus of our efforts to address the impacts of the automobile has shifted to their environmental impact, and a major contender has emerged in the shape of electric vehicles, which seem to do the trick—at least on the surface. The major selling point of this technological refocusing is the switch from gasoline and diesel to electric power, which can be generated by wind, solar, hydro, or another less-polluting source of energy. In parallel, replacing an internal combustion engine with batteries and electric motors means that the experience of driving a vehicle remains largely the same, albeit with a little more range anxiety. As a result, there's been a threefold increase in global electric vehicle sales over a three-year period from 2020. These vehicles solve the oil-based propulsion challenges, but they're not quite an outright panacea. The batteries within electric vehicles require a very specific cocktail of materials to function, and those materials typically come from problematic territories. Take cobalt, for example, which is a primary ingredient in the cathodes of lithium-ion batteries. The largest cobalt reserves in the world are found in the Democratic Republic of Congo, a country ranked 179th out of 191 countries by the Human Development Index and classed as the least-developed country on Earth by the UN. Cobalt is mined there at significant environmental and human cost, including numerous documented cases of child labor, water pollution, air pollution, and corruption. Battery recycling is also notoriously difficult, predominantly due to their bonded laminate construction and the hazardous nature of the materials within them. Numerous companies are developing battery-recycling technologies and standards, but we still face an uncertain future for this looming challenge.

Electric vehicles may not use oil as a means of propulsion, but they commonly use a substantial quantity of petrochemical components in their construction, from paint, lubricants, and films on their exterior to the plastic upholstery, adhesives, and carpets within. Electric vehicles are also heavier than their petrol predecessors, meaning increases in both road and tire wear and a heightened risk of fatality in the event of a pedestrian collision. Importantly, electric vehicles also don't fundamentally alter today's transit models, meaning the smothering effects of congestion in our cities remains unchanged. Our shift to electric motors offers a means to move away from internal combustion, but the web of implications around transportation remains incredibly complex, and will undoubtedly continue to present us with countless challenges in the years to come.

In any significant technological shift, there's always the potential for countless unseen issues or knock-on effects, and foreseeing them can be incredibly difficult. Seemingly positive developments frequently result in complex and even inverse outcomes, an observation ably made by William Jevons, the author of *The Coal Question* I mentioned a little earlier. In 1865, while Jevons was studying figures for the consumption of coal, he realized that increases in the efficiency of steam engines didn't *reduce* coal consumption as expected; rather, they caused an *increase*. At first glance, this seems counterintuitive. If engines become more efficient, then they should use less coal, but this assumes that demand remains constant, which, of course, it doesn't. When something becomes more efficient, it typically becomes cheaper, so we're encouraged to use it more. This disparity between theoretical efficiency gains and actual consumption is what is known as the rebound effect, and when this exceeds 100 percent we find ourselves in what's known as a Jevons paradox. On a more personal level, we're now surrounded by countless "labor-saving" devices, from dishwashers and photocopiers to forklifts and power tools, yet our lives are far from the utopian lands of leisure that we might have imagined or been promised—we've simply added more labor to fill the available space.

In recent years it's become increasingly popular to

think about a future unshackled from our dependence on oil, a future where energy flows plentifully from renewable sources or some inexhaustible wellspring such as nuclear fusion. If this abundant future comes to fruition, the potential benefits to our beleaguered planet seem boundless. But it's also worth remembering that many industries are currently held in check by the associated costs and scarcity of oil. Take mining, for example. If energy supplies become cheap, ubiquitous, and guilt-free, then the corresponding columns in balance sheets all over the world will change, perhaps radically so. Regions that proved too expensive for mining might now start to look viable, previously unprofitable locations might now become profitable, and we might face a significant overall *increase* in the prevalence and impact of extractive industries. For the sake of clarity, the benefits of shifting to electric vehicles and renewable energy sources seem to far outweigh the potential negatives—at least those that we're currently aware of—but how many of us have truly explored beyond the gleaming veneer of optimism and tried to uncover the ripple effects of such shifts? Even seemingly well-intentioned ambitions for the future can often create frustrating and counterintuitive repercussions, yet when we're presented with changes such as these, we're collectively trained to champion the gains while sidelining the costs.

In 2019, my mother died from cancer, and I miss her dearly. The impact on my father, my sister, and our extended family has been profound, and she suffered immeasurably throughout her illness. But let's imagine for a second that we were able to prevent cancer deaths or effectively cure those with cancer symptoms. Families like mine would get extra time with parents, aunts, children, and partners who would otherwise have been cruelly robbed from them by this pernicious disease. This feels like it would be a huge win, but if we think about that idea for a bit longer, things quickly get a little more complex. About 10 million people currently die from cancer every year, which represents around one in every six deaths. If we prevented every cancer death, that would increase the population of our planet by more than a thousand people every hour, each of whom would need a place to live and work, food to eat, clothing, energy, connectivity, holidays, phones, and all the other expected trappings of life on Earth. Not only that, but if we make cancer survivable, we may actually *increase* the strain on our hospitals and care facilities by creating an increasingly elderly population, who may suffer from other degenerative diseases, mental health challenges, or acute cardiovascular issues, all of which would potentially place a catastrophic burden on every nation's insurance and healthcare budgets. Without wanting to sound like Herman Kahn here, that would represent a massive shift in the shape of our society. If the Earth truly does operate as an interconnected system, then a sudden or significant adjustment in one of its key variables would undoubtedly result in shock waves that would travel deep into its complex web of nodes and feedback loops in ways we're probably unable to imagine. Death matters. It's an important, natural part of the cycle of every living thing, yet it's laden with an emotional weight that significantly skews any attempts at rationalism. Such is our desire to rid the world from cancer that we push ahead with our research. The US government increased its funding of the National Cancer Institute to $7.8 billion for 2024. Private donations to cancer charities remain high in almost every country, and as a result we continue to make major strides in cancer survivability. Again, for the sake of clarity, I'm not advocating for a shift from this ambition—I dearly wish my mother was still here—but how many of us can honestly say that we've embraced the full spectrum of impact involved with an end to cancer? If we're successful in eradicating this grim set of diseases, the short-term gains will undoubtedly be incredible, but the longer-term implications could be significantly challenging, precisely because of the outsized role that cancer plays in so many of our lives.

In my industry, these outcomes, knock-on effects, and extra considerations are broadly termed "externalities," and if we're being truly diligent in our quest to identify and illustrate externalities, then we not only need to create a list, we also need to consider how transformations unfold over the arc of time. Every idea, intervention, plan, project, and strategy has a lifespan that evolves, morphs, and decays through the days, months, and years following its introduction. Yet propositions about the future rarely (if ever) factor this in, preferring to focus on launch events, initial transformations, and immediate benefits, rather than describing a lifetime of impact and inevitable deterioration. Some new ideas appear with a brilliant flash followed by a rapid slump (such as the MiniDisc), while others gradually drift into mass use and hang around for generations (such as the telephone), but it's crucial to understand that all ideas about the future have a lifespan. Contemplating that lifespan, its duration, and how anything new will nestle into the existing landscape allows us to better understand the full impact of any new idea and to shape it a little more carefully. Similarly, considering what to trim from an idea through the lens of longevity can actually *increase* the longevity of that idea and help to build a well-rounded, resilient, and durable proposition.

My childhood was spent among the tumbling ruins of the Industrial Revolution; everywhere I went, I was reminded of the disintegration of a once-transformational idea. During Derby's explosive development in the 1800s, I would assume that very little thought was given to what might happen to these huge brick warehouses—or to those who worked in them—when the steam age finally came to an end. We have a tendency to think of future ideas as somehow permanent, that the introduction of any new technology or idea will mark a step change, an enduring metamorphosis, or an irrevocable leap into a bold, new future. But everything has its time. Even transformational, overtly futuristic, Earth-changing revolutions eventually run out of momentum.

On October 14, 1947, around a hundred miles northeast of Los Angeles, Chuck Yeager climbed into a pointy, orange prototypical plane, a Bell X-1 nicknamed the Glamorous Glennis. After being dropped from the belly of a B-29 bomber, the aircraft reached a speed of Mach 1.05, and a sonic boom rang out across the Mojave Desert announcing the moment that humans had mastered the ability to travel faster than sound waves. In commercial air travel, the transition from propellers to jets had happened so swiftly that it seemed plausible that supersonic flights would be the next logical step, and an international race to commercialize supersonic aircraft quickly began between the Americans, Soviets, British, and French. In 1962, the British and French joined forces, signing a treaty to build a supersonic passenger jet appropriately named Concorde. Their decision to share the development costs effectively ended the international competition, and by January 1976 the first Concorde aircraft entered public service. Powered by four Rolls-Royce Olympus engines, Concorde represented a modern-day marvel. A sleek, white aircraft with wings sweeping from tip to tail, capable of flying at an altitude of 60,000 feet at Mach 2.2 (a staggering 1,350 miles per hour, or 22 miles per minute), Concorde could cross the Atlantic in around three hours. It truly felt like a new future had arrived. This gleaming icon of modernity represented a significant change in our ways of thinking about technology, travel, and the overall scale of the world. I remember playing on a Cornish beach as a child and hearing the sonic boom from way above, wondering what it might feel like to be on board, and imagining an elite club in the sky filled with playboys, pop stars, and politicians. Pan Am, TWA, United, Air Canada, and Qantas all put in orders for Concorde aircraft, and by 1980, projected sales were estimated at around 350 planes. At this point it seemed entirely reasonable that all future air travel would be supersonic. But things didn't work out that way.

Sonic booms proved to be incredibly annoying to both people and animals, and were frequently blamed for property damage on the ground. As a result, Concorde was restricted to flying at subsonic speeds over land, and was able to fly at supersonic speeds only over oceans. Traveling by Concorde was also rather uncomfortable, due to the unique design restrictions of supersonic flight. The body of the aircraft was long and slender, and as a result, the interior cabin was only 2.63 meters wide and arranged in a tight two-by-two seating configuration. Concorde also flew at very high altitudes, which created huge pressure differentials between the interior and exterior, so its windows were only slightly larger than a passport. As a result, passengers increasingly chose comfort over speed, preferring to book slower flights on larger wide-bodied aircraft at significantly lower prices. Orders for the aircraft gradually slowed and then stopped, and travel by Concorde quickly became something of a novelty. As a flamboyant luxury for rock stars and the ultrarich, Concorde was impossibly, achingly romantic, but its days were numbered, even before the event that would ultimately mark the aircraft's demise. On the afternoon of July 25, 2000, Air France Flight 4590 taxied out from Paris Charles de Gaulle International Airport. As it sped down the runway, it ran over a small piece of debris, which caused the right front tire to explode, sending out a shock wave that ruptured the number 5 fuel tank at its weakest point and ignited a long fireball that trailed out behind the aircraft. Shortly afterward, Flight 4590 crashed into a hotel near the airport, killing all 109 people on board and 4 people on the ground, a tragic event that ultimately became the epitaph for both the aircraft and the supersonic travel industry.

On October 24, 2003, the last Concorde flew from New

York City to London, and the era of supersonic passenger flight was over. The Paris crash three years earlier was a terrible event, but in truth, the fate of Concorde was already sealed. By the standards of the day, the aircraft was incredibly inefficient with fuel, and maintenance had become a significant issue. What had initially seemed like a vanguard for the future had now come to a complete halt, closing the door on what had seemed a certainty just decades before.

Whenever a future idea is proposed, it's rare that we discuss how it might end. When describing a new idea, product, or scheme, we rarely think about it as something that will one day become invisible or irrelevant. The future is always shown as something new, box-fresh, novel, and shiny, but in truth every product and service has a lifespan and will exist through countless phases, across perhaps many years or decades. We never see images of future products sitting on the shelves of a thrift store, between a Dustbuster and a Sega Genesis, or thrown into a box and shoved up in the attic. But why not? If we're being honest about our future, then confronting the full duration and ultimate decline of an idea might help us to better understand the dent it could make in society and perhaps rethink how we introduce it—or perhaps lead us not to introduce it at all. The designer and writer Joe MacLeod has been steadfastly focusing on this gap, developing a new and rather interesting practice that he calls "Endineering." His approach calls for an active focus on how things stop, the conscious design of "offboarding" alongside "onboarding," and a call for more responsibility in the stewardship of products and services throughout their entire lives. Likewise, in a characteristically acerbic piece of writing in 2022, Cory Doctorow introduced the notion of "enshittification," which describes the ways in which digital platforms evolve and decay: "First, they are good to their users; then they abuse their users to make things better for their business customers; finally, they abuse their business customers to claw back all the value for themselves. Then, they die."

Ultimately, Don't Futurism is focused on exploring the full lifespan of an idea and embracing the full scope of its impact. It helps bring unseen issues, potential downturns, and knock-on effects to the surface. It urges creators to consider curtailing, trimming, or taking full responsibility for their future intervention. I'm aware we've gone quite a long way without really describing how this type of futures work is done professionally or even what it looks like, and I apologize if that's made you impatient. Honestly, those are quite difficult questions. A core challenge when dealing with Don't Futurism is that even if we do take steps to *stop* something, our data doesn't respond particularly well to cessation. Following the launch of a new idea, scheme, or product, we can easily measure sales figures or public interest, and we can simply see how successful or impactful it was, but when we decide to *avoid* something, measurement becomes significantly more difficult. Avoided things quickly become invisible and incalculable, and they exist only in the tales of what might have been or what could have happened. Any notions of measurable change rapidly convert to conjecture, speculation, or hunches when we're talking about all the things we didn't do, which makes this mindset incredibly difficult to promote or structurally formalize. We all have an instinctual ability to identify undesirable outcomes, but this work rarely falls into well-defined professional disciplines. It's rarely taught in classrooms or colleges, and there are very few textbooks that clearly outline the edges of a Don't Futures practice, but there has long existed a community of people eager to extrapolate, hypothesize, and poke at their own work and these kinds of questions.

Don't Futurism can manifest as a simple reflex act, a well-timed question, or a moment of extra thought, but beyond that have emerged a number of more intentional approaches to thinking further, extrapolating deeper, and provoking harder. As one might perhaps expect, this way of thinking can trace its roots back to the creative communities of Italy, those irrepressible cradles of rule-breaking bravado and effortless, shruggy confidence.

EXTRAPOLATORY FUTURES

In the 1950s, Italy was living through a period of rapid growth driven by the postwar boom, known as the *miracolo economico*, which is incredibly fun to say out loud. Swift urban development surged forward, with mass housing units, industrial buildings, and retail complexes rapidly springing up all across the country. By the mid-1960s, Italian cities were filled with these new developments, and Italy had evolved from a largely agrarian society to an industrial powerhouse, much to the consternation of a growing community of designers, many of whom were studying at the University of Florence. These young firebrands rejected contemporary ideas that a city should be a modern, functional machine, and they wanted to challenge the ways in which people thought about their architecture. They also saw the potential of architecture to become a catalyst for change, reflecting the broader social and political developments happening across Europe and North America, and hoped to expand the remit of design beyond capitalism into more provocative territories. Using that uniquely Italian skill of melding design with art, and mixing heavyweight critique with large doses of silliness, they poked at the future of life in their cities. They explored its absurdities through enigmatic and unconventional projects, introducing confrontational new lines of thinking. Out of this nascent period of freewheeling experimentation emerged two hugely influential design collectives—Superstudio and Archizoom—and a movement we refer to as Radical Design.

As with most revolutions, the Italian Radical Design movement had rather humble beginnings. The year 1966 saw the opening of a small exhibition entitled *Superarchitettura*, which brought Superstudio and Archizoom together in public for the first time. Hastily relocated to a tiny gallery in Pistoia—after epic floods wreaked havoc in Florence—the exhibition consisted of two small rooms filled with furniture, lighting, and surface coverings to create a physical manifestation of their ideas about design. The exhibition envisioned new forms for living and unusual arrangements of furniture, made from challenging materials and produced in confrontational colors. Alongside these spaces were essays and propositions that explored the evolution of design and architecture, and the philosophical reasoning behind their work. The show was wildly popular, striking a chord with the growing community of students and protesters in the region and becoming the de facto manifesto for the Radical Design movement. Following the show, numerous pieces of lighting and furniture from the exhibition were produced by the manufacturer Poltronova at the behest of Ettore Sottsass, their effervescent head of design, who had grown tired of the commercial, consumerist world within which he operated.

Perhaps the best-known manifestation of Superstudio's perspective came through their 1969 project *Continuous*

Monument, an extensive photomontage effort featuring a gridded building stretching continuously across the Earth, representing a seemingly infinite model of architecture. In these images, impossibly long, rectilinear constructions strike out across the landscape with little care for the shape or contents of the terrain, driving through mountains, over lakes, and through valleys. This series of images feels relevant over fifty years later, and it still provokes questions about modern urbanization, consumerism, and the homogenization of culture. It's difficult to look at this project and not see a comparison to the Saudi Arabian Line construction effort that I mentioned earlier. The *Continuous Monument* was intended to fill us with questions and concerns about the trajectory of the world and the role of architecture in society, yet Saudi Arabia appears to have considered it something of a brief.

Archizoom would also riff on the future of urban life with their provocation the *No-Stop City*, which proposed a diffuse metropolis that could be reconfigured at will, moving and reordering itself to suit the evolving needs of its inhabitants. The purpose of this project was to act not as a blueprint for a future utopia, but more as a means to place something alongside the status quo and ask which one felt more absurd. It envisioned a city without predefined forms, iconic buildings, or hierarchical organization, asking us to look toward the future and to question the ways we live in the present. The work of these groups was contrarian and transformational, and led to a significant reassessment of the role and implications of public design work. One of the founders of Superstudio, Adolfo Natalini (a man whose face was permanently arranged with one doubtfully arched eyebrow), called for an end to design until it could become something more than a commercial tool. Writing in *Avvicinamenti all'architettura* in 1971, he declared, "If design is merely an inducement to consume, then we must reject design; if architecture is merely the codifying of bourgeois model of ownership and society, then we must reject architecture; if architecture and town planning is merely the formalization of present unjust social divisions, then we must reject town planning and its cities . . . until all design activities are aimed towards meeting primary needs. Until then, design must disappear. We can live without architecture."

The Radical Design movement largely collapsed as an organized effort by 1974, and Superstudio abandoned working as a collective in 1978, but the effects of their work on the shape of design have been profound, and their storytelling techniques are enduringly popular with a great many people to this day. Theirs was a way of thinking about the future that wasn't utopian—nor financially or commercially oriented—but that spurred the viewer to stop and think about where we might be headed, that proposed new ways of thinking, and that shocked the system into acknowledging the present. Their work contributed to the notion that design could be more than a crucible for capitalism, that it could be a means to provoke, to change perspectives, and to act in a more responsible (rather than responsive) manner. The highly critical and playfully absurd output of the Radicals encouraged people to explore other possibilities—alternatives to the prevailing state of the world or the potential pitfalls of our contemporary obsessions—and introduced a new way of thinking about the future that continues to echo through design education to this day.

I'm a firm believer that *when* one studies is just as important as *where* one studies, and I consider myself incredibly fortunate not only to have been accepted into the Royal College of Art, but also to have started studying there in 1999, a pivotal moment in technology, society, culture, and design. The impending rollover of the millennial clock served to remind us of our place in history, and a feeling of positivity, hope, and invention had crept up on us all. Tony Blair's Labour government was two years into its modernizing agenda, hosting Britpop bands at Downing Street and building huge domes on the banks of the River Thames. At that time the iPhone didn't exist, smartphones were in their infancy, and the biggest-selling cellular device was the virtually indestructible Nokia 3310. This was the world before Wi-Fi. There was barely any Bluetooth, and the internet came spluttering into our laptops through umbilical ethernet cables that tethered us to our desks. By today's standards we were living in a technological dark age, but it felt like something interesting was happening, and everything around us seemed to be changing remarkably quickly. Digital cameras started cropping up in more places, as did broadband internet, DVD players, GPS, and Skype. This rapid parade of new technologies flickered through the minds of me and my peers, and the possibilities of this new world seemed limitless, strange, and otherworldly. Ideas that had remained in the realm of fantasy were suddenly becoming almost possible, and all around me people were experimenting, exploring, and building interesting things.

In parallel—as the college was populated by artists, contrarians, and theorists—the implications of this abundant change became fertile ground for discussion and debate. Alongside this rising tide of potential and excitement about the future came questions, cautions, and uncertainties.

Two of my tutors at the time were a pair of soft-spoken, affable, and immensely thoughtful people named Anthony Dunne and Fiona Raby. They approached this torrent of new technology not with the sparkly-eyed excitement that was so prevalent at the time but with an air of deep intrigue and questioning skepticism. Curious to identify how this emergent machinery might be misused, how it might lead to strange habits and subcultures, and how it might redraw our ideas of personal and private space, they undertook a series of highly influential projects that still resonate today. Their explorations looked at how the signals from baby monitors might be heard through the radios of passing cars and what the cultural implications of that leakage could mean; how the robotic dreams of previous generations might *actually* manifest in our lives and perhaps develop personalities of their own; and how furniture might address more of our psychological needs. Through these projects the pair danced gleefully across the boundaries between fact and fiction, creating objects and stories to pick at the uncomfortable space between the poetic and the provocative. Dunne's 1999 book, *Hertzian Tales*, and the couple's subsequent publication *Speculative Everything* cemented a way of working that made its way deep into the conscience of their students. They use the term "Critical Design" to describe their work, which is now considered part of a much broader Speculative Design movement that has since emerged. As with any influential movement, the roots of Critical Design are a little uncertain, but it clearly owes a significant debt of gratitude to the Italian Radicals of the 1960s and 1970s. It aims to poke and provoke, to encourage discussion and reflection, and to focus on the implications of emerging technology and societal change. In turn, this kind of work can help us move forward into the future with a little more awareness of the full scope of what we might be putting in motion.

One of Dunne and Raby's most celebrated and arresting projects is the Faraday chair. Over the last fifty years, humanity has created a host of new products whose effective presence expands well beyond their physical edges, from the unnatural magnetic fields created by electrical currents to Wi-Fi, Bluetooth, and infrared technologies, whose signals pass through walls, floors, and our own bodies. The Faraday chair consists of a rectangular box of transparent orange plastic that sits on a simple metal support. Within the box are a small pillow and a breathing tube to give a little comfort to the inhabitant, who is typically pictured curled up in the fetal position inside. The object is intended to represent something of a secure refuge from these emissions, and while it's not intended to be a viable product proposition, its ability to help us stop and reflect on what these signals might be doing to us, or on how people might react to them, is notable. For good reason, this project has become somewhat emblematic of the Critical Design movement, and it now forms part of the permanent collection at the Victoria and Albert Museum in London.

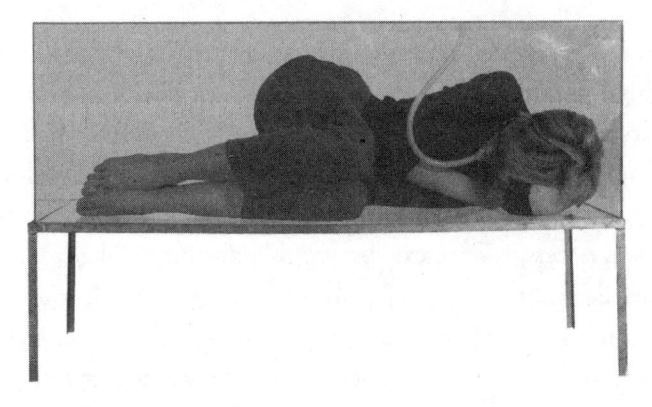

Faraday chair—Anthony Dunne and Fiona Raby—1995 (Photo: Lubna Hammoud)

Many of my fellow graduates from the Royal College of Art—and students of Dunne and Raby—would go on to fundamentally change the role of design in critical thinking over the next two decades, producing work that picked at the future, pointed out uncomfortable truths, uncovered problematic motives, and extrapolated further than almost all other types of futurism that had come before. This new generation of creative people embraces the responsibility that comes with making something new. They explore and illustrate the ethical, social, and political implications of the things we produce and attempt to unpick, rewire, and redefine the purpose of design in the modern world.

It's heady stuff, and in its purest forms Critical Design has found a natural home in galleries and museums, in the pages of inscrutable pamphlets, and in the work of activists. The majority of Critical Design practitioners wouldn't be caught dead working within established commercial environments or taking money from the large corporations against which they so often campaign. I obviously feel differently, and I think this abstraction represents something of a weakness for the Critical Design movement. When this work is undertaken from a willfully extrinsic perspective, it can operate with a kind of pomposity that can be difficult to digest. Critical Design perspectives can be highly effective at identifying and illustrating the implications of change and asking us to reconsider the future but can also produce work that feels sanctimonious, that wags its finger judgmentally and often carries with it an air of effortless superiority. Whether this kind of work will be integrated into broader commercial use remains to be seen; I've never seen a Critical Design role advertised by any major organization. Design—which has long been a tool of positivity, productivity, and aspiration—struggles particularly in this regard, as Dunne and Raby said: "Dark, complex emotions are usually ignored in design; nearly every other area of culture accepts that people are complicated, contradictory, and even neurotic, but not design." Introducing this kind of work within fast-moving, positive environments can be tricky, but I've actually been surprised by how willing some of my employers have been to adopt a more self-aware stance, to reflect on the impact of their work and accept an increasing level of responsibility for their output.

I have a personal tale to tell here.

In the summer of 2016, I was working with a team at Google exploring new ways of building computer operating systems. In such a broad and expansive area of exploration, you can imagine there were a great deal of ideas, opinions, and assertions that swirled through the team with alarming regularity. The effect of all this uncertainty was bewildering, and we struggled to get a handle on how the team felt about almost anything. I'm not attempting to paint a picture of a dysfunctional group here—this is fairly typical of this kind of work, particularly in its earliest stages. Conversations flare wildly between applications, implications, near-term goals, long-term ambitions, research outcomes, and product ideas. It can all get a bit messy, but that's part of the process. What was abundantly clear was that we needed some way of focusing our discussions. Sometimes this can be a simple essay, a manifesto, a series of principles, or some sort of semifunctional prototype around which people can gather and discuss. This can help team members see where they agree or point directly at the parts where they disagree, and can help to make some sort of sense of the mess and uncover a collective logic. In this case, the subject we were discussing was the long-term implications of unfettered access to user data, a topic so loose and nebulous that it was difficult to focus on any single thing, so I gathered together a couple of colleagues to try to tell a story instead.

We set about creating a short movie built around a gradually escalating scenario, made to look like a series of product pitches or vision videos. The movie began by illustrating a few simple, benign, and inoffensive applications of the technologies we were discussing, but as things progressed, the products began accessing increasing amounts of user data and gradually becoming more self-oriented and pernicious. The film began treading into more uncomfortable territory until it reached a conclusion where users were being unconsciously conditioned and the products were almost entirely autonomous. It was intended to spark a discussion around where each member of the team began to feel uncomfortable, and acted as a piece of Don't Futurism by giving us a way to safely explore what we were putting in motion and discuss what we might choose *not* to do.

A couple of years later, I received a frantic call from the Google press team asking about the project. I was a little befuddled, as the film had long since served its purpose and been archived, but it transpired that another employee—in a totally different part of the organization—had discovered the film, watched it without any accompanying context, and evidently been outraged. They made a decision to share it with the press, at a moment when Google was under significant scrutiny about its approach to user data and privacy. The technology blog *The Verge* broke the story with a long essay that was featured on their front page, and other networks quickly picked up the thread. Fox News, CNN, and Infowars ran increasingly breathless editorial pieces, chat rooms buzzed, and conspiracy theories flared across Twitter and Facebook—it seemed that here was evidence of Google's dystopian master plan for total control over users. Finally! Proof that they want to create a world of total surveillance and turn everyone into servile robots!

Life became quite tense for a week or so.

Thankfully, the news cycle moved on. The story eventually dipped below the horizon, and I continued to work at Google until 2023, but I hope this tale illustrates the risk and complexity that comes with doing this kind of self-critical work. The tone of the film was deliberately misleading: it acted as a tool to facilitate uncomfortable conversations and to highlight chain reactions and the sequences of events that may unfurl if we set certain decisions in motion. Evidently, without that context it seemed implausible that a company like Google would undertake such an act of self-reflection, that it would contemplate, explore, and illustrate the potentially negative outcomes of its ideas to help shape its decisions in the present. It might surprise you to hear that I've never worked with a group of more ethically attuned people than during my time at Google. The company has a long way to go, but Google is well aware of its impact on the world and appears to be working hard to embrace this kind of thinking.

A desire to look to the future and envisage negative outcomes may not be one that comes naturally to many organizations, but this behavior exists in pockets all over the world: it helps teams to get ahead of potential issues in their future and embrace the full impact of the things they're doing in the present. Like many of the ideas throughout this book, the term "red team" is a descendant of the work of RAND and Herman Kahn, where it was used to denote a group that represented the enemy (in their case Soviet Russia, hence "red," as opposed to the United States, the "blue" team). Today, the purpose of red team work is to think and act as an adversary, to play out any number of scenarios from an oppositional perspective in order to break free from positivist thinking and develop more detailed and more well-rounded strategies. In contemporary software development, it's now commonplace to have a red team during the development of a new platform, application, or service, including at Google. These "ethical hackers" exist to attempt all the wrong and naughty things, to try to break the system, to make it do what it isn't supposed to do in order to develop more robust software or prevent future infiltrations. The US Federal Aviation Administration introduced red team exercises following the bombing of Pan Am Flight 103 over Lockerbie. Today, red teams conduct tests at around a hundred US airports annually, role-playing as bad actors or terrorists in order to identify weaknesses in the physical design or digital systems in use at America's major airports.

As the world begins to slowly recalibrate its priorities, we've witnessed the emergence of more educated, motivated, and empowered citizens. In advanced democracies, populations are starting to demand more from their manufacturers, governments, and service providers, leveraging both their purchasing and voting clout to stand up for their "don'ts" and drive meaningful change. In parallel, enlightened organizations are beginning to embrace a newfound sense of conscience and responsibility for their actions, and operate in ways that would have seemed counterintuitive a mere decade ago. Take, for instance, Yvon Chouinard, the visionary founder of outdoor retailer Patagonia, who is bequeathing his $3 billion company and its future earnings to the fight against climate change, stating in a press release that "Earth is now the company's only shareholder." A growing number of corporations now offer recycling initiatives for their products, device buyback schemes, and outreach programs to aid those displaced or disenfranchised by their actions.

While the integration of ethics teams and corporate social responsibility divisions into large-scale enterprises represents a noteworthy shift, these efforts often fall short in effecting substantive change amid the relentless pressures of capitalism and growth. Organizations appear to need not only to feel the pressure of Don't Futurism before they act, but also to see a clearly defined business motivation before making any sort of meaningful change. Pressure alone can only stimulate dialogue to a certain extent; true transformation demands the conversion of that pressure into *opportunity*. As Don't Futurism finds its way into more corners of our lives and begins to more accurately define its role, it will need to find ways to address this issue. If it's successful in developing methods to entice resistant organizations toward embracing the full impact of their actions, it will be rewarded with a more important role, and be more capable of generating the changes it wishes to see.

•

If you drive south along Interstate 580 in Berkeley, California—directly across the Bay from San Francisco—you'll pass under countless bridges that are permanently festooned with all manner of political and campaign-oriented banners. Such is the culture of Berkeley. One hand-painted notice currently zip-tied to the chain-link fence ominously reads ALL IN ON CLIMATE—TRUST YOUR DESPAIR.

As I write this book, it feels like we're entering something of a golden age of dread about the future. Our bright, excited, positive attitudes toward the future feel as if they've fallen away far behind us. We appear to have largely traded hope and excitement for anxiety and fear, and the future increasingly feels like a foreboding and terrifying place. The systems of capitalism we have relied on for generations have resulted in alarming disparities in wealth on both a local and a global scale, yet we seem collectively incapable of proposing meaningful alternatives. As the American philosopher and political theorist Fredric Jameson identified so clearly, it's now easier for us to imagine the end of the world than an alternative to capitalism. Our industrial systems also appear unable or unwilling to make the difficult choices needed to avert an apocalyptic climate disaster, quarreling and quibbling with one another while the world gets warmer. Speaking on the subject of climate change, the naturalist Sir David Attenborough put it starkly: "If we don't take action, the collapse of our civilizations and the extinction of much of the natural world is on the horizon." Our governments appear increasingly divided and divisive, unable to work together in meaningful ways to tackle the complex global societal challenges we face. Even technology appears to be losing its luster as the great solutions machine of generations past. Sam Altman, the CEO of OpenAI, joined hundreds of scientists, researchers, and business leaders in signing a letter that stated that "mitigating the risk of extinction from AI should be a global priority alongside other societal-scale risks such as pandemics and nuclear war." Nevertheless, development in this field continues apace, unconstrained by the normal frictions of the world and moving faster than our legal systems are able to recalibrate. The conference panels I'm invited to speak on these days are now increasingly focused on "saving," "preventing," or "averting" any number of ghoulish specters lurking just around the corner.

Many people now feel so strongly about a certain topic that they define themselves not by what they're in favor of, but by what they oppose. We've become more familiar with terms like "anticapitalist," "antifascist," "anticonsumerist," "antiabortionist," "antiglobalist," "anti-imperialist," "antimonopolist," "anti-Zionist," "antinationalist," and "antimilitarist," which we see pasted into countless social media bios and profile pages. The age of freewheeling future positivity appears to have been largely replaced by a sense of fear and oppositional contrarianism—perhaps a symptom of our inability to exert meaningful change or a brooding frustration with society's inaction. The future, as Chuck Palahniuk so deftly articulated, has transitioned from a *promise* to a *threat*.

This never-ending tide of fear about the future may have led to a palpable sense of ambient despair, but there's increasing evidence that our obsessions with worst-case scenarios, dystopias, and extinctions might be affecting us more fundamentally. Clinicians and psychologists are increasingly noting cases of unrelenting low spirits, dysthymia, and persistent depressive disorders in their patients. Our perspective on the future has, in a relatively short space of time, become dominated by disaster porn, collapsitarianism, and a bewildering tsunami of terrifying data on any number of subjects. But a consistent, pervasive, heightened sense of fear cannot possibly be good for our well-being. Even in highly motivated people, endlessly apocalyptic rhetoric often does little more than generate feelings of paralysis, yet our world seems to be increasingly focused on pointing out everything that is going wrong. In response, there's been an increasingly discernible thread of strident Don't Futurism emerging in communities all across the world. The desire to scream against entrenched norms, to campaign and protest against injustices and futures that seem impossibly awful, is one with which I can empathize. The increasingly radical rhetoric of protesters, campaigners, and activists worldwide often reflects the exasperation they experience when faced with what feels like apathy and inaction. But here's where Don't Futurism faces something of a challenge.

Don't Futurism is difficult—mostly because it wants to be. It enjoys being the fly in the ointment, pointing out negative outcomes, long-tail implications, and unseen hazards, but pushing this thinking beyond an initial scream or shout is remarkably complex. Don't Futurism often backs itself into a contrarian corner, intentionally seeking positions of opposition rather than finding ways to integrate its ideas into the ongoing flow of business, policy, or technology. To produce work that is well researched and well balanced, and that *actually leads to meaningful change* is significantly more intellectually challenging than the creation of even the most extreme projections of flying cars or humanoid robots. Hard stops, U-turns, and shutdowns are difficult in almost every circumstance. There are often countless reasons why such actions may even be as problematic as continuing on the current course. But when Don't Futurism is at its best, it embraces notions of transition and integration. Finding ways to actively consider implications, present them in balanced ways, and propose elegant alternatives or off-ramps is when this work finds its feet. When it's done well, Don't Futurism can be remarkably persuasive, and for this reason I believe in it, or at least in its ambitions. If we can find ways to meaningfully integrate these mindsets into more of our thinking alongside our coulds, shoulds, and mights, we stand a chance of getting beyond the short-term, blindingly positive, solutions-oriented mindsets that have led us to this point.

I'm excited by the new generation of future-oriented people emerging from our universities and schools. They seem to be thinking about the future from a position of responsibility and long-termism, which wasn't the case when I graduated. They seem more able to identify and articulate potential future issues, and are focused on using their creative acuity and intellect to propose alternatives and coax change from resistant organizations. As I age, I'm trying to resist the urge to hark back to the "good old days" and am focusing more on listening to young people and trying to understand their ways of working, not least because they'll be in charge of my future healthcare. One thing is clear to me: the next half century will bring with it significant challenges, and perhaps now is the time to make a conscious pivot to a different way of thinking about the future, one that is less about more, and more about less.

...

AND SO . . .

Over the chapters of this book, I've outlined what I believe to be the four main varieties of futures work that take place in corporations, creative industries, governments, and your own life, each of which exhibits its own unique and alluring strengths. Could Futurism strides confidently through our world, wielding its breathless imagination with exuberant glee. It builds excitement about the future and offers a form of unconstrained optimism that can occasionally lead to genuinely compelling ideas and can motivate people to take action. Should Futurism builds a bridge of soothing confidence over the unknown chasm of the future. It gives us the encouragement to move ahead with a little more certainty, converting our visions into actions and helping us move steadfastly toward our stated goal. Might Futurism dramatically increases the scope of our thinking, highlighting new avenues, uncovering hidden pathways, and revealing undiscovered opportunities in a territory. It helps identify multiple possible outcomes and brings methodological, rational structure to any debate about the future. Don't Futurism brings its strong biceps of diligence and responsibility to the party, helping us to think through the unintended consequences of our ideas, identifying areas we might want to avoid and highlighting potential bumps in the road. Of course, these represent caricatures that I've drawn out to give some sort of structure to our topic, but this segmentation undoubtedly exists, and each of us has our preferences.

Unfortunately, each of these mindsets also has its own significant weaknesses, which are frequently overlooked. Could Futurism is often loud, brash, and simplistic, offering vacuous, escapist nonsense to thirsty media outlets that offer little pushback and demand even less detail. Should Futurism can be self-assured and cocky, relying heavily on its numeric projections or its dogmatic predictions to drive decisions and make self-serving assertions. Might Futurism pores over endless reams of analysis, techniques, and models but often struggles to imagine sufficiently broadly, and leaves us with more work to do rather than any firm answers. Don't Futurism loves to scold us, leaning back in its chair and judging us while smugly brandishing its intellect about the place. It fills us with dread and demands immediate and often impossible action on a major scale. What results from this situation is a feudal futures landscape comprising factions that don't (and in many cases can't) work well together.

We all go through life grabbing snippets of futurism from anywhere we can, and these sit in the back rooms of our minds to be trotted out as convenient punctuation marks in conversation. We're drawn to unsettling tidbits, inspirational quotes, eye-widening statistics, and arresting nuggets of insight, and we use them as salacious, provocative scaffolding to prop up our opinions. For the majority of us, this is where our work on the future ends, but occasionally some of us are required to deliver some deeper thinking, and it's hardly surprising that all of us seem to struggle to put this discordant mess into some sort of coherent whole.

As we saw at the outset of this book, our ideas about the future typically begin as a belief that we've absorbed from elsewhere or been drawn toward through our societal, cultural, political, or corporate ambitions. Once that starting point is in place, there's a temptation to seek more data, more evidence, or more projections that might give this belief some heft or make it feel a little more rational, and there's plenty to pick from. Following that, a couple of persuasive quotes from an authority figure, a trusted organization, or an accommodating expert can also help make everything feel a little more rational and well considered, and nudge an idea a little closer toward the plausible. In recent years, there's also been a tendency to add a few existential threats or elements of societal duty into the mix, to give an argument an air of selfless, grown-up responsibility. Once that's done, we'll season our work with a sprinkling of futuristic images from Google or type a prompt into the latest generative AI tool to get some appropriately enticing yet inevitably clichéd illustrations, and our work is pretty much done. In professional circles, this happens frequently, resulting in haphazard collages of content that are positioned as insight and presented as strategy.

The truth is, you're not very good at thinking about the future. None of us are, really. It's not something we've found a way to prioritize nor trained ourselves to do effectively. Thinking about the future with rigor and sophistication isn't something many of us have come even close to achieving. This inability is a significant factor underlying many of the issues we're grappling with today, but it feels like this might evolve into a definitive and crippling shortcoming in the years to come.

In order to improve the quality of our collective thinking about the future, we all need to become significantly better at recognizing the shortcomings of each of the four approaches I have outlined, and the perils of sticking too firmly to just one of them. We need to bring depth, nuance, detail, and uncertainty into our conversations alongside confidence, surety, and pithiness, and that will require us all to push ourselves significantly harder. I'm reluctant to tie a neat bow around this book with some sort of methodological conclusion for you to adopt, or to add myself to the overwhelming mountain of self-proclaimed experts who seem to dominate our bookshelves, websites, and podcasts. It doesn't feel like we need any more six-step plans, manifestos, mapping exercises, or analytic structures—and I've never found much use for that kind of approach in my career—but I would like to see a meaningful shift in the ways we approach this type of thinking, and perhaps you'd like a little more detail on how I bring rigor to my own work.

THE FUTURE MUNDANE

You can tell a lot about a person by the way they treat waiters and shop assistants, especially when you are one.
—CHARLIE BROOKER

As I mentioned earlier, when I was a young designer, I frequently fell into the familiar traps of futures design, creating glossy, energetic, and ambitious work, and telling tall tales of extreme experiences to wide-eyed clients and colleagues. Very quickly, however, this work started to feel flat, hollow, and rather meaningless. It all felt somehow abstract, as if it were living in its own world that was deliberately removed from the reality that surrounded it—and that it purported to be interested in. I just couldn't see how that kind of work interleaved with the present in any meaningful way, and this disjointedness began to bother me. At some point around 2008, I began thinking about the future a little differently. I felt a strong desire to bring new levels of detail and reality to my work, and a motivation to draw my projects significantly closer to the world that I knew. You may (I hope) have picked up a strong whiff of everyday rationalism throughout this book, and if I have an internal ideology, this is probably it.

Like most teenagers, I spent my summers doing whatever temporary jobs I could find to generate a little spending money. I worked in an old-fashioned tailoring shop, which was owned by a stern Victorianesque man who referred to me all summer long as "Boy." I worked in an abattoir, where I cut steaks for chain restaurants and pushed carcasses around in a huge freezer. I washed and counted golf balls at a driving range, and for one glorious summer I scratched imperial measurements from old engineering drawings with a scalpel and neatly wrote metric conversions in their place. These jobs were fairly monotonous, but I found moments of interest in them, and my enduring memories are centered on the people I met, many of whom told me stories that still sit with me today. Stories of saving all year for a week in the sun. Stories of sharing a car between three families. Stories of paying for a tattoo in monthly installments. Stories of beers on a Friday, hangovers on a Saturday, and fry-ups on a Sunday. Stories of messy divorces, hand-me-down jackets, flooded basements, scrap metal scams, kitchen haircuts, benefit frauds, bus trips, bad dates, petty thefts, and dodgy pills.

As I progressed through my professional life, these stories increasingly crept back into my subconscious and nagged at my work. During discussions and conversations with clients and colleagues, I began to think more about these people and how they seemed ignored, irrelevant, and utterly overlooked. Will this technology we're discussing *actually* be of any use to Dennis the forklift driver? Would Amir *really* pay for this idea you're presenting? What will Sally do with her old thing when you launch this *new* thing? What might Gordon and Mary do if this bank *does* actually shut its branches? What happens when we imagine this VR headset in Derek's backpack rather than in the hands of a scientist in a pristine white laboratory? As I started to more intentionally bring my own life experiences—and those of my family, friends, and colleagues—into my work, something started to click. The future stopped being a lofty, unattainable, and abstract place; instead, it became an extension of *our* world, with all its complexities, fascinations, challenges, and priorities. The future stopped being something mythical, extreme, or transformational, it became something mundane.

I've been thinking about the word "mundane" for many years, and it's followed me around like a pebble in my shoe. It's a word that has undoubtedly developed negative cultural connotations, but I've grown to adore it, and I've adopted it deep within my work. Our world almost always skirts around anything mundane, and to be mundane is to be almost invisible. The mundane is ordinary, everyday, boring, humdrum, middling, and basic. It's banal, prosaic, commonplace, grounded, and bland, but here's where it finds its power, especially when we are thinking about the future. As I explained earlier, futures work loves to occupy the thin ends of a bell curve, where expectations and experiences are extreme yet unlikely. Escapist, heroic futures can help drive the imagination, but they ultimately create ideas that feel like fantasies—aspirational yet out of reach or impossible. Likewise, dystopian futures help warn us of epic misfortune and potential collapse but can often act as little more than gloomy fearmongering, which can lead to deep feelings of paralysis and a general loss of hope.

The middle is unremarkable, ordinary, and normal, but as much as we'd like to think otherwise it's where the overwhelming majority of us will live. That's exactly why a bell curve is shaped like a bell. Our lives, our incomes, our hobbies, our habits, our products, our height, our weight, our spending, our education, our health, and our diet will all fall somewhere pretty close to the statistically swollen middle. Lives filled with commuting and work, yearly vacations, birthday parties, fast food, and moments of good fortune paired with the occasional canceled train, traffic jam, twisted knee, or missed payment. The characters in our future will not necessarily need to save the world at every turn—most of them will simply live in it, quietly getting through each day.

Whenever new future narratives come along, I have an urge to rip them from their Silicon Valley stages, strategic foresight decks, terrifying TV shows, or political launch parties and imagine them in this kind of context. I've found that pushing conversations toward this type of mundanity offers not only a point of provocative differentiation (which can be a lot of fun), but also an incredibly powerful way to develop engaging rigor in any thinking about the future. It puts the future in living rooms and bathrooms, on buses and in pockets. It sees the future saving for childcare and doing night shifts. It takes the future to the mall, the queue at the supermarket, and the elementary school parking lot. It places the future in food trucks, on economy airlines, in taxis, and slumped on the couch. It can absorb complex projections or exciting product pitches and help them feel embedded and normalized. It can help us move the conversation beyond what something might *be* and toward what it might *mean*. In adopting this mindset—and actively rejecting the allure of extremes—I've been able to change the way I frame the future, which noticeably changes the ways in which people consume my work. If successful, even the most disruptive, transformative new technology, policy, or societal intervention will find its way into mass culture and become a normal, embedded, perhaps invisible part of everyday life. Here's my one piece of advice: when thinking about the future, try to think less about what you saw in a sci-fi movie and more about where you buy your chewing gum.

I've been fortunate to have visited a great many different places on Earth, and I've found that one of the quickest ways to uncover what life is like for the local population is not to visit the local museums or cultural centers, but to spend time in a neighborhood convenience store. Whether you call them bodegas, 24-hour garages, 7-Elevens, mini-marts, or corner shops, you're undoubtedly familiar with these ubiquitous neon-lit outlets that sell snacks, magazines, lottery tickets, household essentials, canned food, cigarettes, and booze. These stores can be found all over the planet, and they have a habit of laying everyday life bare. Through the products stacked on their shelves, they show what the local community eats and drinks, and what influences they may have adopted from elsewhere. The faces that feature on the packaging of toothpaste, cosmetics, and domestic cleaning products show us what the population finds beautiful or alluring. Coca-Cola, Kinder, and Heineken are almost ubiquitous, but look a little closer and you'll find Almdudler herbal lemonade in Austria, Alyonka calcium-fortified chocolate in Russia, and cans of Modelo beer flavored with chili, tomato, and clam juice in California (which, though I've lived here for more than a decade, I still can't quite understand). Every culture is drawn toward different things and finds different things delicious, from pickled fish potato chips in China's humid south to sweet potato KitKats in Okinawa. Between diapers and motor oil, you'll see phone chargers, USB cables, batteries, reading glasses, SIM cards, laser pointers, and Tetris key rings jangling from little metal rails, all of which were technological marvels not so long ago but have now been value-engineered down to a pocket-change price point. These humble items utterly reek of normalcy, reflecting the desires, habits, routines, necessities, and ambitions of the region's mass population. When viewed through an anthropological gaze, these mundane artifacts tell us much more about a foreign land than the ceremonial relics that sit in the region's museums ever could.

If we begin to imagine these places in ten years' time, an engaging new way to think about the future emerges. New stories appear, and new ideas along with them. I've found that picking one of these everyday objects—such as dish soap, motor oil, or canned soup—and viewing it through an analytical gaze can help to provoke deeper questions about change. These everyday archetypes can help us get beyond the hand-waving and generalization that is so rife in futures work and situate a new idea, technology, or industry into our lives in a doggedly normal way. Consider the work of archaeologists for a moment. They dig around in the dirt to find small shards of broken pottery, a piece of discarded cutlery, or a scrap of clothing from which they begin building an understanding of how an ancient society functioned, what it struggled with, and what its priorities were. I believe it's possible to take this approach and point it at the future.

Let's take a humble box of cereal, for example. We all know what a box of cereal looks like, and can easily imagine one right now, but when was the last time you *really* looked at a cereal box in detail? If we think like archaeologists or crime scene investigators and examine it forensically, what quickly emerges is a dazzling array of signals that tell us what life is like for the community in which this cereal box exists. First, and most obviously, there's the branding, graphic design, and visual style of the box, which gives us an idea of the appealing aesthetics of the day. Look closer and the language featured on the packaging tells us how people speak, what social structures may be in place, or what constitutes humor or levity. The ingredients, allergy warnings, and nutritional claims show us the state of public health and the contemporary understanding of diet. Look closer still and you'll see barcodes, QR codes, or internet links that help us understand what technologies and infrastructures exist at this moment. Look even closer and you'll find small traces of government intervention, global compliance certifications, approval organizations, and quality assurance policies. Look again and you'll be able to understand which materials, printing techniques, and construction technologies are currently suitably priced for use in a piece of disposable packaging. I could go on, but you get the idea.

If we hold on to all of this detail, what happens when we

project forward? How might these details change, and why? Perhaps more importantly, what might remain the same? If VR starts to really take off, if homeschooling becomes the norm, if America adopts a universal basic income or our homes become filled with domestic robots, will this packaging change? And if so, how? How would these huge societal and technological developments actually find their way into our lives through the cereal we eat every morning? This is an approach known as Design Fiction, which I've used frequently to great effect. It stops conversations

Cricket Crunch breakfast cereal. Design Fiction prototype (Nick Foster, 2020)

about the future from feeling abstract, lofty, and vague, and drops them into our kitchens, living rooms, and late-night supermarkets. If considered in sufficient detail, a prototypical box of cereal from the future can tell us much more than just what people might eat in years to come. It can open our eyes to everything from the future of manufacturing, government, and industry to where technology, culture, language, fashion, and society might be headed. In exploring the future of a new technology, for example, there's a tendency to approach it head-on, to illustrate the exciting direct impact it will have or the incredible new gizmos we might make. But what's much more useful is to project forward and explore the full network of impact that might occur following its introduction, which tangential changes might be set in motion, and how other, seemingly unrelated industries, communities, and products might be affected. When I talk about adding rigor to our explorations of the future, this is the kind of thing I mean.

This obsession with detail is, in truth, the core feature of *all* good fiction. Whenever we engage with anything beyond the present, in whatever form, we're creating some sort of story, and for any story to be effective it needs to be believable. By leaning on things we're already familiar with, we can start our story from a position of common understanding, which makes a concept significantly easier to digest, but also draws our eyes to whatever might be different or new. This is why I struggle with escapist science fiction that builds entirely new worlds, and why I find it much less interesting and impactful than stories which build upon the world we currently live in. We can explore complex ideas like predictive technologies or universal biometric profiles without resorting to off-world colonies, autocratic dystopias, cybernetic implants, or flying cars. We can think about how these things might change an after-dinner fortune cookie, or the pills we buy from our local pharmacy, which I think helps us wrap our heads around these ideas a little more effectively.

Of course, not every change in our future might seem like it fits into this "humdrum" framing. Significant moments of major change or radical invention do occasionally occur, and they arrive in our lives with a thunderclap. But even when this kind of change comes our way, we've proved to be remarkably skilled at adapting to it—and remarkably quickly. I recall, quite vividly, sitting in a train in 2008, watching a small blue dot creep its way across my phone as we meandered through the countryside. Cell phones now had real-time directions, and GPS coordinates could be pulled from thin air and projected onto my little portable screen. It was as though I'd stumbled upon something from a Bond film or a high-tech military documentary, and I remember being absolutely transfixed. But before long, this became completely normal. Within mere weeks, I was walking through the streets of London, following the blue lines on my map, and when I found myself in a connectivity dead zone, cursing the very device that had seemed like a marvel only days before.

Major change can often catch us unawares, but we're remarkably good at catching up and absorbing it into our lives. Take the recent coronavirus pandemic, for example: an event of gargantuan global disruption that we haven't experienced in a lifetime, and whose full impact may be

Fortune cookie from a predictive future. Design Fiction prototype (Nick Foster, 2020)

Domingo's nightstand. Design Fiction prototype (Nick Foster, 2020)

immeasurable when viewed at an international scale. Businesses and economies collapsed, medical systems were taken to their breaking points, and a great many people died, but the overwhelming majority of people found ways to normalize the disruption remarkably quickly, and concerns rapidly pivoted from the catastrophic to the mundane. People cobbled together rudimentary home offices, took up new hobbies, began baking bread, and switched their sessions at the gym for YouTube workouts. Even in this environment of significant uncertainty, hardship, and change, we made space for Zoom quiz nights, distanced happy hours, and children's drawing parties. We shifted from shopping at the grocery store to food delivery services, started hiking, and arranged cooking contests with friends as we attempted to find ways to make this extraordinary situation more habitable.

One of the reasons for the ongoing success of our species is this kind of adaptability. Any new event, technology, disruption, or intervention will always create some form of instability, but it will rapidly become part of the normalized, ongoing fabric that we call "the present," and we'll experience it as an embedded, everyday reality. We know this to be true, yet we all struggle to think of the future in this way. At the start of 2024, I took my first ride in one of the self-driving taxis in San Francisco, which—after decades of tenacious work—are now available for public use. I pulled out my smartphone, jabbed at the appropriate app, and within moments a shiny white vehicle bristling with sensors pulled up to my location with no one inside. For the first five minutes of the ride, my fellow passengers and I marveled at the technological miracle we were experiencing. The steering wheel turned all by itself as we navigated the city streets! When a cyclist pulled out from between parked cars, our taxi gently applied the brakes! The turn signals went clickety-clack all by themselves! We changed lanes! We even passed another vehicle! There were a couple of moments where we felt unsure—and even a little unsafe—but these feelings soon passed, and we came to trust the vehicle and the systems running within it. Ultimately there wasn't much else to talk about, so the conversation drifted toward the restaurant where we were headed and what we were about to eat. Everything soon felt incredibly normal; I even began to daydream a little and started looking at the stickers on the window and the construction site outside. What had been incredibly futuristic and achingly modern just moments ago had transitioned to something almost banal within the space of a single ride. In a word, it became *mundane*.

In 2010, I wrote a short essay around this subject titled "The Future Mundane"; it's probably become what I'm best known for in futurist circles, and conveniently it's something of which I'm immensely proud. I think it's a helpful framing for thinking about the future—and, thankfully, other people seem to find value in it too—but more importantly, it feels genuine, authentic, and honest. It's taken me a remarkably long time, but I've discovered that when you're being honest about how you feel, people pick up on that, and it comes across as confidence. The reason I'm telling you this is not to encourage you to adopt the tenets of "The Future Mundane," but more to give you the confidence to explore how *you* view the future, through your *own* lens, on your *own* terms. You should feel empowered to develop ways of shaping what's out there that feel genuine to you rather than simply adopting what you think you're supposed to say or going along with whatever gets thrust at you. But please, I urge you, do so with rigor. Get into the weeds. Get beyond the headlines, flashy images, jaw-dropping statistics, and provocative think pieces, and truly engage with the meat of the issue. Think about how an idea will *actually* appear in the world, and the steps through which society might need to pass in order to get there. I can't stress this strongly enough: the more detail you can add (or the more detail you demand), the better these stories will be.

I recently watched a short film from 1921 that featured a train full of people arriving for a fun day on a Dutch beach. As was normal for the time, the clip was shot in monochrome at a comparatively low resolution, with a low frame rate and erratic exposure levels. As a result, it's hard to make out the features of the people, and they all move in that fast, jerky, and rather humorous way we've become accustomed to from period footage. In this case, however, the clip was part of an ongoing experiment with emerging video enhancement technologies, and it had been utterly transformed. The frames had been automatically colorized, stabilized, and balanced. Each image had been analyzed and enhanced to increase its levels of detail and consistency, and interstitial frames had been created to produce a bright, sharp, stable version of the clip in 4K resolution, playing at sixty frames per second. The result was astounding. Suddenly, all this extra detail made everything feel significantly richer and more *real* somehow. These people moved like real humans. They had heft and depth as they hugged, paddled, and frolicked in the surf. The wind blew their hair, their clothing had a visible weave to it, their skin had creases and blemishes, and their sandwiches looked delicious. While far from perfect, this huge amount of additional information and detail had the cumulative effect of significantly closing the gap between their world and mine. These people—who just moments before had felt like abstract artifacts from a different world—instantly felt more like me, more relatable, and somehow more relevant. This had the effect of stopping me from seeing the participants of this film as distant specimens and helped me to consider what it might have felt like to *actually be there*.

This also applies to our stories about the future. The more detail we add, the more time we spend contemplating the full shape of our stories and rendering the future in excruciating, exacting, precise, and exhausting detail, the more it will feel relevant and relatable to those viewing it. Every project I have ever worked on has started with some sort of lofty statement, assertive prediction, or grand ambition, but very quickly—sometimes within hours—the true shape of the work, which lies just under the surface, is revealed. It's relatively straightforward to imagine, for example, a futuristic device based on whatever the latest exciting technology might be. We can make a cool image of it, explain what we hope it will do, justify its existence with statistics, point at trends that show its likelihood, or identify its transformative power and potential, but if we truly want to bring that thing into existence, if we truly believe that's where the future is headed, then we very quickly have a lot more work to do. We have to think about compatibility, usability, security, disposal, packaging, legislation, charging, assembly, disassembly, ethics, safety, marketing, advertising, branding, retailing, pricing, distribution, competition, standards, legal requirements, sourcing, testing, and a million other annoying yet essential details. The same goes for services, policies, interventions, or any other story we tell about the future—once we crack the surface, it's details all the way down—a long, arduous, and relentless journey from audacity to pragmatism. Of course, a futures project needn't necessarily *solve* all of these things, but providing some idea of how they might be solved, or at the very least acknowledging that they exist, will help immensely. By omitting this level of detail or by waving off anything tricky or willfully pretending it doesn't exist, we risk perpetuating the bombastic yet ultimately hollow reputation of today's futurism, which simply isn't good enough.

Critics of my desire for this level of detail frequently remind me that the future should be the one place where we needn't let ourselves be tied down by the complexities of the present. In many respects, the future is a place where we can let our imaginations gambol freely, a place where we can dream about other ways of being or push ourselves to imagine ambitious change. To be clear, I'm absolutely in favor of that. A key part of any creative process (be that within art, design, policy, or business) lies in the removal of restrictive shackles. But if the output of these exercises is to have any kind of meaningful impact, the translation back down to Earth will have to take place at some point. I happen to prefer doing that work as early as possible.

I appreciate that considering the future as a humdrum place filled with ordinary experiences and everyday people isn't how most of us think—or, more accurately, isn't how we've been *trained* to think. Judging by the overwhelming majority of our literature, television shows, movies, press articles, presentations, essays, and manifestos it seems that the future isn't a place where people will make breakfast, clean shoes, paint sheds, or sweep stairs—but why not? All of us have become attuned to thinking about the future through the lenses of major change, epic transformations, or significant disruptions, but we have to understand that this monocultural diet of turbocharged content is unhelpfully shaping, conditioning, and programming us all. Even if there *are* huge upsets or incredible changes ahead, they'll be experienced by a population made up of people just like you and me, with all our painful knees, expired credit cards, bad jokes, and favorite jackets. Far from improving our ability to think, this torrent of titillating content is suffocating the machinery of innovation, hampering our ability to imagine expansively, and unhelpfully squeezing new thoughts into old templates. If we're going to get more transformative ideas about the future out of these brains of ours, we'll need to start by putting different ingredients in there. When we create new ideas about the future, we need to figure out how they'll fit into the communities, businesses, and cultures we already know rather than standing alone in the distance and waving back at us, hoping that we'll make it there someday.

Whenever I have been invited to give lectures, no matter where in the world I might be speaking, I typically deliver presentations that explore the idea of the future as a quotidian, lived-in evolution of the present, but I often get the feeling that the organizers and attendees expected something different. Whenever there's a futurist on a stage, podcast, or TV screen, they seem to have been invited in order to deliver the same old whizzbang fantasies, strident ideological visions, or terrifying statistics that can whip audiences into an excitable frenzy or shock them into an anxious mess. Audiences frequently stare up at me from the darkness, expectant and curious, and I can feel the energy in them. Sitting there in neat little rows, they're clearly hoping for miraculous insights, yoga-mat utopianism, exuberant sci-fi imaginings, or nuggets of data that they can repeat over coffees with friends. I recently gave a lecture at a futures event in Stockholm during which I outlined the positive benefits of thinking about the future as an ordinary place, and talked a little about the Future Mundane. Throughout my talk I was pleasantly surprised to find the audience engaged and apparently drawn into the idea. They nodded along to the examples I presented and laughed politely at my quips, all of which gave me hope that I'd made some sort of meaningful impact on at least some of them. When my time was up, I walked offstage and was whisked away to give a short interview with the event's media team, but when I returned to the arena shortly afterward, I was disappointed to see the act that had followed me. The lights had been dramatically dimmed, and sitting there beneath a purple laser show in the center of the stage was a cello being played by two robots.

When it comes to thinking about the future, we clearly still have a long, long way to go.

THERE'S PLENTY OF FUTURE LEFT

I know what's coming. I know no one beats these odds. And it's a matter of getting used to that and growing up and realizing that you're expelled from your mother's uterus as if shot from a cannon, towards a barn door studded with old nail files and rusty hooks. It's a matter of how you use up the intervening time in an intelligent and ironic way . . . and try not to do anything ghastly to your fellow creatures.
—CHRISTOPHER HITCHENS

At the 2014 World Economic Forum in Davos, Tim Brown, the former chief executive of IDEO stated boldly that "everyone is a designer." The driving force behind this statement is somewhat understandable—perhaps it was an attempt to demystify the practice of design and encourage participation—but it fairly demands the question, *If everyone is a designer, then is it really even a job?* For this reason, I'm cautious of making a similar mistake in calling everyone a futurist. It isn't for everyone, but that shouldn't preclude anyone from wanting to try. All of us think about the future in some way or other. We all harbor dreams and wishes, ideas and fears about what's to come, but only a very privileged few are given the opportunity to turn this into a career—and that feels like it needs to change. For me, this is more than just a call for inclusivity and diversity—and I'll not be launching a LinkedIn campaign anytime soon—but it's hard to believe that our ideas about the future and the stories we tell wouldn't be richer, more detailed, and more encompassing if a broader collection of people were involved in their creation.

I began this book by recounting my own somewhat unlikely route into this industry, which I think has helped me bring something different to the conversation. At the same time, I'm conscious that my perspectives are riddled with biases, many of which I'm aware of, and surely many of which I'm not. Futures work is typically undertaken by confident, self-starting individuals working with large, successful organizations, in the corridors of power or the halls of academia. As a result, it has largely been the domain of wealthy, privileged individuals with the scope, resources, and time to undertake such work. It's difficult to do any sort of accurate survey here, but my gut tells me that the overwhelming bulk of futures work has historically been created, championed, and delivered by white men like me, in just a few select corners of this expansive planet. This undoubtedly affects the scope, tone, and focus of the work, and perpetuates many of the issues I've covered in this book.

But that's not to say that historically marginalized and underrepresented communities haven't made significant contributions to the futures scene. Afrofuturism has been around since the early twentieth century (beginning, perhaps, with W. E. B. Du Bois's postapocalyptic racism story "The Comet"). The subsequent works of Sun Ra, Octavia E. Butler, and Marvel's hugely popular *Black Panther* franchise, to name but a few, have absolutely broadened our perspective on the future and opened the world to new possibilities. Indigenous and Latinx futurists are also on the rise, as are queer, trans, feminist, and gay futures communities. There are also burgeoning groups of practitioners exploring posthumanist, transhumanist, postcolonialist, Middle Eastern, Asiacentric, decentralized, elder-oriented, migratory, regenerative, postlegal, and psychoactive futures. This work isn't restricted to cities like London, San Francisco, and New York either. Interesting futures work is emerging from places like Mumbai, Lagos, Mexico City, and even farther afield. These perspectives are incredibly useful and inspiring in the creation of well-rounded reasoning about the future, offering new lenses through which to see the world and reshuffling the dominant order of things. If you're struggling to find a new angle to approach a conversation, these mindsets can undoubtedly offer new ways of framing old problems and new ideas about everything from the shape and trajectory of technology to the structure of society and government. The persistent challenge within these focused strains of futurism is in avoiding single-issue representation, or producing strident, blinkered pieces of Don't Futurism. As with all perspectives on the future, this kind of work is always more effective when integrated into the ongoing stream of things and incorporated into broader explorations rather than being siloed off into a "special project."

There are probably a great number of you reading this

book who have no interest in becoming a practicing futurist, and that's almost certainly a good thing, but one thing I hope to have achieved here is to provide a way to navigate this kind of work as it crops up in your life. This is a vast subject, and we've moved through things at a fair rate, but I hope I've at least sparked a curiosity in you and given you some context for this increasingly important part of all of our lives. If you aren't (and don't want to be) a creator of futures provocations, projections, or pitches, then I suggest you focus on becoming a significantly better consumer of them. I hope you feel better prepared to deconstruct what type of future is being presented to you and identify its weaknesses, recognizing when it feels imbalanced or biased and what it might be missing. When you notice these things, I encourage you to speak up and ask for more detail; you might be surprised at just how little there is under the surface. Daily life can be all-consuming, encouraging us to look down at our feet rather than up at the horizon. We all get caught up in headlines, celebrity gossip, school runs, errands, pings, posts, messages, notifications, and whether to have a salad or sandwich for lunch. Many of us feel that our lives have become dominated by chasing those little neon rectangles through our calendars, with a short break on the weekend before everything starts again on Monday. Before we know it, it's winter again. Before we know it, we're turning fifty. Before we know it, we're retired, and the cycle of life moves on. It can be difficult to rise above all this noise and get a bit of perspective, or to stop and think about what we're all doing and why, but each of us occasionally finds that place.

For me, this happens most often on long flights. "The overview effect" is a term used to describe that wistful feeling one gets when looking out of an aircraft window at the majestic towering clouds and the patchwork of human life laid out below. On planes, I find myself drifting off and thinking at an entirely different scale. Long-term thoughts about work, relationships, ambitions, and retirement come easily here, perhaps due to the abstraction of time and place one finds on an aircraft, or perhaps due to the copious quantities of free gin available. I can't help thinking this was the motivation for the design of that *Futurama* exhibit at the 1939 World's Fair, which elevated visitors high above the intricate city model laid out below, giving them an opportunity to zoom out of their daily routines and snatch a few precious moments of reflection. Wherever you find yourself experiencing these kinds of emotions, I encourage you to go there more often. Find ways to get lost in thought about where things might be heading, what you'd like to see, and what it might feel like. Start to build a more rounded idea of the future. Really think about it. Concentrate on developing your own personal perspectives rather than photocopies of something you've been sold, told, or encouraged to believe. Try to shake off those adopted opinions, dig below the headlines, and flex your own imagination muscles.

When futures work crops up in your life, resist the urge to swoon, nod along, or recoil in horror. Instead, have a think about what it might actually feel like, and how your family, friends, colleagues, and neighbors might experience it. When you're presented with an amazing new thing, think about how it might look with Malcolm sitting next to it, or how Sally from yoga might use it, or what Brian from the office might think of it. Train yourself to see the future as an evolution of the present rather than somewhere far off in the distance, and try to figure out how we might get there. When someone is presenting their idea of the future, try asking "And then what?" or "Why?" over and over again, just to see how deep the thinking goes. And don't settle for hand-waving or approximations. Our collective thinking about the future will improve only if we all get much better at critically assessing the stories we're being told, and that's where you can play a vital role. Don't settle. Push for better and expect more.

•

On Friday, August 4, 2017, a cheery German man injected my left arm with a chemical agent that stopped my heart from beating. For the first time since its creation, my body lay utterly still. My heart sat idle, my lungs stopped filling with air, and my blood was pumped through a machine plugged into the artery at the top of my right leg. For the next couple of hours, a huge team of talented people piloted a delicate robot through tiny incisions in my right armpit, underneath my rib cage, and into my heart, where they installed tiny strings of Gore-Tex into its muscle fibers. A routine health examination months prior had revealed a birth defect in my mitral valve that, if left unattended, would have led to an unannounced and almost certainly fatal heart attack. I'm the beneficiary of centuries of technological and intellectual progress, and without those machines and the diligent work of my surgeons, technicians, and carers, there's a reasonable chance I wouldn't be here today. Following procedures such as this, many people describe experiencing religious epiphanies, celestial awakenings, or eschatological reflections, but none of that happened for me. I feel neither debt to a creator nor any spiritual interconnectedness, and I remain convinced that humans represent little more than clever sacks of biology. One thing that did change, however, is that I became a little more aware of my own window of time here on Earth. As a young man, I didn't think much about a world without me in it, but as the years tick by, these thoughts come more frequently and more vividly.

At the outset of this book, I asked you to imagine a metaphorical flag in the distance that marks the end of your life. If you look again, it's still there fluttering in the breeze, but you're ever so slightly closer to it now than when you started reading. Once you reach this flag, you'll pass away and the tally of your life experiences will come to an end, but the landscape itself will continue onward long after both you and I are gone, and for much longer than you probably think. In roughly 5 billion years, the star at the center of our solar system will finally run out of hydrogen, causing it to expand into a red giant and engulf the inner planets, including Earth. Life on our little globe will likely come to an end much sooner than that though, as the oceans will evaporate and our planet will become unbearably hot in a mere 2 billion years. Even so, that's still a remarkable amount of time. Two billion years. Think about it. Two billion years ago, we weren't even close to being human. Our ancestors were nothing more than bacteria bubbling away in some primordial puddle. But that's the glorious thing about the future: there's just so much of it.

It's unlikely that many of us think about what the world will be like 2 billion years from now, or even two thousand or two hundred years hence, but the closer years of this timeline are absolutely crammed full of conjecture, ideas, and proposals. Through this book, I hope I've given you some sort of rudimentary grounding to help you carve this body of work into more manageable pieces, or at least provided you with some useful labels for what you see and hear. There's a huge amount of complexity facing us in the future, perhaps more than ever before. It's easy to become weighed down by the scale and severity of the challenges that we all face, but we also have to understand that there's a significantly larger amount of potential. Humans are uniquely positioned to define our own future. We have incredible amounts of agency, creativity, and resources to play with, and we can bend and modify this world into whatever shape we wish. I'm not here to tell you what that should be, but if you can define your idea clearly enough—and get enough people to agree with you—I'm sure it's possible.

Whatever your aspirations may be—for humanity, for life on our planet, for your industry, for your family, or for yourself—I'm convinced that we can all improve the quality of our thinking when it comes to what might lie beyond the horizon. Let's move forward with our eyes open, with an acknowledgment of the implications in the things we're creating, and with an air of responsibility about what we're doing in the present. Let's recognize when we're being hoodwinked or pushed into avenues of thinking. Let's propose more alternatives for our future and think about the different paths we could take and what they might allow us to do. Let's get more people from different backgrounds thinking about the future, in more locations and in much more detail. Let's get comfortable with the unknown and remain open to other possibilities. Let's create a generation of people who can differentiate between entertainment and ideas, who can ask better questions and demand more rigor in the messages being presented to them.

Let's raise the quality of the stories we tell ourselves about the future, and perhaps then we might improve the things we leave behind for those who will follow.

A list of references and further reading may be found at www.couldshouldmightdont.com.

THANK YOU

This book is for Jayne.

I'd like to extend my sincere gratitude to Jamie Byng and Sean McDonald, who showed significant trust in me to deliver this book, and whose belief and support brought it to this point. I couldn't have completed this project without the generosity and advice of Patrick Pittman, and significant thanks must go to Antony Topping and Zoë Pagnamenta, who helped me navigate unknown waters. I'd also like to acknowledge the following, without whose collaboration, conversations, disagreements, education, and advice this book would not exist:

Marko Ahtisaari, Rafi Ajl, Alex Aldridge, Beth Aldridge, Evie Aldridge, Stuart Aldridge, Molly Anderson, Pascal Anson, Ron Arad, Adi Aron-Gilat, Casper Asmussen, Paul Backett, Phil Balagtas, Brian Ballard, Neil Baron, Tommaso Bartalucci, Anderson Bartlett, Philip Battin, Garrett Berg, Durrell Bishop, Julian Bleecker, Jenny Bone, James Bridle, Matt Brown, Chris Butler, Tod Butler, James Cadogan, David Cameron, Geoffrey Camm, Alistair Campbell, David Campbell, Joanne Campbell, Rachel Campbell, Earl Carlson, Benjamin Christian, Chas Christiansen, Aldo Cibic, Mike Colville, Jordan Crane, Alastair Curtis, Claire Davies, Matt Day, Mark Delaney, Mae Delaney-Reid, Bill Dellinger, Alice

Duggan, Anthony Duggan, Anthony Dunne, Hugo Eccles, Emily Eisen, Christian Ervin, David Fisher, Graham Foster, Margaret Foster, Chris Frey, Christian Friessler, Stephen Fry, Susanna Georgiades, Philip Gilsenan, Fabien Girardin, Charlie Gower, Nestor Grace, Mark Grainger, Sir Kenneth Grange, Dan Gratiot, Christoph Gredler, Dionne Griffith, Gill Hadley, Jo Hankar, Patricia Hankar, Eric Hardrath, Brian Haynes, Hilary Haynes, Stephanie Henkle, Dan Hill, Charlie Humble-Thomas, Anna Hustler, Warren Hutchinson, Angus Hyland, Kaz Ichikawa, Cassie Isherwood, Gareth Jones, Matt Jones, Nooka Jones, Joseph Kable, Tin Kadoic, Alexis Kay, Bobby Kim, Cliff Kuang, Simon Lamason, Sara Liebert, KR Liu, Tom Lloyd, Matteo Loglio, Emma Lundgren, Tessa Mansfield, Chris Matthews, Kevin McCullagh, Jason Mesut, Gary Miller, James Milne, Julinka Mistzal, James Molyneux, Jan Moolsintong, David Murphy, J. Paul Neeley, Rhys Newman, Henry Newton-Dunn, Melinda Nokes, Nicolas Nova, Harold Offeh, Katey Osborn, Stefan Pannenbecker, Ben Pawle, Luke Pearson, Kathleen Pekkola, Boris Pluskowski, Dick Powell, Brigit Powers, Helen Protheroe, Fiona Raby, Simone Rebaudengo, James Reid, Tobias Revell, Joe Rickerby, Eugénie Rives, Jason Rugolo, Peter Russell-Clarke, Sasha Samochina, Benoit Schillings, Uli Schöberl, Richard Seymour, Fredrik Silfver, Kate Smaby, Scott Smith, Bruce Sterling, Andy Stewart, Sandy Suffield, Charlie Sutton, Hirotaka Tako, Paul Thornton-Jones, Paul Turnock, Alex Valdman, Georgina Voss, Matt Wade, Matt Ward, Simon Waterfall, Matt Webb, Mike Webster, Jan Weeks, Raymond Weeks, Chris Weightman, Jonah Weiner, Simon Wells, Robert-Jay Wharmby, Ben White, Stephen White, Will Widera, Alex Williams, Paul

Wolfson, Erin Wylie, Kenichi Yoneda, Pete Ziegler, Paula Zucotti-Webster.

You've got to pick some people up.
You've got to let some people go.
—DAVID GEDGE

A NOTE ABOUT THE AUTHOR

Nick Foster is a designer and writer based in Oakland, California. He has spent his career exploring the future for technology companies including Google, Nokia, Sony, and Dyson, and has established himself as a leading figure in the field of Futures Design. In 2021 he was awarded the title Royal Designer for Industry—the highest accolade for a British designer—in recognition of his significant contributions to the discipline. Foster is also a public speaker, delivering talks and lectures to share his thinking with audiences around the globe. He earned his master's degree from London's Royal College of Art in 2001, and in 2018 he was made a fellow of the Royal Society of Arts. He has lived in the United States since 2012 with his wife, Jayne.